The Vietnam War Reexamined

Going beyond the dominant orthodox narrative to incorporate insight from revisionist scholarship on the Vietnam War, Michael G. Kort presents the case that the United States should have been able to win the war, and at a much lower cost than it suffered in defeat. Presenting a study that is both historiographic and a narrative history, Kort analyzes important factors such as the strong nationalist credentials and leadership qualities of South Vietnam's Ngo Dinh Diem, the flawed military strategy of "graduated response" developed by Robert McNamara, and the real reasons South Vietnam collapsed in the face of a massive North Vietnamese invasion in 1975. Kort shows how the US commitment to defend South Vietnam was not a strategic error but a policy consistent with US security interests during the Cold War, and that there were potentially viable strategic approaches to the war that might have saved South Vietnam.

Michael G. Kort is Professor in the Division of Social Sciences at Boston University. He is the author of several books, including *The Soviet Colossus: History and Aftermath*, *The Columbia Guide to the Cold War*, and *A Brief History of Russia*.

Cambridge Essential Histories

Cambridge Essential Histories is devoted to introducing critical events, periods, or individuals in history to students. Volumes in this series emphasize narrative as a means of familiarizing students with historical analysis. In this series, leading scholars focus on topics in European, American, Asian, Latin American, Middle Eastern, African, and World History through thesis-driven, concise volumes designed for survey and upper-division undergraduate history courses. The books contain an introduction that acquaints readers with the historical event and reveals the book's thesis; narrative chapters that cover the chronology of the event or problem; and a concluding summary that provides the historical interpretation and analysis.

Editors

General Editor: Donald T. Critchlow, Arizona State University

Other books in the series:
Edward D. Berkowitz, *Mass Appeal: The Formative Age of the Movies, Radio, and TV*
Howard Brick and Christopher Phelps, *Radicals in America: The U.S. Left since the Second World War*
Sean P. Cunningham, *American Politics in the Postwar Sunbelt*
Ian Dowbiggin, *The Quest for Mental Health: A Tale of Science, Medicine, Scandal, Sorrow, and Mass Society*
Maura Jane Farrelly, *Anti-Catholicism in America, 1620–1860*
John Earl Haynes and Harvey Klehr, *Early Cold War Spies: The Espionage Trials that Shaped American Politics*
James H. Hutson, *Church and State in America: The First Two Centuries*
Maury Klein, *The Genesis of Industrial America, 1870–1920*
John Lauritz Larson, *The Market Revolution in America: Liberty, Ambition, and the Eclipse of the Common Good*
Wilson D. Miscamble, *The Most Controversial Decision: Truman, the Atomic Bombs, and the Defeat of Japan*
Mark E. Neely Jr., *Lincoln and the Democrats: The Politics of Opposition in the Civil War*
Charles H. Parker, *Global Interactions in the Early Modern Age, 1400–1800*
Stanley G. Payne, *The Spanish Civil War*
W. J. Rorabaugh, *American Hippies*
Jason Scott Smith, *A Concise History of the New Deal*
David M. Wrobel, *America's West: A History, 1890–1950*

The Vietnam War Reexamined

MICHAEL G. KORT

Boston University

CAMBRIDGE
UNIVERSITY PRESS

University Printing House, Cambridge CB2 8BS, United Kingdom

One Liberty Plaza, 20th Floor, New York, NY 10006, USA

477 Williamstown Road, Port Melbourne, VIC 3207, Australia

314–321, 3rd Floor, Plot 3, Splendor Forum, Jasola District Centre,
New Delhi – 110025, India

79 Anson Road, #06–04/06, Singapore 079906

Cambridge University Press is part of the University of Cambridge.

It furthers the University's mission by disseminating knowledge in the pursuit of
education, learning, and research at the highest international levels of excellence.

www.cambridge.org
Information on this title: www.cambridge.org/9781107046405
DOI: 10.1017/9781107110199

© Michael G. Kort 2018

First published 2018

Printed in the United Kingdom by Clays, St Ives plc

A catalogue record for this publication is available from the British Library.

Library of Congress Cataloging-in-Publication Data
Names: Kort, Michael, 1944– author.
Title: The Vietnam War re-examined / Michael G. Kort, Boston University.
Description: Cambridge ; New York, NY : Cambridge University Press, 2017. |
Series: Cambridge essential histories | Includes index.
Identifiers: LCCN 2017028182| ISBN 9781107046405 (hardback) |
ISBN 9781107628175 (paperback)
Subjects: LCSH: Vietnam War, 1961–1975.
Classification: LCC DS557.7 .K68 2017 | DDC 959.704/3–dc23
LC record available at https://lccn.loc.gov/2017028182

ISBN 978-1-107-04640-5 Hardback
ISBN 978-1-107-62817-5 Paperback

In memory of my parents
And for Maya

Contents

Maps

Acknowledgments

I am deeply indebted to military historian D. M. Giangreco, who not only read and critiqued the entire manuscript but also offered his irrepressible brand of encouragement from the inception of this project to its completion and, during lengthy phone conversations, provided me with invaluable tutorials on technical military matters. James H. Willbanks, Vietnam War veteran and now one of the leading historians of that conflict, on short notice, read the manuscript and provided extremely helpful comments. Cathal Nolan, my colleague at Boston University and also a military historian, likewise on short notice, provided a valuable critique of the entire manuscript. Robert Wexelblatt, also my colleague at Boston University, read and then reread large sections of the manuscript and offered key suggestions that helped me move forward when I seemed stuck in Chapter 1. William Tilchin, Jay Corrin, and June Grasso, my colleagues in Boston University's Division of Social Sciences, evaluated or discussed parts of this manuscript with me and were always available for consultations when needed. My thanks to Lewis Bateman, the editor at Cambridge University Press who was willing to take a chance on this project; to the anonymous evaluators enlisted by Cambridge University Press for comments and criticism that guided me in crafting and completing this project; and to Kristina Deusch, copy editor Linda Benson, Saranya Jeeva Nath Singh, Robert Judkins, and the staff at CUP for their hard work in helping bring this project to fruition.

I owe a special thanks to my wonderful daughters, Eleza and Tamara, for their unconditional love and support regardless of my many moods. My wife, Carol, took on the tedious job of proofreading the final version of the manuscript before I sent it to the publisher. More important, as she has done for half a century, she held body and soul together as I struggled to complete a project that turned out to be far more difficult than I had originally anticipated. As always, my deepest gratitude is reserved for her.

A Note on Vietnamese Names, Military Ranks, and the Spelling of the Words "Communist" and "Communism"

Vietnamese names begin with the family name. That name usually is followed by a middle name and then the given name. The middle name can indicate the generation to which a person belongs, which is one, but not the only, reason siblings often share that name. For example, the brothers Ngo Dinh Diem and Ngo Dinh Nhu (and their two other brothers) had the same middle name. Complicating matters further, Vietnamese refer to each other formally by the given name. That is why, for example, following accepted practice, in this volume Ngo Dinh Diem is referred to as "Diem"; Vo Nguyen Giap, the North Vietnamese general, is referred to as "Giap"; and Nguyen Van Thieu, the president of South Vietnam, is referred to as "Thieu." The one exception to this system, admittedly a major one, is Ho Chi Minh, who, again following accepted practice, is referred to as "Ho." As in most recently published books, Vietnamese individuals are indexed in this volume according to their family names. Thus in the index Ngo Dinh Diem is followed by Ngo Dinh Nhu under the letter "N," General Giap is listed under the letter "V" as Vo Nguyen Giap, and, not an exception in this case, Ho is listed under "H" as Ho Chi Minh. Some important individuals are listed both ways: for example, Ngo Dinh Diem is found under his full name and under "Diem." Readers of this volume also will notice a large number of people named Nguyen. This is not because they were related but rather because Nguyen is the most common family name in Vietnam; in fact, almost 40 percent of the people in Vietnam carry the family name Nguyen. It was Ho Chi Minh's real family name (Nguyen Sinh Cung) as well as the family name of the alias (Nguyen Ai Quoc) he used for many years before becoming "Ho Chi Minh."

Many of the books and articles that served as sources for this volume were written by serving or retired officers in the US military. In referring to them in the text for the first time, I have used the highest rank they reached of which I am aware. For example, Dave Richard Palmer, a colonel when he wrote *Summons of the Trumpet*, later became a general and is referred to as "General Dave Richard Palmer" in this volume, and James H. Willbanks, who published his major works after retiring from the US Army as a lieutenant colonel, is referred to by that rank when first mentioned in the text.

With regard to the spelling of the words "communism" and "communist," my system is to spell them with a lowercase "c" when referring to that concept in the generic sense and with an uppercase "C" when referring to the Soviet variant and its various offshoots.

Abbreviations

APC	Accelerated Pacification Campaign
ARVN	Army of the Republic of Vietnam
DMZ	Demilitarized Zone
CCP	Chinese Communist Party
CIA	Central Intelligence Agency
CMAC	Chinese Military Advisory Group
CORDS	Civil Operations and Revolutionary (later changed to Rural) Development Support
COSVN	Central Office for South Vietnam
CPSU	Communist Party of the Soviet Union
DAO	Defense Attaché Office
DIA	Defense Intelligence Agency
DVN	Democratic Republic of Vietnam
GVN	Government of (South) Vietnam
ICP	Indochinese Communist Party
JCS	U. S. Joint Chiefs of Staff
MACV	Military Assistance Command, Vietnam
NATO	North Atlantic Treaty Organization
NLF	National Liberation Front
POL	Petroleum, Oil, Lubricants
PPBS	Planning Programming and Budgeting Systems
PRC	People's Republic of China
PSDF	People's Self Defense Force
ROEs	Rules of Engagement
RVN	Republic of Vietnam (South Vietnam)
RVNAF	Republic of Vietnam (South Vietnam) Armed Forces

SAM	Surface to Air Missile
SEATO	Southeast Asia Treaty Organization
VCI	Vietcong Infrastructure
VNQDD	Vietnam Nationalist Party
VWP	Vietnamese Workers' Party

INTRODUCTION

Understanding the Vietnam War

Like all wars, the war the United States fought to preserve the independence of South Vietnam as a non-Communist state has its terrible statistics. It lasted eight years, from 1965, when the first American combat units arrived in Vietnam, to 1973, when the last US combat troops left the country, twice as long as any previous American war other than this country's fight for independence. If, as some historians have done, one goes back to 1950, when the United States began its involvement in Vietnam by making a major financial commitment to help the French retain control of Indochina, then one has what General Bruce Palmer Jr. called "The 25-Year War" or what historian George Herring calls "America's Longest War."[1] More than 58,000 American soldiers died fighting in Vietnam, and more than 300,000 were wounded. More than three million Vietnamese lost their lives in that conflict, almost two-thirds of them civilians.[2] During the fighting the United States employed more explosives in Vietnam than had previously been used in all of human

---

[1] General Bruce Palmer Jr., *The 25-Year War: America's Military Role in Vietnam* (Lexington: The University Press of Kentucky, 1984); George C. Herring, *America's Longest War: The United States and Vietnam* (New York: Alfred A. Knopf, 1979). As of this writing, the US combat role in Afghanistan, with 8,000 troops still in that country, has exceeded in length this country's combat role in Vietnam. Since there was no official declaration of war in the cases of either Vietnam or Afghanistan, determining which conflict was America's longest war depends on how one does the dating.

[2] Vietnamese losses increase significantly if one goes back to 1945, the beginning of fighting between the Communist-dominated Vietminh and the French, who were attempting to reestablish their colonial control of Vietnam after Japan's surrender ended World War II. The Vietminh-French struggle, which lasted from 1946 to 1954, often is called the "First Indochina War." This in turn makes the subsequent military struggle that involved the United States the "second" such war.

history, the equivalent of more than 450 Hiroshima atomic bombs. Yet this enormous effort turned out to be a war that the United States was unable to win.

These grim statistics are only part of the story. There are scars as well. The Vietnam War strained and distorted the American economy; it opened social and political fissures and defeated attempts to close them; it sapped the country's will, eroded its confidence, and frayed its nerves; it addicted many of its soldiers to drugs and damaged its military establishment. Perhaps worst of all, it embittered Americans against one another. The Vietnam War became the first American war since the Civil War to spawn what might reasonably be called a secondary war at home, a national fracturing at once political and personal complete with riots, mass demonstrations, arrests, bitter family feuds, and shattered relationships of all sorts. In short, the Vietnam War was an American tragedy, an ordeal that left far more Americans sadder than it did wiser.

The Vietnam War also spawned a debate, one that erupted well before American combat troops became involved in the fighting, before the United States actually was at war in Vietnam. It began as a disagreement over why the American effort to help the government of South Vietnam defeat the Communist insurgency it faced was going badly and what could be done to remedy that situation. Like the war itself, the debate about what the United States should do in Vietnam escalated in scope and intensity as the question of how US ground troops and air power should be employed became a major point of contention. The war ended for the United States with the signing of the Paris Peace Accords and withdrawal of all American military forces from Vietnam in early 1973 and for the people of Vietnam when the North Vietnamese army finally overwhelmed South Vietnamese's weakened and demoralized military forces in April 1975. But the debate in the United States over the war continued, having now expanded to include a clash of views over why the American effort to stem the advance of Communism in Vietnam had ended in defeat. It continues to this day.

The debate over the Vietnam War was and remains multi-faceted, a controversy that has gone on for decades and produced literally thousands of books and uncounted scholarly and journalistic articles. Ultimately, however, it breaks down into two primary questions. First, was it necessary and wise – that is, vital to American security interests – for the United States to get involved in Vietnam with its own military forces, the goal being to guarantee the survival of a non-Communist South Vietnam? Put another way, should the United States have applied its

Cold War policy of containment, which was designed to limit the expansion of the influence of the Soviet Union and prevent the spread of Communism, to Vietnam and Southeast Asia? Second, having become involved, and consequently gotten into a war in which American and South Vietnamese government forces were matched against southern Communist guerrillas and regular North Vietnamese army troops, was that war winnable?

In the end, notwithstanding the enormous variety of ways those questions have been answered, the bulk of the responses may be loosely classified into two competing narratives: the orthodox and the revisionist. The orthodox narrative, which also often carries the label "liberal realist," is the prevailing viewpoint most college and university students encounter in their US and international history courses, and it answers both questions firmly in the negative. This narrative has a pedigree that goes back to well before the United States withdrew from Vietnam and has featured as articulate proponents some of the most prominent American journalists who covered the war, including four who wrote best-selling and influential books during the 1970s and 1980s: David Halberstam (*The Best and the Brightest*, 1972), Frances Fitzgerald (*Fire in the Lake*, 1972), Stanley Karnow (*Vietnam A History*, 1983), and Neil Sheehan (*A Bright Shining Lie: John Paul Vann and America in Vietnam*, 1988).[3] It achieved the status of orthodoxy in large part for several reasons. Over time, albeit with modifications, it became and remained the predominant outlook among journalists who had covered the war and then added critical commentary in books and articles after it was over. It also became the prevailing viewpoint among American academics, the people who since

---

[3] David Halberstam, *The Best and the Brightest* (New York: Random House, 1972); Frances Fitzgerald, *Fire in the Lake: The Vietnamese and Americans in Vietnam* (Boston: Vintage, 1972); Stanley Karnow, *Vietnam: A History* (New York: Penguin Books, 1983); Neil Sheehan, *A Bright Shining Lie: John Paul Vann and America in Vietnam* (New York: Random House, 1988). The outstanding early correspondent of the Vietnam War was Bernard B. Fall, who was born and raised in France but received his graduate education in the United States. Fall covered both the French and the American efforts between his first visit to Vietnam in 1953 and his death in 1967. (He was killed while on patrol with US Marines when the jeep he was riding in hit a land mine.) Fall's work later provided ammunition for commentators on both sides of the Vietnam debate, as he was staunchly anti-Communist but also argued that the United States was repeating the mistakes made by the French and, in addition, that America's reliance on high-tech military methods was so destructive as to alienate most Vietnamese and therefore ultimately futile. Among his highly respected books are *Street Without Joy* (1961), *Hell in a Very Small Place: The Siege of Dien Bien Phu* (1967), *The Two Vietnams: A Political and Military Analysis* (2nd rev. ed., 1967), and *Last Reflections on a War* (1967).

the end of the Vietnam War have produced most of the scholarly books and articles on the subject and, significantly, written the textbooks students read in courses on American foreign policy in general and on the Vietnam War in particular. More generally, it became the prevailing outlook among Western intellectuals. As Andrew Wiest, author of *Vietnam's Forgotten Army: Heroism and Betrayal in the ARVN* (2008) and coeditor of *Triumph Revisited: Historians Battle for the Vietnam War* (2010), has observed, "It became accepted wisdom that America's war in Vietnam had been a mistake and a tragedy."[4] This remained the case even as this "wisdom" evolved and branched off into many directions as new participants proliferated and added their research and commentary to the debate. As a result most students of American foreign policy are unlikely to encounter in their course assignments a sympathetic or even a reasonably impartial overview of the revisionist narrative, which in contrast to the orthodox/liberal realist narrative answers the two questions listed earlier in the affirmative.[5]

However, the revisionist narrative includes many compelling arguments. They are grounded on two basic premises: first, that the United States became engaged in fighting in Vietnam with good reason in terms of national interest given the context of the Cold War, and, second, that it did so without first developing a strategy for victory and therefore squandered opportunities that in fact existed to secure victory at a far lower price than it ultimately paid in defeat. The premise that the Cold War provided a compelling justification for the United States to defend South Vietnam was argued from the very beginning of the US commitment in the 1950s when the ultimate results of that decision could not be known, and it retains merit despite the fact that the United States and its allies lost their battle in Vietnam while still winning the larger Cold War. The premise that the United States lacked a sound strategy for dealing with Vietnam

[4] Andrew Wiest, "Introduction," in *Triumph Revisited: Historians Battle for the Vietnam War*, eds. Andrew Wiest and Michael J. Doidge (New York and London: Routledge, 2010), 8. Wiest uses the term "traditional" rather than "orthodox" to describe that "accepted wisdom." Unfortunately, when it comes to the Cold War in general, the "orthodox" and "revisionist" terminology is reversed. In that case, "orthodox" commentators in most cases support US post–World War II foreign policy, including the effort to preserve a non-Communist South Vietnam while "revisionist" commentators in most cases are critical of many aspects of US foreign policy. The Cold War debate also includes the "post-revisionist" camp, which lies somewhere between the other two camps.

[5] One notable exception is a thematically organized textbook by Gary R Hess, *Vietnam: Explaining America's Lost War* (2009), which, while finding for the orthodox side on each of seven issues it examines, treats the revisionist narrative seriously throughout.

emerged and then gained support as the conflict deepened in the early 1960s. One might note here that the belief that a sound strategy is vital to success in war is a fundamental military precept with a venerable pedigree. As the Chinese thinker Sun Tzu cautioned more than 2,500 years ago, "Tactics without strategy is the noise before defeat." In retrospect, it seems difficult to deny that the American strategic approach to the Vietnam War was deeply flawed and, at a minimum, that approach yielded what was close to a worst-case scenario, at least in Vietnam itself.

An understanding of what revisionist historians have to say about the Vietnam War is essential if students engaged in a serious investigation into that conflict are to have to the background they need to render their own informed judgment on that war, whatever that may turn out to be. This volume will attempt to provide such an understanding. It will do so not only by presenting what the revisionists have to say but also by citing the historical record as presented by orthodox commentators, whose own evidence not infrequently supports arguments made by revisionists. At the same time, it will examine many issues on which the revisionists themselves disagree, including the key question of which strategic approach to the war the United States could have taken that might have produced better and perhaps decisive results on the battlefield and thereby preserved the independence of South Vietnam.

It is important to remember that there is no one or sole orthodox or revisionist case but rather a great variety of analyses, most of which can, with approximation, be placed in one camp or the other. With regard to revisionism, the characteristic that places a given work in that camp is that, in one way or another, it supports the premise that the United States had military options it did not employ that could have enabled it, along with South Vietnam and other countries that contributed to South Vietnam's defense, to win the Vietnam War at less cost than was suffered in defeat. With this caveat in place, it is hoped that this volume will contribute to a more balanced discussion of the Vietnam War.

The Vietnam War in History

The two major narratives regarding the American effort to defeat communist forces in South Vietnam are by necessity artificial constructs. Each narrative is a large tent that houses many points of view. Each, therefore, inevitably includes works by authors who have a wide variety of disagreements, even as they agree on the larger issues of whether the United States should have intervened in Vietnam and whether it could have won the war that followed. For example, one major issue that sharply divides orthodox historians is whether John F. Kennedy was planning to withdraw from Vietnam had he won the 1964 election. Among the prominent historians who argue that Kennedy planned to disengage from Vietnam are David Kaiser (*American Tragedy: Kennedy, Johnson, and the Origins of the Vietnam War*, 2000) and Fredrik Longevall (*Choosing War: The Last Chance for Peace and the Escalation of War in Vietnam*, 1999). Those who disagree include Robert Schulzinger (*A Time for War: The United States and Vietnam, 1941–1975*, 1997) and George McT. Kahin (*Intervention: How America Became Involved in Vietnam*, 1986). Revisionist historians have their own disagreements, including on the vital issue of how the ground war in South Vietnam should have been fought. For example, two major works by serving US Army officers are often juxtaposed because they advocate diametrically opposing approaches and were published relatively soon after the war: *On Strategy: A Critical Analysis of the Vietnam War* (1982), by Colonel Harry Summers Jr., and *The Army and Vietnam* (1986), by Lt. Colonel Andrew F. Krepinevich Jr. Summers argues that the United States failed in Vietnam because it did not sufficiently stress conventional warfare and that the US military effort should have been concentrated against North

Vietnam, which controlled the Communist insurgency in the South. In sharp contrast, Krepinevich argues that the US military overemphasized conventional warfare when it faced a guerrilla war in South Vietnam that required a multi-faceted counterinsurgency strategy to produce victory. These and other internal differences notwithstanding, the orthodox and revisionist narratives together provide the best available framework for understanding the historiography and key issues of the Vietnam War.

ORTHODOXY

Orthodox historians argue that it was a major mistake for the United States to get involved in Vietnam and once this country found itself at war, that war was unwinnable. Thus John Prados titled his history of the war *Vietnam: The History of an Unwinnable War, 1945–1975* (2009). Or, as Robert Schulzinger put it somewhat earlier in *A Time for War*, "The United States embarked on the impossible task of creating a separate state and society in the southern part of a single land."[1] This perspective almost invariably is grounded on two fundamental assumptions: first, Communist forces led by Ho Chi Minh represented the only authentic and viable form of Vietnamese nationalism; second, the war in the South, notwithstanding the fact that North Vietnam ultimately controlled and directed the Communist insurgency there, began as a spontaneous response to local inequities – most notably in land ownership – and to repression by the regime headed by Ngo Dinh Diem that was attempting to maintain those inequities. The first assumption has remained relatively consistent over time, although in recent years some orthodox scholars have granted Ngo Dinh Diem a limited measure of nationalist legitimacy. The second assumption, however, has evolved in one significant way. Initially, the orthodox narrative maintained that the Communist insurgency in South Vietnam was an indigenous rebellion. For example, in 1962 the French scholar and expert on Vietnam Phillipe Devillers claimed that "the insurrection existed before the Communists decided to take part" and that "the people were literally driven by Diem to take up arms in self defense." In the United States, historians George McT. Kahin and John W. Lewis wrote in 1967 that "insurrectionary activity" started in South Vietnam "under Southern leadership not as

---

[1] Robert D. Schulzinger, *A Time for War: The United States and Vietnam, 1941–1975* (New York: Oxford University Press, 1997), 96; see also John Prados, *Vietnam, The History of an Unwinnable War* (Lawrence: University Press of Kansas, 2009).

a consequence of any dictate from Hanoi, but contrary to Hanoi's injunctions." Once the war was over and more information became available, it quickly became clear to many orthodox observers that this narrative was inaccurate. Thus in 1976 Jean Lacouture, a French expert on Vietnam who had believed that the Communists in South Vietnam enjoyed considerable autonomy, acknowledged that they were "piloted, directed, and inspired by the political bureau of the Lao Dong [Communist] Party, whose chief was and remains in Hanoi." Currently, the prevailing orthodox narrative, while stressing grievances in the South and the crucial role of local Communists, accepts that the insurrection in the South was controlled from Hanoi virtually from the beginning. William J. Duiker therefore speaks for many orthodox commentators when he claims that "the insurgency was a genuine revolt based in the South, but it was organized and directed from the North."[2]

The orthodox outlook prevails in most of the major textbooks on the war. One of the most widely assigned textbooks in college and university courses on the war is *America's Longest War: The United States and Vietnam, 1950–1975*, by George Herring. Herring is one of the most respected historians of the Vietnam War – see his *LBJ and Vietnam: A Different Kind of War* (1991) – and his textbook has earned a reputation for comprehensiveness and balance. *America's Longest War* therefore carries a lot of weight when it informs its readers that the American effort to maintain an independent non-Communist South Vietnam "probably was doomed from the start." This was the case because the United States was attempting to preserve a flawed social order in South Vietnam, "and there was no long-range hope of stability without revolutionary change." Turning to the issue of containment, the fundamental American policy for dealing with the Soviet Union and the rest of the Communist world during the Cold War, Herring argues that regardless of how one evaluates containment as a whole, "that containment was misapplied in Vietnam ... seems beyond debate." On the matter of the origins of the rebellion in the South, Herring quotes Duiker while adding that there was more "complexity" to the issue because the Communist Lao Dong Party in Hanoi was a unified national party

---

[2] Philippe Devillers, "The Struggle for Unification in Vietnam," in *North Vietnam Today: Profile of a Communist Satellite*, ed. P. J. Honey (New York and Washington: Frederick A. Praeger, 1962), 42. The Kahin/Lewis quotation and the Lacouture quotation are in Guenter Lewy, *America in Vietnam* (Oxford: Oxford University Press, 1978), 15, 18; William J. Duiker, *The Communist Road to Power in Vietnam* (Boulder: Westview Press, 1981), 198.

whose members came from all parts of the country.[3] Another widely used and well-crafted textbook, *Vietnam: An American Ordeal*, by George Donelson Moss, notes under the heading "Why We Lost and They Won" that the "creation of an independent South Vietnam was doomed to fail from the outset. The Republic of South Vietnam could never have become a viable nation-state." Moss adds that because of the weaknesses of the South Vietnamese government and the inability of American planners to come up with a successful strategy, "only a Communist triumph could bring peace to southern Vietnam." With regard to containment, "the outcome of the American Indochina war invalidated its prime ideological justifications and suggested that the containment ideology itself had been misapplied." Moss quotes and generally follows Duiker on the matter of the origins of the rebellion in South Vietnam.[4]

According to the orthodox narrative, Vietnam, and indeed all of Indochina, lacked strategic importance in the Cold War and therefore did not merit direct American engagement. This narrative also rejects the validity of the domino theory, made famous by a metaphor President Dwight Eisenhower used in explaining his administration's commitment to defend South Vietnam in 1954, according to which the fall to Communism of one country victimized by subversion or attack could lead to the rapid collapse of its neighbors. Further, in committing the United States to maintain a non-Communist South Vietnam, American policy makers did not appreciate the strength and determination of the North Vietnamese regime or the Communist Vietcong guerrillas fighting in the South, or that their Marxist program had a strong nationalist component and therefore considerable popularity. North Vietnamese president Ho Chi Minh, the orthodox narrative maintains, was a nationalist, and in fact a nationalist first, as well as a Communist. Ho had led the struggle that drove the French from Vietnam in a war that lasted from 1946 to 1954; as a result, he had nationalist credentials and personal popularity unmatched by any non-Communist Vietnamese leader. Nor did the United States sufficiently examine the weaknesses of its South Vietnamese clients, beginning with the government headed by Ngo Dinh Diem from 1954 to 1963 and continuing with its successors through 1975, and therefore it did not grasp their vulnerability to an insurgency that at its core was provoked by inequities in South Vietnam. Indeed,

[3] Herring, *America's Longest War*, 5, 339, 357, 80.
[4] George Donelson Moss, *Vietnam: An American Ordeal*, Fifth Edition (Upper Saddle River, NJ: Pearson/Prentice Hall, 2006), 29, 421, 425, 102.

a common orthodox claim is that the South Vietnamese regime from the start was essentially an American creation and therefore lacked any legitimacy. An important corollary of the orthodox position that the Vietnam War was unwise and unwinnable is that the entire tragedy could have been avoided had American policy makers correctly assessed their country's vital interests and understood the limits of its power, especially in a place such as Vietnam, where the odds were stacked so strongly against a non-Communist alternative.

With regard to the years 1965 to 1973, when US combat forces were directly involved in the fighting, orthodox historians generally agree that America's military strategy was unsuited to the conditions in Vietnam. Between 1965 and 1968 the US ground campaign in South Vietnam produced a highly destructive war of attrition incapable of securing anything more than a bloody stalemate. Extensive bombing added to the destruction but could not break the stalemate. Meanwhile, the bombing campaign directed against North Vietnam failed to achieve its goal of forcing Hanoi to end its effort to take over the South. All this in the end eroded the American public's support for the war. These historians further argue that the Tet Offensive of 1968, in which Communist Vietcong guerrillas and North Vietnamese troops carried out attacks against more than 100 cities and towns, demonstrated the futility of American policy in Vietnam. Even though Communist forces in the end were repulsed with staggering losses – the Vietcong, who did most of the fighting, were largely destroyed – those losses over time were replaceable. The war itself overall had become a quagmire with no end in sight, and the American people were correct to intensify their demand that it be brought to an end. Nor did the improved military situation between 1968 and 1972 and the 1973 Paris Peace Accords under which the United States withdrew its remaining military forces from Vietnam solve South Vietnam's fundamental social and political weaknesses, and it was those weaknesses, not America's failure to back the South Vietnamese regime with sufficient aid over the next several years, that led to that regime's defeat and collapse in 1975.

Among the many ironies of the Vietnam War and the debate that surrounds it is that one of the most forceful expositions of the orthodox case against America's effort in Vietnam was made by none other than Robert S. McNamara, who as secretary of defense to Presidents John F. Kennedy and Lyndon B. Johnson from January 1961 through February 1968 was the chief strategist of that involvement, to the point where critics often referred to it as "McNamara's War." That exposition was a long time coming, as McNamara did not make it until the publication of his memoir, *In Retrospect: The Tragedy and Lessons of Vietnam* (1995), more than a quarter century after he left his post at the Pentagon and two decades after the war had ended with a Communist victory. McNamara's belated retrospective provoked widespread anger and/or contempt from, among others, both orthodox and revisionist historians of the war. For different reasons, to be sure, historians in both camps blamed McNamara for mismanaging American foreign policy in the 1960s. Again for different reasons, both sides rejected what they regarded as his effort, even as he admitted to having made errors, to somehow exculpate himself for that mismanagement. At the same time, notwithstanding what many hostile orthodox historians thought of McNamara's decision to speak up after so many years, *In Retrospect* seemed to validate the orthodox side in the Vietnam debate.

Even before getting to the body of his argument, a clearly apologetic McNamara, in a single six-word sentence, in effect repudiated just about everything he and the other architects of US policy in Vietnam had done for seven years: "Yet we were wrong, terribly wrong," he confessed.[5] And why did the McNamara and his colleagues go so wrong? According to McNamara, now armed with the invaluable perspective of hindsight, he and his fellow American policy makers had attempted to deal with the complex crisis they faced in Southeast Asia with "sparse knowledge, scant experience, and simplistic assumptions."[6] Those assumptions included accepting the notion of the monolithic nature of international Communism and the validity of the domino theory. American policy makers in addition had failed to ask a number of the "most basic" questions, including whether the fall of South Vietnam would lead to the fall of the rest of Southeast Asia, whether that development was a threat to Western security, and what kind of war (conventional or guerrilla) would develop if the United States sent combat troops to Vietnam.[7]

McNamara also retrospectively instructed his readers on the lessons he had learned from America's Vietnam experience. During the Vietnam War era, America's leaders failed to understand the "geopolitical intentions" of their adversaries – North Vietnam, the Vietcong, the Soviet Union, and China – a failure that included totally underestimating the

---

[5] Robert S. McNamara, *In Retrospect: The Tragedy and Lessons of Vietnam* (New York: Times Books, 1995), xvi.
[6] Ibid., 29.   [7] Ibid., 39, 101.

"nationalistic aspect of Ho Chi Minh." Nor did they understand the South Vietnamese leaders whose cause this country was supporting, beginning with Ngo Dinh Diem, a man McNamara calls an "enigma to me and ... virtually every American who met him." American leaders did not appreciate the power of nationalism and compounded that lack of insight by being woefully ignorant of Vietnamese history, culture, and politics. They did not recognize the limits of modern, high-technology military weaponry or appreciate the challenges of dealing with unconventional warfare. Finally, they did not appreciate that there are some problems in international affairs "for which there are no immediate solutions."[8] There was nothing new in McNamara's "lessons": they already were and have remained central to the orthodox analysis. However, few of the volumes by the vast legion of McNamara's orthodox critics have provided a more comprehensive critique of what he did as secretary of defense than he does himself in the pages of *In Retrospect*.

Marxism and Neo-Marxism

One segment of the Vietnam debate does not fit easily into the orthodox/revisionist categorization: the Marxist perspective, along with its offshoots that are sometimes labeled neo-Marxist and/or the New Left school. Works based on Marxist or neo-Marxist/New Left assumptions are sometimes grouped with the mainstream orthodox narrative works because they share the assumption that the Vietnam War was unwinnable for the United States. Marxists also condemn America's intervention in Vietnam on moral grounds, another point of commonality with some, though certainly not all, orthodox historians. However, Marxist historiography differs in a crucial way from the orthodox liberal realist narrative because it is rooted in the notion of inevitability: in this case the assumption that the United States as the world's leading capitalist power was driven by imperialist economic imperatives to intervene in Indochina to stop the advance of Communism and/or radical nationalist movements. This determinism in effect renders moot any discussion of what the United States might or should have done by denying the possibility of alternative options its policy makers might realistically have chosen. The Marxist analysis also renders any serious debate moot by tending to condemn *a priori* virtually any action the United States took during the Cold War (and before and after it as well) while whitewashing or ignoring completely

[8] Ibid., 41–43, 321–23.

the violence and repression committed by Communist regimes since a group of Marxists led by Vladimir Lenin established the world's first such regime in Russia in November 1917. In the case of the Vietnam War, those getting a pass, presumably for representing the "people" and promoting historical progress toward the realization of socialism, are the North Vietnamese government and the guerrilla forces in South Vietnam that operated under its control as well as North Vietnam's two main backers, the Soviet Union and the People's Republic of China. The traditional Marxist perspective with regard to the Vietnam War is probably best represented by Gabrial Kolko's *Anatomy of a War: The United States and the Modern Historical Experience* (1985). One volume often used as a textbook that reflects the neo-Marxist/New Left perspective is Marilyn B. Young's *The Vietnam Wars, 1945–1990* (1991).[9]

REVISIONISM

The revisionist narrative on the Vietnam War matches the orthodox approach in terms of variety and complexity. More to t he point, however, is that the revisionist case is more difficult to make. The reason is that orthodox commentators – often leaving unexamined some of their key assumptions such as the stakes in Vietnam were minor and the war in any event could not have been won – basically can limit their focus to the question of why the United States failed in Vietnam. Revisionists must confront that question, but then they must venture afield from the relatively firm ground of historical fact – America's failure in Vietnam – to the quicksand-laced swamp of what historians call counterfactual history to explain how, in their judgment, the United States could have succeeded in

---

[9] See Marilyn B. Young, *The Vietnam Wars, 1945–1990* (New York: HarperCollins, 1991). Seth Jacobs, author of a volume on Ngo Dinh Diem that supports the orthodox position, notes that Young "can fairly be said to represent the far-left position on Vietnam" (http://bcm.bc.edu/issues/fall_2012/linden_lane/assigned-reading.html). David G. Marr, who likewise cannot be considered a revisionist, notes in his review of Young's book that "Young romanticizes the followers of the Democratic Republic of Vietnam ... and the National Liberation Front, portraying them as if they always treated each other with care and respect, endured endless privations cheerfully, never doubted their cause, never acted brutally." See David G. Marr, review of *The Vietnam Wars, 1945–1990*, by Marilyn B. Young, *Pacific Historical Review* 62, no. 3 (August 1993): 393–95. Not everyone places the Marxist narrative in or near the orthodox camp. Gary Hess calls it "a more radical version of revisionism." See Gary Hess, *Vietnam: Explaining America's Lost War* (Malden, MA, and Oxford: Blackwell, 2009), 47, n.24.

Vietnam. This formulation of counterfactual arguments regarding the Vietnam War becomes even more problematic because revisionists, however strongly they dissent from the orthodox narrative, disagree among themselves about how the war could have been won. They disagree, often very strongly, on which aspects of the American war effort were faulty and on what alternative strategy and tactics were needed to correct those faults. And, inevitably, by offering counterfactuals, revisionist commentators are burdened by arguments that can never be proven. That said, there is a great deal one can point to in terms of faulty judgment and errors made by both civilian and military policy makers who were in charge of America's effort on behalf of South Vietnam to lend credence to the case that viable alternatives existed to what the United States did in Vietnam, and that therefore the mission to defend South Vietnam from Communism could have succeeded there.

Vietnam, the "Lesson of Munich," the Cold War, and Containment

The anchor of the revisionist narrative is its defense of the application of America's Cold War policy containment to Vietnam, a policy dating from the presidency of Harry Truman. The key postulate here is that this commitment cannot be viewed in isolation but only in the international context of the time: that is, containment was a necessary response to a genuine global Communist threat; and, at a time of great peril and uncertainty, Communist initiatives – both Soviet and Chinese – turned Vietnam into one of several Cold War fronts where containment was required. As Guenther Lewy notes in *America in Vietnam* (1978), his groundbreaking defense of America's effort to defend the independence of South Vietnam, from the early days of the Cold War immediately after World War II into the 1960s, "the fear of communism was not an irrational obsession." The post–World War II expansion of Soviet power into central Europe cast what Lewy accurately calls "a menacing shadow over Western Europe" that by 1947 had given the United States good reason to implement containment in the first place. The Communist victory in China in 1949; the Sino-Soviet alliance of February 1950; and, in June of that same year, the invasion by North Korea of South Korea and the resultant Korean War (1950–1953) had by necessity brought containment to Asia. Within a short time, with the support of several Southeast Asian countries and American allies farther afield, containment was extended to Vietnam. This was a reasonable response. The world of the 1950s and early 1960s was highly unstable, a place in which, Lewy asserts, "a Communist victory anywhere appeared to threaten the U.S. because it represented a further extension of Soviet power."[10] In terms of South Vietnam itself, while pointing to the shortcomings of the Diem regime and significant opposition to it, Lewy rejects the orthodox contention that the Communist insurrection arose spontaneously from conditions in the South. As he puts it, and as revisionists generally have agreed, "the decision to begin the armed struggle in the South was made by the Central Committee of the ... communist party of Vietnam, in Hanoi in 1959."[11]

In defending the extension of containment to Vietnam, Lewy does not argue for that country's vital strategic importance to the United States. Indeed, he concedes that the United States exaggerated the geopolitical importance not only of Vietnam but also of Southeast Asia. He is not alone among revisionists in making this point. R. B. Smith, author of the three-volume study *An International History of the Vietnam War*, agrees about Vietnam's place in the world, adding that ultimately not only the Americans but also the Soviets and Chinese attributed to Vietnam "an international significance out of all proportion to its size."[12] C. Dale Walton, author of *The Myth of Inevitable U.S. Defeat in Vietnam* (2002), observes that "there was little about South Vietnam, or even all of Indochina, to indicate that the area was particularly vital to US interests."[13] But, as these and other revisionists point out, the Cold War context raised the stakes involved in what happened to Vietnam well beyond that country itself.

The argument for containment in Vietnam has been made comprehensively by Michael Lind in *Vietnam, The Necessary War: An Interpretation of America's Most Disastrous Military Conflict* (1999). According to Lind, on one level the Cold War "was the third world war of the twentieth century." In particular, it was "a contest for global and military primacy" between the United States and the Soviet Union, the two military superpowers of the second half of that century. More fundamentally, Lind joins with other revisionist scholars in stressing that at its core the Cold War was much more than a geopolitical conflict between the leading military

---

[10] Lewy, *America in Vietnam* 420–21.   [11] Ibid., 15.

[12] R. B. Smith, *An International History of the Vietnam War*, vol. 2, *Kennedy Strategy* (New York: St. Martin's Press, 1985), 1.

[13] C. Dale Walton, *The Myth of Inevitable U.S. Defeat in Vietnam* (London and Portland, OR: Frank Cass, 2002), 18. Walton cites a May 1954 memo from the Joint Chiefs of Staff to Secretary of Defense Charles E. Wilson to this effect.

powers of the age: it was an *ideological* conflict between totalitarian Communist societies led by the Soviet Union and democratic capitalist societies led by the United States, with the Soviet Union committed to a program of global expansionism that would eliminate free societies and make Marxist socialism the world's dominant economic and social system. As Lind puts it, "The Soviet Union was not only a superpower but the headquarters of the global religion of Marxism-Leninism, with zealous adherents in dozens of countries who looked to Moscow not only for military and economic support but for ideological guidance." This ideological commitment to revolutionary Marxism in turn explains why after World War II the Soviet Union, rather than simply establishing a sphere of influence in Eastern Europe, forcibly imposed Communist totalitarian regimes based on the Soviet model throughout that region.[14]

It is worth noting that revisionist scholars writing about Vietnam are hardly alone in affirming this view of the Cold War. Many experts on Soviet history or Marxism with no involvement in the Vietnam debate have argued much the same thing. None has done so more trenchantly than the distinguished historian of Russia Martin Malia. For Malia, the Soviet Union was the fountainhead of international Marxism whose mission was nothing less than world revolution and the destruction of those nations and societies standing in the way of that revolution. This mission gave the Soviet regime, from its founding in 1917, a unique foreign policy that permitted temporary truces but not permanent peace with its capitalist adversaries. Hence the nature of the Cold War, a struggle with the highest possible stakes in which conventional strategic assumptions about defining and defending American national interests did not always apply:

The Cold War ... became the Third World War that never took place. But it was a real world war all the same, with stakes as high as in its two predecessors. Since this war could not be waged in actual battles, it was fought through endless logistical preparations for these non-battles – the increasing refinement of nuclear and conventional weapons, the building of permanent alliances within each bloc, and rival programs of economic aid to Third World clients. Even more of a novelty, this contest was not about tangible national interests. Russia and America certainly had no conflicting territorial or economic interests; and Russia and the states of Western Europe, once partition of the continent had given Moscow an ample security glacis, were in a similar relationship.

The source of the conflict, rather, was ideological, or, in Moscow's terminology, "the international class struggle between the two social systems." Indeed, the

---

[14] Michael Lind, *Vietnam, The Necessary War* (New York: Free Press, 1999), 4–5, 62–66.

Cold War is *the* great example in modern history of the power of "irrational," cultural forces in international affairs ... [T]he Cold War continued the prewar anomaly of Soviet Russia's dual nature as both a sovereign state and the leader of an international revolutionary movement, an anomaly magnified many times over by the Soviet Union's new status as a superpower.[15]

It is against this background that the strategic importance of Vietnam emerges. The "third world war of the twentieth century," Lind notes, aside from its particular ideological component, differed crucially in a military sense from the two world wars that preceded it. This, of course, was because of nuclear weapons, which required the superpowers to avoid a direct military conflict lest they risk a general war and mutual annihilation. That in turn precluded any effort to break the deadlock that by the late 1940s existed in Europe, the "primary front" of the Cold War. Direct confrontations, including proxy wars and other duels of various sorts, therefore had to be relegated to "peripheral areas," one of which turned out to be Indochina, and in particular the country that after 1954 was known as South Vietnam. Indochina was not the only area in Asia that, while peripheral in a conventional strategic sense, became a Cold War battleground. Mao Zedong, the leader of the People's Republic of China (PRC) and thus a speaker of some authority on the subject, argued that there were three Cold War "fronts" in Asia, territories where Communist and non-Communist countries faced each other directly across a contested border: Korea, Taiwan, and Vietnam. And that is precisely what gave them a strategic significance far beyond what they normally would have merited in terms of conventional geographic, economic, military, or political considerations. As Lind observes, "These three regions were not contested because they were important. *They were important because they were contested.*"[16]

As to why, Lind turns for an explanation to the lessons of history and the nature of how states behave in the anarchic international system. Following Norman Podhoretz, author of *Why We Were in Vietnam* (1982), Lind draws on the "lesson of Munich" – a reference to what happened after the 1938 international conference in that German city when the leaders of Great Britain and France attempted to avoid war with Nazi Germany by caving in to Hitler's territorial demands on

---

[15] Martin Malia, *Russia Under Western Eyes: From the Bronze Horseman to the Lenin Mausoleum* (Cambridge, MA: The Belknap Press of Harvard University Press, 1999), 352–54, 359–60.
[16] Lind, *Vietnam, The Necessary War*, 4–5, 64–66.

Czechoslovakia. The catastrophe of appeasement at Munich – the weakness of Europe's leading democracies emboldened Hitler, who soon made additional territorial demands that led directly to World War II – had an impact that outlasted World War II. On several occasions during the Cold War, American leaders, beginning with President Harry Truman, cited Munich and its consequences to justify resisting aggression early. The objective was to act when the possibility of deterrence – as in Greece in 1947 – or at least avoiding a general war – as in the case of Korea in 1950 – still existed, rather than attempting to appease aggressive nations by retreating, only to be forced to fight a major war later under less favorable conditions. This application of the lesson of Munich to South Vietnam, Lind insists, was valid. Lind acknowledges that no analogy of this sort is "perfect" and stresses that in applying the Munich lesson to Vietnam it is not Ho Chi Minh's North Vietnam that plays the role of Hitler's Nazi Germany. That role belongs to North Vietnam's totalitarian sponsors, the Soviet Union and the PRC, which together were attempting to subvert the West wherever they could. Ho himself was merely an ally or client of the two Communist superpowers, much as Franco and Mussolini were to Hitler in the 1930s.[17] Podhoretz sums up this matter well:

In other words, in Vietnam now as in Central Europe then, a totalitarian political force – Nazism then, Communism now – was attempting to expand the area under its control. A relatively limited degree of resistance then would have precluded the need for massive resistance afterward. This was the lesson of Munich, and it already had been applied successfully in Western Europe in the forties and Korea in the fifties. Surely it was applicable to Vietnam as well.[18]

Again, one does not have to rely on revisionist Vietnam historians to back up this assessment. As historian Qiang Zhai documents in *China and the Vietnam Wars, 1950–1975* (2000), China began sending large quantities of aid to Ho's military forces as early as April 1950, just months after the Chinese Communist Party (CCP) won its civil war in China. Mao did so even as he was consolidating his party's rule in China because, Qiang notes, he was "determined to transform not only China but also the world." Nor, as would later happen, was Mao thinking and acting in more radical ways than other CCP leaders. He in fact was following an internal party directive dating from March 1950 that called for the PRC to "assist in every possible way the Communist parties and people in all

---

[17] Ibid., 41–43; Norman Podhoretz, *Why We Were in Vietnam* (New York: Simon and Schuster, 1982), 11–12.
[18] Podhoretz, *Why We Were in Vietnam*, 11.

oppressed nations in Asia to win their liberation." The CCP's second in command, Liu Shaoqi, had already made essentially the same point in a public address delivered in November 1949 to Communists from several countries; its publication in January 1950 in *Pravda*, the official newspaper of the Communist Party of the Soviet Union (CPSU), as Qiang observes, "confirm[ed] Stalin's approval" for all to read. Whatever problems developed later between Communism's two great powers – which in February 1950 signed their Treaty of Friendship, Alliance, and Mutual Assistance – Qiang maintains that there was "an international division of labor within the Communist world at this time." Stalin thus informed Liu in July 1949 that the center of world revolution had moved eastward to Asia, and while the Soviet Union would carry the major burden of promoting revolution in the West, he expected his Chinese comrades to do the same in the colonial and semicolonial countries.[19]

This in turn brings the revisionist case to the argument over the so-called domino theory and the closely related question of the importance of American credibility and the ultimate course of the Cold War. While the actual term "domino theory" was Eisenhower's 1954 metaphor, the concept, and, more significantly, its role in US foreign policy, dates from the years immediately after World War II. The concern that the fall of one country to Communism could precipitate the fall of vulnerable neighboring countries as well was central to President Truman's decisions to support the non-Communist government of Greece against a Communist insurgency in 1947 and to send American troops to defend South Korea after that country was invaded by North Korea in 1950. Today both of those decisions are widely viewed as having been correct, even though neither the Greek nor South Korean governments had serious democratic credentials at the time. Although most orthodox historians in the Vietnam debate reject the domino theory, both with regard to its application during the Cold War in general and to Vietnam in particular, many revisionist historians vigorously defend its validity. They do so with regard to Truman's decision to aid the French in 1950, the far more significant decision to become directly involved in Vietnam by the Eisenhower administration during 1954–1955, and the even more serious decisions in terms of their ultimate impact by both Presidents Kennedy and Johnson that deepened US involvement in the early and mid-1960s.

[19] Qiang Zhai, *China and the Vietnam Wars, 1950–1975* (Chapel Hill and London: University of North Carolina Press, 2000), 20–24.

Thus Mark Moyar, author of *Triumph Forsaken: The Vietnam War, 1954–1965*, points out that when Truman decided to aid the French in Vietnam there already were Communist insurgencies in Malaya, Burma, and Indonesia, and contemporary developments "readily supported the domino theory."[20] Moving forward in time, he adds that had the United States not continued its commitment to South Vietnam in 1965, Laos, Thailand, Burma, and Malaysia were "dominoes likely to fall first," while Cambodia and Indonesia were already "tipping forward." This was a concern not only in Washington but in other national capitals as well. The list of countries at that time supporting American efforts on behalf of South Vietnam included Laos, Thailand, Malaysia, South Korea, the Philippines, Burma, Taiwan (the Republic of China), and India in Asia; most of the countries of the NATO alliance, including Great Britain and West Germany; and, in the Pacific, Australia and New Zealand.[21] Nor does the fact that Thailand, Burma, Malaysia, and Indonesia did not fall to Communism in 1975 when South Vietnam finally succumbed invalidate the domino theory since by then those four countries had evolved to the point where they were strong enough to resist Communist pressures and were, in a sense, no longer dominos. In fact, two small dominoes did fall in 1975, as Communist forces triumphed in both Laos and Cambodia. As Moyar concludes, "An assessment of the domino theory, therefore, demands a close investigation of the dominoes and the would-be topplers in 1965, not 1975."[22]

In the revisionist narrative the domino theory in turn is linked to the broader issue of American credibility, not only in Southeast Asia but also worldwide, and thus to matters of strategic importance in the Cold War as a whole. In terms of Southeast Asia, Smith points out that by the early 1960s an American defeat in Vietnam would have been viewed by other countries in the region "as evidence of a lack of commitment to South-East Asia as a whole." In other words, "What was at stake was not merely the future of South Vietnam but that of Indonesia and the whole region." As for the argument that South Vietnam was the wrong place to demonstrate that commitment, Smith responds – having noted earlier that Truman's "emergency" decision to help the French was made under conditions that were not "the ideal state of affairs" – that in turning to

---

[20] Mark Moyar, *Triumph Forsaken: The Vietnam War, 1954–1965* (New York: Cambridge University Press, 2006), 24.

[21] Ibid., 377–88.

[22] Ibid., 378–79, 388. See also Moyar, "Section III Response," in *Triumph Revisited*, 205.

a strategy of counterinsurgency to defeat Communist guerrillas in South Vietnam, President Kennedy was "responding to a situation where most of the initiative lay with the Communist side." Smith points out that the struggle in Vietnam could have been avoided only "by surrender," an option he notes likewise was available, and rejected, in the case of Korea. Smith therefore concludes that the war in Vietnam was fought because "that was where the challenge arose, at a moment when Kennedy could not ignore that challenge."[23]

Lewy likewise stresses that the issue of credibility actually was global in extent. For example, he argues that along with President Kennedy's promise to defend West Berlin and his stand against the Soviet attempt to station missiles in Cuba, his decision to stand firm in Indochina was meant to demonstrate American resolve and thereby discourage Soviet expansionist pressures elsewhere.[24] The issue of American credibility worldwide being at stake in South Vietnam was well understood by Johnson and his key advisors. One of the best-known and most frequently quoted memos of that era, written in 1965 by Defense Department official John McNaughton, stressed that 70 percent of US aims in Indochina were to "avoid a humiliating US defeat (to our reputation as a guarantor)."[25] Lewy also approaches the importance of credibility in another way. He argues that once three American presidents (Eisenhower, Kennedy, and Johnson) had committed the United States to defending the independence of South Vietnam, that in itself created a vital national interest given the importance of a great power's prestige and credibility.[26] Actually, Henry Kissinger made the same point back in 1969, just as he was assuming the post of national security advisor to Richard Nixon and, with it, the burden of unraveling a knot others had tied. As Kissinger saw it:

But the commitment of 500,000 Americans has settled the issue of the importance of Viet Nam. For what is involved now is the confidence in American promises. However fashionable it is to ridicule the terms "credibility" and "prestige," they are not empty phrases; other nations can gear their actions to ours only if they can count on our steadiness. The collapse of the American effort in Viet Nam would not mollify many critics ... Those whose safety or national goals depend on American commitments could only be dismayed ... Unilateral withdrawal, or

[23] Smith, *An International History of the Vietnam War*, vol. 2, 14, 359; R. B. Smith, *An International History of the Vietnam War*, vol. 1: *Revolution Versus Containment, 1955–1961* (Basingstoke: Macmillan, 1983), 261. The comments on Truman are from vol. 1, 36–38.
[24] Lewy, *America in Vietnam*, 420.   [25] Cited in Lind, *Vietnam: The Necessary War*, 41.
[26] Lewy, *America in Vietnam*, 425.

a settlement which unintentionally amounts to the same thing, could therefore lead to the erosion of restraints and to an even more dangerous international situation. No American policymaker can simply dismiss these dangers.[27]

In Lind's telling, the most important thing at stake for the United States in Vietnam was its credibility as a military power and reliable ally, which had to be demonstrated globally to friend and foe alike. The greatest danger for the United States was that if the Soviet Union and China could enable one of their client states to destroy an American protectorate, they would be "dangerously emboldened" while some American allies and neutral countries would be intimidated and decide their best option was to appease one of the two Communist great powers. This "bandwagon effect" might well have undermined the unity and strength of America's relationship with Great Britain, France, West Germany, and its other democratic allies and thereby negated what Lind calls "the first condition of western success in the Cold War."[28] In particular, West Germany and Japan might have turned to neutrality had they lost faith in America's commitment to defend their fundamental interests. In short, the loss of US credibility and the resultant bandwagon effect could have changed the ultimate resolution of the Cold War as a whole. In this regard Lind concludes:

The Cold War was most likely to end with a rapid and more or less bloodless diplomatic realignment in favor of the superpower that was perceived as the most militarily powerful and most politically determined. We know this is how the Cold War would have ended had the United States lost, because this is how it ended when the Soviet Union lost.[29]

On this point, it is interesting to note the irony that the single most compelling, and dramatic, vindication of the domino theory – and its link with great power credibility – involves not non-Communist states falling one after another to Communism but the very opposite: Communist regimes toppling in rapid succession after one of them succumbed to democracy. This is what happened to the Soviet Union's system of satellite states in Eastern Europe, where Communist dictatorships had been imposed by Stalin in the aftermath of World War II, an act of expansionism that in fact started the Cold War. These regimes never succeeded in winning legitimacy and survived only because they were backed by Soviet

[27] Henry Kissinger, "The Viet Nam Negotiations," *Foreign Affairs* 47, no. 2 (January 1969): 218–19.
[28] Lind, *Vietnam, The Necessary War*, 38–39.
[29] Ibid., 54–58. The quotation is on page 54.

military might. Indeed, it took Soviet threats to preserve Poland's Communist regime on several occasions beginning in 1956 as well as direct military intervention to preserve the Communist regimes in East Germany in 1953, Hungary in 1956, and Czechoslovakia in 1968. Still, whatever its chronic troubles, the Soviet satellite system stood intact for four decades. Then a process of collapse took place over a matter of months during 1989, the so-called Year of the People.

The collapse began, as might have been expected, in Poland, whose Communist regime tottered in April and then collapsed in August in the face of mass popular opposition and the withdrawal of support by Soviet leader Mikhail Gorbachev, who as part of his reform effort at home was determined to end the Soviet Union's long confrontation with the West. Gorbachev's willingness to allow Poland's Communist regime to be swept away simultaneously swept away Soviet credibility as the defender of last resort of any of these satellite regimes, despite the fact that Soviet troops were stationed in every one of them except Romania. The consequences came quickly. The collapse of Communism spread from Poland to Hungary, East Germany, Bulgaria, Czechoslovakia, and, finally, Romania. By the end of December, the entire Soviet system of satellite Communist regimes was gone. The postwar wave of Communist expansion that had given birth to containment four decades earlier finally receded, and since Moscow had made no effort to prevent that reversal, the Cold War was over.

Two other dominoes of sorts, the militant Communist regime in Albania (which rejected both the Soviet and Chinese versions of communism as insufficiently pure) and the neutralist semi-Communist regime in Yugoslavia, remained precariously upright until 1991, when they also fell. By then the Soviet Union, the main block of the system that had supported all the rest, itself was being whittled down into a domino by the combination of its internal weaknesses and Gorbachev's reforms and was beginning to shake and tilt. In December 1991 it keeled over and broke into fifteen parts, the largest of which became the Russian Federation. An imposing and highly symbolic physical domino also went down as part of this continental Communist collapse, the Berlin Wall, which Germans living to its west as well as its east finally breached and began to dismantle on November 9, 1989.

Vietnamese Nationalism, Ho Chi Minh, and Ngo Dinh Diem

One reason the revisionists can justify and defend the application of containment to Vietnam is that they generally reject two key orthodox premises about Vietnamese nationalism. They are that Ho Chi Minh and his Communist colleagues in Vietnam were nationalists first and Communists second and that there was no viable alternative to their version of Vietnamese nationalism.

The first premise, revisionists argue, is inconsistent with the historical record on two counts: Ho Chi Minh's personal career and how under his leadership the Vietnamese Communists treated other Vietnamese political groups. To be sure, Ho, who lived abroad for three decades after 1911, began his political career as a nationalist. However, by 1921 he had become a committed Marxist-Leninist who loyally and without question served the Third International (or Comintern), the worldwide organization of Communist parties controlled from Moscow, as a full-time agent. Ho served the Comintern in several Asian locales before finally returning to his own country during World War II to direct the struggle for Communism there. In fact, in 1930, just a few months after he presided over the formation of the Vietnamese Communist Party, on Comintern orders Ho did the same for fellow Communists from Siam (today, Thailand) and Malaya. For Ho and his colleagues, the struggle to drive the French from Vietnam and then to unite the country under Communist rule was part of a larger and primary effort to promote a world Communist revolution. As Smith points out, the "nationalism" of Ho and his fellow Vietnamese Communists "found expression in a sense of pride that the Vietnamese revolution has been of major historical significance" in the international struggle against capitalism.[30] As for non-Communist Vietnamese nationalist groups, from the early 1920s onward Ho fought them ruthlessly from abroad, and he continued to do so upon his return to Vietnam. This did not change after Ho, always acting on Comintern orders, in 1941 formed the Vietnamese Independence League (Vietminh), a supposedly broad-based organization committed to securing independence from France that in fact was under tight Communist control. Ho and the Vietminh had the blood of tens of thousands of non-Communist Vietnamese nationalists on their hands before they started their rebellion against French colonial rule in December 1946, hardly

---

[30] Smith, *An International History of the Vietnam War*, vol. 1, 10.

a record characteristic of people who were nationalists first and Communists second. The case against the "nationalists first, Communists second" thesis is further strengthened by two sets of policies: what Ho and his colleagues did after their victory over the French and the establishment of North Vietnam in 1954, beginning with their brutal "land reform" campaign that led to the deaths of thousands of peasants; and, after Ho's death, what his successors did after the victory that brought all of Vietnam under their control in 1975.

The second premise likewise does not stand up to the historical record, as there was no shortage of alternatives to the Vietminh's Communism-first version of Vietnamese nationalism. Non-Communist Vietnamese nationalists came in many forms and, to be sure, often were hostile to one another and varied in their popular appeal and long-term viability. What they had in common was a degree of loyalty to traditional Vietnamese society and culture, an attitude the revolutionary Communists, with their determination to bring a totally new way of life to Vietnam, did not share. That the Vietminh considered some of these rival political groups serious potential challengers, in contrast to what many orthodox historians have maintained, is demonstrated by the reign of terror and murder Ho's minions waged against their non-Communist nationalist countrymen during 1945 and 1946, before the war of independence against the French.

In considering America's involvement in Vietnam, the key question with regard to Vietnamese nationalism is whether any of the South Vietnamese regimes after 1954, beginning with that of Ngo Dinh Diem, were viable. Historian Keith W. Taylor has observed that the "war of 1955–1975 was a war between two Vietnamese versions of the future of the country," and he is among those who argue that the non-Communist version that existed in South Vietnam during those years was both legitimate and had a chance of success.[31] Others – from Pulitzer Prize–winning journalist Marguerite Higgins, who covered events in Vietnam from the early 1950s to the mid-1960s; to historian Ellen Hammer, one of the first American scholars to become a specialist on Vietnamese history back in the 1950s; to William Colby, who served in South Vietnam in several major civilian positions, knew Diem well, and eventually headed the CIA; to historian Mark Moyar, author of *Triumph Forsaken* – have over the years provided considerable evidence

[31] Keith W. Taylor, "The Vietnamese Civil War in Historical Perspective," in *Triumph Revisited*, 18, 27. The quotation is on page 18.

for the viability of the Diem regime in particular and/or that of non-Communist Vietnamese nationalism in general. Diem himself, whatever his flaws, far from being a rigid and inept reactionary isolated from the Vietnamese people, emerges in these authors' discussions as a genuine nationalist and modernizer who understood South Vietnam and the problems it faced better than his American critics. Interestingly, Moyar cites recent scholarship by orthodox historians who have focused on Diem and his regime, while acknowledging that their ultimate conclusions differ from his, to back up his positive assessment of Diem and the regime he led.[32]

Any assessment of the viability of the Diem regime must consider the origins of the Communist insurgency against it that began in the late 1950s. The revisionist position on the question of the origins of the insurgency in South Vietnam is reasonably well summed up by the title of a State Department white paper issued in 1965: *Aggression from the North: The Record of North Vietnam's Campaign to Conquer South Vietnam*. The case that the insurgency was initiated and controlled by Hanoi from the very beginning has been made repeatedly, more recently with the benefit of new and formidable documentation from Communist sources, by revisionist commentators from Guenter Lewy to Mark Moyar.[33]

The subject of non-Communist and anti-Communist Vietnamese nationalism through Ngo Dinh Diem's time in power will be reviewed in greater detail in Chapters 3 and 4. Later governments, in particular the one led by Nguyen Van Thieu, will be discussed in subsequent chapters.

---

[32] See Marguerite Higgins, *Our Vietnam Nightmare: The Story of U.S. Involvement in the Vietnamese Tragedy with Thoughts on a Future Policy* (New York: Harper and Row, 1965); Ellen Hammer, *A Death in November: America in Vietnam, 1963* (New York: E. P. Dutton, 1987); William Colby, *Lost Victory: A Firsthand Account of America's Sixteen-Year Involvement in Vietnam* (Chicago: Contemporary Books, 1989); and Moyar, *Triumph Forsaken*. For more recent and more positive overviews of Diem than the entirely negative one-dimensional view normally provided by orthodox historians, see Philip E. Catton, *Diem's Final Failure: Prelude to America's War in Vietnam* (Lawrence: University Press of Kansas, 2002) and Edward Miller, *Misalliance: Ngo Dinh Diem, the United States, and the Fate of South Vietnam* (Cambridge, MA: Harvard University Press, 2013).

[33] United State Department of State, *Aggression from the North: The Record of North Vietnam's Campaign to Conquer South Vietnam* (Washington, DC: US Department of State Publication 7839, Far Eastern Series 130, February 1965); Lewy, *America in Vietnam*, 10–18; Moyar, *Triumph Forsaken*, 79–86.

The American Military Effort in Vietnam

As already noted, revisionist commentators often disagree on how the United States should have fought the Vietnam War. They cite a variety of military errors the United States allegedly made in Vietnam, sometimes disagreeing about what they were and, if in agreement on that point, assigning different levels of importance to errors they agree were made. While this complicates any effort to explain how the United States could have been successful in its military effort, it does not invalidate the thesis that the war could have been won at a cost far less than was incurred in defeat. Perhaps more to the point, there is not necessarily only one strategy that can be used to win a given war. For example, at various points during World War II several military strategies were available to the United States and its allies to achieve victory, in both the European and Pacific theaters. This was understood at the time and remains the prevailing outlook in retrospect. It also is generally accepted that had the Allies made certain strategic errors – or had Nazi Germany avoided certain strategic errors – the war could have ended differently, with dreadful implications for freedom in the world. As Richard Overy has stressed, "Though from today's perspective the Allied victory might seem somehow inevitable, the conflict was poised on a knife's edge in the middle years of the war."[34] One might add that Overy's "knife's edge" observation can be applied to many other wars, including World War I, the American war of independence, and the US Civil War. In the case of Vietnam, a strong case can be made that, first, the overall American strategic approach to the war was seriously flawed and, second, there were a variety of options that the United States did not take that plausibly could have brought success. Thus C. Dale Walton argues in *The Myth of Inevitable Defeat in Vietnam* that "there were *numerous* roads to victory, but ... Washington chose none of them."[35] The result, according to military historian and Army lieutenant colonel Robert E. Morris, was "one of the most inept military campaigns in history."[36]

---

[34] Richard Overy, *Why the Allies Won* (New York: Norton, 1996), 325. Overy also notes that to win World War II "the Allies had to learn to fight more effectively," an observation that can easily be applied to Vietnam. With regard to individual battles, with the battles of Midway and Stalingrad in mind, Overy writes, "Battles are not preordained. If they were, no one would bother to fight them." See pages 317 and 320.

[35] Walton, *The Myth of Inevitable U.S. Defeat in Vietnam*, 2.

[36] Robert E. Morris, "Why We Lost the War in Vietnam: An Analysis," in *The Real Lessons of the Vietnam War: Reflections Twenty-Five Years After the Fall of Saigon*, eds. John Norton Moore and Robert F. Turner (Durham: Carolina Academic Press, 2002), 385.

The Rationalist Approach, Systems Analysis, Graduated Pressure, and Gradual Escalation

In the welter of disagreement that characterizes the revisionist analysis of the American military effort in Vietnam, the premise that probably enjoys the most support is that the policy of gradual escalation, the approach to the war followed under President Lyndon Johnson, was a fatal and inexcusable blunder. Gradual escalation was the fundamental principle that guided American military policy after the overthrow of the Diem regime in 1963. Indeed, to the extent the United States had a strategy for fighting in Vietnam, gradual escalation was it. It evolved out of the concept of "limited war," a popular concept among social scientists and academics during the 1950s and 1960s, in large part because of the understandable fear that a military conflict between nuclear powers could lead to a total war of nuclear annihilation. Crises therefore had to be prevented from escalating out of control. Limited war, like any other doctrine, came in many versions, and it did not necessarily imply the policy of gradualism ultimately used in Vietnam. For example, General Mathew Ridgway, a World War II veteran who led U.N. forces in Korea after 1951 and who later became the US Army chief of staff, thought of limited war as nonnuclear war. In his view, and to many others of similar mind, there was no contradiction between fighting a limited war while also using decisive military force to achieve the desired objectives. In sharp contrast, as political scientist Christopher M. Gacek points out, certain civilian writers argued for strategies "in which the means used in war were kept below a specified level and decisive military victory was not necessarily achieved or sought."[37]

Prominent civilian limited war advocates often drew heavily on what is known as systems analysis: studying the purposes and goals of an

---

[37] Christopher M. Gacek, *The Logic of Force: The Dilemma of Limited War in American Foreign Policy* (New York: Columbia University Press, 1994), 143–44. Total war is a conflict in which the entire resources and populations of the combatants are committed to winning a complete victory, with the result that the distinction between civilian and soldier is eliminated and the former become legitimate military targets. It is a term that most frequently is applied to the two world wars of the twentieth century. Military historians agree that, with a few exceptions, pre-twentieth-century wars were limited wars. The fear after World War II was that a total, or nuclear, war between the United States and the Soviet Union would destroy civilization. See Hugh Bicheno, "Total War," *The Oxford Companion to Military History*, eds. Richard Holmes, Hew Strachan, and Chris Bellamy (Oxford: Oxford University Press, 2001). Available online at www.oxfordreference.com.ezproxy.bu.edu/view/10.1093/acref/9780198606963.001.0001/acref-9780198606963-e-1290?rskey= ue99ht&result=1304

institution or procedure to create systems that will achieve those objectives efficiently. Systems analysis in turn draws heavily from the economic concept of "cost-benefit analysis." The result of applying systems analysis to matters of war is what defense analyst Gregory Palmer calls the "rationalist approach" to national defense policy. The most influential advocate of this way of thinking in the government was Secretary of Defense Robert McNamara, who brought several limited war theorists to the Pentagon when he took office in 1961. These theorists argued that actors in a military conflict acted rationally. This meant that they could be restrained by a limited use of force that, as it was increased in a precisely calibrated and focused manner, would demonstrate to them that promoting a conflict was against their interests. This cost-benefit analysis mode of thinking therefore would allow the United States to apply "maximum pressure with minimum risk" on North Vietnam. The object of this gradually increasing pressure, Palmer explains, was to "affect the calculations of future costs and benefits being made in Hanoi in a way that the best possible ratio of costs and benefits would be obtained by ceasing to support the Vietcong."[38] In other words, McNamara and his colleagues in Washington assumed that the Communist leaders in Hanoi thought and made decisions about their effort to conquer South Vietnam in the same way as American bureaucrats did in managing the Pentagon. Therefore by gradually increasing military pressure, initially through the use of air power and then, when that did not produce the desired results, by introducing US combat forces into the mix (although air attacks on North Vietnam clearly remained the main method of applying pressure on Ho Chi Minh and his colleagues), Washington could convince Hanoi that the cost of its effort to conquer South Vietnam outweighed the benefits of

---

[38] Gregory Palmer, *The McNamara Strategy and the Vietnam War: Program Budgeting in the Pentagon, 1960–1968* (Westport, CT and London: Greenwood Press, 1978), 3–7, 108–12. The basis of McNamara's war planning was the Planning Programming Budgeting System that he brought to the Pentagon upon becoming secretary of defense in 1961. It was based on the thinking of a small group of economists at the Rand Corporation who are sometimes referred to as "the defense economists." See Palmer, pages 3–7. See also Mark Moyar, *Triumph Forsaken*, 306. Moyar mentions Thomas Schelling's *Strategy of Conflict* (Cambridge, MA: Harvard University Press, 1960) as the "most influential" book produced by limited war theorists. Shelling was a professor at Harvard University at the time. Colonel Harry G. Summers calls a volume published about a decade later, Alain C. Enthoven and K. Wayne Smith *How Much Is Enough? Shaping the Defense Program, 1961–1969* (Santa Monica, CA: RAND, 1971), the "bible of the limited war theorists." See Harry G. Summers Jr., *On Strategy: A Critical Analysis of the Vietnam War* (New York: Dell, 1982), 77.

unifying Vietnam under Communist rule. Having reached that conclusion Hanoi would abandon that effort.

McNamara's approach to the war in Vietnam grew out of his jaundiced view of traditional military thinking. As military historian Lieutenant General H. R. McMaster has noted, McNamara and his advisors were "convinced that traditional military conceptions of the use of force were irrelevant to contemporary strategic and political realities." McNamara's confidence that he and other civilian advocates of what he called "graduated pressure" in Vietnam were better qualified to craft a strategy for coping with the situation there was reinforced by the Kennedy administration's handling of the Cuban Missile Crisis of 1962. In particular President Kennedy had rejected military advice from the Joint Chiefs of Staff for an attack against Soviet missiles being installed in Cuba in favor of blockading Cuba and gradually increasing the pressure on Soviet leaders in Moscow, an approach that McNamara and other top Kennedy advisors argued was the key to the peaceful resolution of the crisis. McNamara's assessment of the Cuban Missile Crisis has merits, although some scholars assign less credit to graduated pressure for resolving the crisis than does McNamara.[39] Whatever one's assessment of that crisis, McNamara apparently did not allow two important considerations to influence his assessment of what would work for the United States in Vietnam: first, that the Cuban Missile Crisis was a diplomatic confrontation in which the goal was to defuse a crisis and avoid a nuclear war while in Vietnam a war involving conventional and guerrilla forces already was

[39] H. R. McMaster, *Dereliction of Duty: Lyndon Johnson, Robert McNamara, the Joint Chiefs of Staff, and the Lies That Led to Vietnam* (New York: HarperCollins, 1997), 62; Moyar, *Triumph Forsaken*, pp. 306–7. Moyar's sources on this point are two books published in the mid-1990s: Vladislav Zubok and Constantine Pleshakov, *Inside the Kremlin's Cold War: From Stalin to Khrushchev* (Cambridge, MA and London: Harvard University Press, 1996) and Aleksandr Fursenko, *"'One Hell of a Gamble': Khrushchev, Castro, and Kennedy, 1958–1964* (New York and London: Norton, 1997). McNamara's recounting of his own role in the Cuban Missile Crisis is not consistent with some important evidence: the tape recordings of the meetings of the ExComm, the committee of top officials that Kennedy formed to advise him during the crisis. See Sheldon M. Stern, *The Cuban Missile Crisis in American Memory: Myth Versus Reality* (Stanford: Stanford University Press, 2012). Stern, formerly the historian at the John F. Kennedy Library and the leading expert on the tapes, characterizes McNamara's conduct and advice during those meetings as "erratic and inconsistent" (56). McNamara's exact phrase was "Graduated Overt Military Pressure." See Robert McNamara, "Memo for the President," March 16, 1964, *The Pentagon Papers: The Defense Department History of United States Decisionmaking on Vietnam,* Senator Gravel Edition (Boston: Beacon Press, 1972): 1: 499–510.

going on; and, second, that the relationship of the Soviet Union to Cuba and the Soviet stake in keeping nuclear missiles in Cuba bore no resemblance to relationship between North Vietnam and South Vietnam and North Vietnam's determination to control all of Vietnam. Rather, the outlook of McNamara and his colleagues was as described in 1970 by Cyrus Vance, who held high positions under both Kennedy and Johnson: "We had seen the gradual application of force applied in the Cuban Missile Crisis and had seen a very successful result. We believed that, if this same gradual and restrained application of force were applied in South Vietnam, that one could expect the same result."[40]

McNamara was not entirely without professional military support for his policy of graduated pressure. His most important backer by far was General Maxwell Taylor, who served as chairman of the Joint Chiefs of Staff under Kennedy and Johnson from 1962 to 1964 and then as ambassador to South Vietnam from 1964 to 1965.[41] Taylor in effect became an advocate of limited war during the 1950s when he criticized the Eisenhower policy of relying on the threat of massive nuclear retaliation to contain the Soviet Union. Taylor advocated what he called "flexible response," which meant having sufficient conventional military forces available to meet Soviet challenges at any level to ensure that no conflict or crisis would escalate into a disastrous nuclear exchange. Among the American politicians Taylor impressed was Senator John F. Kennedy, and flexible response became the term that Kennedy would use when he became president in 1961 to describe his overall strategy for containing Communism. That said, McMaster points out that flexible response as initially conceived did not mandate graduated pressure when dealing with a particular military crisis; rather, it advocated applying military force at a necessary and appropriate level. In contrast, graduated pressure meant beginning the application of force at a low level and gradually increasing its scale and intensity. While Taylor's advice changed as the situation changed in Vietnam, his notion of applying flexible response to Vietnam during the 1960s generally paralleled McNamara's notion of graduated pressure, a position that put him out of step with the other Joint Chiefs. Thus in 1965,

---

[40] Quoted in McMaster, *Dereliction of Duty*, 62.
[41] Taylor compiled a distinguished record during World War II, including commanding the Army's 101st Airborne Division. He served in Korea and as army chief of staff from 1955 to 1959. His book, *The Uncertain Trumpet* (1960), outlined his critique of massive retaliation and ideas about flexible response.

according to the *New York Times*, Taylor stated that "our objective is limited – namely, to oblige Hanoi, to persuade Hanoi, to desist in its efforts to maintain an insurgency." A year later he testified at a Senate hearing that rather than trying to defeat North Vietnam the United States was trying to "cause them to mend their ways."[42]

When it came to defending South Vietnam from Communism in practice, the rationalist approach to war and its corollary graduated pressure gave birth to gradual escalation. Gradual escalation was the policy of the Johnson administration beginning in 1965 once it committed US forces to fighting directly in Vietnam, a policy that lasted amid stalemate and criticism until 1968. One of the most effective and best-known critics of the rationalist approach to war in general and its offspring of gradual escalation in Vietnam in particular is Colonel Harry Summers. Summers's critique of the American effort in Vietnam is based on the ideas of the renowned nineteenth-century German military thinker Carl von Clausewitz (and in particular his classic treatise *On War*). Summers grants that McNamara's system of running the Pentagon, officially known as the Planning, Programming, and Budgeting System (PPBS), was useful as a means of making the Defense Department more efficient in managing its resources, that is, in preparing for war. The trouble is that the PPBS approach was "only half the equation." Summers stresses the crucial distinction between what Clausewitz called "preparation for war" and "war proper" and argues that while PPBS was "efficient in structuring forces in preparing for war, it was neither designed for, nor was it capable of, fighting the war itself."[43] Clausewitz had no use for theorists who "aimed to equip the conduct of war with principles, rules, or even systems, and thus considered only factors that could be mathematically calculated (e.g., numerical superiority; supply; the base; interior lines)." He argued that rules and systems do not work because "they aim at fixed values. In war everything is uncertain and variable, intertwined with psychological forces and effects, and the product of a continuous interaction of opposites." Yet rules and systems were the basis for what Summers calls "the theory of graduated response," which he states had "a devastating effect" on the US military effort in Vietnam.[44]

[42] Taylor quoted in Gacek, *Logic of Force*, 198 and 143; McMaster, *Dereliction of Duty*, 74.

[43] Summers, *On Strategy*, 75.

[44] Ibid., 74, 80–82, 163. Summers uses a different translation of the Clausewitz's work than the one cited here. I have used this one, which comes from the translation of *On War* by

Other revisionist commentators have pointed out the same thing with different words. According to Robert E. Morris, gradual escalation "violated a fundamental precept of waging war," which, he argues, is to dislocate and destroy the willpower of the enemy. Military strategy, Morris continues, must be designed "to meet the enemy with overwhelming force ... [that] finally destroys their will to fight." But gradual escalation meant that the United States did not employ the force required to break North Vietnam's will to fight. America's gradual increase in its use of force enabled North Vietnam to engage in "a total effort that matched our buildup."[45] And that, according to Admiral U. S. Grant Sharpe, who was in overall command of US forces in the Pacific (including Vietnam) from 1964 to 1968, was why graduated pressure under President Johnson failed. Sharpe complains that American military leaders during the war "were never allowed to move decisively with our tremendous air and naval power." It was, he continues, "folly" for the United States to commit troops to combat and then not use the means it had to win an "early victory." Instead of using the means that could have produced such a victory, the United States "increased the pressure on North Vietnam in a series of nibbles that permitted them to build up their defenses and to anticipate every move we made." Or as General Philip Davidson, who served from 1967 to 1969 as chief US intelligence officer in South Vietnam, has noted, the policy of gradualism "played into the hands of Giap [Vo Nguyen Giap, North Vietnam's leading general and strategist] and his strategy of revolutionary war." It allowed Giap to prolong the war, strengthen North Vietnam's forces, and at the same time erode American morale and will. As for the "signals" the United States assumed it was sending to Hanoi, in fact they were read there as a "sign of weakness or lack of national resolve." At home, as the war dragged on, these "signals" helped convince the American people that the war was

---

Michael Howard and Peter Paret (Princeton: Princeton University Press, 1976, 84) because I believe it is clearer. It may be found online at The Clausewitz Homepage (www .clausewitz.com/readings/Cquotations.htm). Summers's translation of these passages is on page 82 of *On Strategy*.

[45] Robert E. Morris, "Why We Lost the War in Vietnam," 390–91. It is important to understand that there is no contradiction between the use of overwhelming force and another classic principle of warfare, what Gregory Palmer, following Clausewitz, calls "economy of force." It states that the "minimum possible force should be used in obtaining an objective." See Gregory Palmer, *The McNamara Strategy*, 18–19. The problem is that gradual escalation made it impossible to achieve victory and over time forced the United States to resort to more and more force in a fruitless endeavor.

unwinnable and should be abandoned.[46] Dale Walton, in discussing the air campaign against North Vietnam, argues that by attempting to implement "the seemingly elegant theory of graduated pressure, US policy makers outsmarted themselves" because they did not attack the appropriate targets and thereby hamstrung the entire effort.[47]

McMaster makes an important point by viewing graduated pressure from the North Vietnamese side. He points out that while McNamara and his colleagues considered the carefully calibrated and therefore limited bombing raids on North Vietnam to be a form of "coercion and communication short of war," to Ho and his comrades those attacks were acts of war. And war, McMaster stresses, following Summers's use of Clausewitz against systems analysis, "unleashes a dynamic that defies systems analysis quantification." In this case, McMaster observes, "linear thinking" prevented McNamara and his systems analysis advisors from understanding that they might not be able to predict the enemy's reaction to graduated pressure, and hence the future course of events.[48] Interestingly, in 1969 General Giap himself echoed this critique when he noted that US strategy was based on "arithmetic." American strategists, he said, "question the computers, add and subtract, extract square roots, and then go into action." The problem for them was that "arithmetical strategy doesn't work here. If it did, they'd already have exterminated us."[49] As it turned out, McMaster concludes, North Vietnam's response to Washington's carefully calibrated graduated pressure during 1964 and 1965 – the infiltration of full divisions of the North Vietnamese army into South Vietnam – forced the United States to commit its own combat troops to the struggle, "precisely the action that graduated pressure was designed to avoid."[50]

---

[46] U. S. Grant Sharpe, *Strategy for Defeat: Vietnam in Retrospect* (San Rafael and London: Presidio Press, 1978), 2; Phillip B. Davidson, *Vietnam at War: The History, 1946–1975* (New York and Oxford: Oxford University Press, 1988), 806–7.

[47] Walton, *The Myth of Inevitable US Defeat in Vietnam*, 110.

[48] McMaster, "Crack in the Foundation: Defense Transformation and the Underlying Assumption of Dominant Knowledge in Future War," Center for Strategic Leadership. U.S. Army War College (November 2003, Volume SO3-03), 77–78.

[49] Quoted in James S. Robbins, *This Time We Win: Revisiting the Tet Offensive* (New York and London: Encounter Books, 2010), 40. Regarding McNamara and his systems analysis experts, Robbins quotes John P. Roach, a special advisor to President Johnson from 1966 to 1968, to the effect "the problem with McNamara and Co. was that they could never distinguish between a war and a war game" (32).

[50] McMaster, "Crack in the Foundation," 78.

It is ironic as well as instructive to read what Taylor had to say on this subject once the war had continued into the 1970s. By 1972 he was having what may be called "second thoughts" about gradualism. In his memoir (*Swords and Plowshares*, 1972), published before the United States withdrew its last combat forces from Vietnam, Taylor wrote, "carefully controlled violence ... ended by defeating its own purposes. Designed to limit the dangers of expanded war, it ended by assuring a prolonged war which carried with it the dangers of expansion." He added that gradualism "violated the military principles of surprise and mass as means to gain prompt success with minimum loss." In short, long before McNamara repudiated his approach to the Vietnam War by penning *In Retrospect*, Taylor in his memoir acknowledged the shortcomings of gradual escalation.[51] Commenting on how graduated escalation was actually implemented, Robert E. Morris takes the critique of that strategy one step further. He argues that in fact US policy was not, as advertised, "even gradual escalation; that is, a progressive and increasing application of force to strangle the enemy." Rather it was a policy of "escalation and de-escalation, an 'on again, off again' knee-jerk reaction that varied with the intuitive whims of President Johnson and his advisors."[52] And those shortcomings, as Admiral Sharpe put it succinctly when he chose the title of his book on the war, were what made graduated escalation in Vietnam a "strategy for defeat."

Gradual Escalation, Tet, Vietnamization, and the Abandonment of Vietnam

Gradual escalation and the events that occurred after it was abandoned will be covered in detail later in this volume. Although gradual escalation, which lasted from 1965 until 1968, had many facets, its two main pillars were the Rolling Thunder bombing campaign against North Vietnam (officially: Operation Rolling Thunder) and the search and destroy ground campaign against Communist forces in South Vietnam. Revisionist commentators generally agree on the faults of Rolling Thunder and on the reasons it failed, with the main culprits being President Johnson and

---

[51] Quoted in Gacek, 400. Gacek notes that Taylor did not abandon the concept of limited war. That, however, is not a contradiction, as the views of General Matthew Ridgeway, among others, clearly demonstrate that limited war and gradualism in applying the use of force are far from the same thing.

[52] Morris, "Why We Lost the War in Vietnam," 391.

Secretary of Defense McNamara and the restrictions they placed on that campaign. Such a consensus does not exist with regard to search and destroy, which was devised by General William Westmoreland, commander of the Military Assistance Command, Vietnam (MACV) and therefore the commander of US forces in South Vietnam from 1964 to 1968. Instead, a variety of positions exist between two poles – one arguing that search and destroy did not respond properly to what was primarily a guerrilla insurgency and the other that it did not respond properly to what was primarily a conventional invasion – that in many ways are diametrically opposed to each other. A revisionist consensus emerges again regarding the 1968 Tet Offensive: that an overwhelming US/South Vietnamese military victory which should have been exploited was turned into a political defeat that in turn badly undermined the US effort in Vietnam. There is also a general, though hardly unanimous, consensus regarding Vietnamization, the overall policy of the Nixon administration from 1969 through the signing of the Paris Peace Accords in January 1973 that included the gradual withdrawal of US combat troops from South Vietnam. It is that in the wake of the Tet victory and by employing different tactics, the new team on the ground in South Vietnam of MACV commander General Creighton Abrams, Ambassador Ellsworth Bunker, and Bunker's deputy in charge of pacification William Colby achieved considerable success and that by 1972 the military and political situation favored the South Vietnamese government. However, because of what transpired beginning in 1973, following the title of Colby's book, the improved situation that existed in 1972 by 1975 was turned into a *Lost Victory*. Victory was lost because after Nixon's resignation the United States cut its support of the South Vietnamese government to the point where it was unable to bear the burden of resisting renewed North Vietnamese aggression, which was lavishly backed by the Soviet Union. In other words, as many revisionists put it, the United States "abandoned" South Vietnam. The result, and the title of the definitive book on the subject by George J. Veith (*Black April: The Fall of South Vietnam, 1973–1975*) was "Black April": the collapse of the South Vietnamese government and the unification of Vietnam under a one-party dictatorship that rules there to this day.

2

Vietnam 101: Origins to 1946

The debate over the American effort in Vietnam has a feature rarely, if ever, found when discussing modern wars: while inevitably focused on the period from 1954 to 1975, this debate also involves looking back two millennia in the history of the Vietnamese people. One reason for this journey into the distant past, which may seem an irrelevant digression to those new to the subject, is the widely accepted portrayal of the Vietnamese as a people who for centuries resisted Chinese aggression and/or attempts at assimilation and in the process forged a national identity with a powerful tradition of fiercely opposing any and all foreign efforts to compromise their independence.[1] With regard to the Vietnam War, this heroic David versus Goliath narrative implicitly supports the orthodox argument that the United States, as part of its worldwide effort to contain Communism, erred by intervening in what essentially was an internal fight in a country whose people were intensely averse to interference by foreigners. This error presumably was compounded by the fact that in siding with the non-Communist South Vietnamese, the United States was supporting the weaker side in that struggle. Orthodox commentators then often link this presumed US error to how they assess the relationship between Communism and nationalism in Vietnam and therefore to what they see as another mistake: the failure to recognize the true nature of Vietnamese Communism as led by Ho Chi Minh. They stress that immediately after World War II and subsequently during the Cold War, it was local Communists who led the struggle against the foreign

---

[1] For example, George Herring states in the first chapter of *America's Longest War*, "the Vietnamese during much of this millennium [approximately 208 BC to AD 939] fiercely resisted the rule of their larger northern neighbor." Herring, *America's Longest War*, 4.

presence in Vietnam. Between 1946 and 1954 Vietnamese Communists fought against France, which was trying to retain de facto colonial control of Vietnam, and between 1954 and 1975 against the United States, which in effect was preventing the unification of Vietnam by supporting a weak and illegitimate non-Communist regime in the southern half of the country. Impressed by this effort and by the strength of the Communists as opposed to the weakness of their opponents, orthodox commentators tend to conclude that Vietnamese Communism was the only legitimate expression of Vietnamese nationalism during those years.[2] They therefore argue that the United States erred, to its detriment and to the great misfortune of Vietnam, by not recognizing that fundamental reality.

Revisionists challenge the validity of this narrative. To be sure, the saga of steadfast Vietnamese resistance to constant pressure from mighty China and their resultant national identity that proved impervious to accepting any foreign rule does draw on actual events scattered throughout a historical record of two millennia. And between 1946 and 1975 Vietnamese Communists did lead the struggle in their country against, first, French colonialism and, next, American anti-Communism. But these facts constitute only threads and patches of the complete historical tapestry, and revisionists justifiably argue that by themselves, and in the absence of other pertinent information, they constitute an inaccurate picture of the historical record.

With regard to Vietnam and China, a thorough examination of that long relationship reveals its complexity and, most notably, that it involved significant benefits to the Vietnamese as well as hardships. Indeed, Chinese influence was central to the development of the culture and identity of the Vietnamese people. Furthermore, the Vietnamese, far from always battling outside interference, at times not only allowed but invited China, and at times other foreign powers, to intervene in their domestic affairs, most notably during disputes between rival claimants to their country's throne. Turning to Vietnamese identity, there has not consistently been what can be called one Vietnam or one vision of how Vietnamese life should be organized; indeed, after 1500 for about two centuries there were, at least de facto, two Vietnamese kingdoms with decidedly different ways of life.

---

[2] For example, see Moss, *Vietnam: An American Ordeal*, 28–29. In discussing the events of late 1945, Moss says that with the coup by the Vietminh in August 1945, the "Vietnamese people had reclaimed their national identity" after eighty years of French and Japanese colonialism. He then bemoans the failure of the United States to support the Vietminh by arguing, "If there ever was a time when Washington could have aligned itself with the forces of Vietnamese nationalism, it failed to grasp it."

Not coincidentally, the border between those kingdoms ran very close to the 17th parallel, the line that divided North and South Vietnam between 1954 and 1975. Finally, the claim that Vietnamese Communism as formulated by Ho Chi Minh and his comrades represented the only legitimate or viable form of Vietnamese nationalism from the mid-1940s through the mid-1970s is contradicted by the actual history of Vietnamese nationalism as it evolved during the twentieth century. Vietnamese nationalism came in a variety of forms; while the Communists excelled when it came to organization, propaganda skills, and military prowess, those qualities are hardly a reasonable basis on which to crown one political movement with legitimacy at the expense of rival movements whose agendas may have more closely corresponded to the overall interests and desires of the people of Vietnam.

THE VIETNAMESE AND CHINA

The Vietnamese under Chinese Rule

The Vietnamese people have spent their entire history living under the shadow of China. Their original homeland placed them cheek by jowl with the Chinese. It centered on the Red River plain along the Gulf of Tonkin, which amounts to approximately the northern quarter of the area that currently makes up Vietnam. When Vietnam later expanded southward, that region was referred to as Tonkin, with the central part of the country known as Annam and the far south as Cochinchina. The arrival in the Tonkin region of the Chinese from the north about three millennia ago meant that the people of the Red River delta – who are most accurately described as proto-Vietnamese – found themselves living next to a giant that was by far the most powerful and advanced society in East Asia. From the first quarter of the second century BC to AD 939, the Vietnamese lived under the control of Chinese states, which were either centralized dynastic empires or regional kingdoms during times of Chinese disunity. The first Chinese state to rule over the Vietnamese, known as Nam Viet (Chinese: Nam Yu), was in fact a regional state that emerged under the leadership of a Chinese general in the wake of the collapse of the China's Qin dynasty (221–206 BC).[3] Nam Viet controlled territory on both sides of the current Chinese/Vietnamese border and had a composite Chinese/Vietnamese

---

[3] Nam Viet means "land of the southern Viets," with the term "Viets" referring to tribes that at the time lived in what today is southern China.

population. Its capital was near today's Chinese city of Guangzhou. Chinese imperial rule came to the Vietnamese when Nam Viet was incorporated into the Chinese empire by the Han dynasty in 111 BC, that is, when the Chinese Empire conquered a Chinese regional state.

In any event, as noted earlier, living under Chinese rule for a millennium does not mean that the Vietnamese were always in conflict with their Chinese overlords or that they developed a particularly powerful tendency to resist foreign interference in their affairs because of that presumed conflict. Indeed, one does not have to be a revisionist commentator on the Vietnam War to make that point. For example, David G. Marr, an expert on Vietnamese resistance to French colonial rule, while noting the "major strains" in the relationship between Vietnam and China, also points out: "A more general account of Sino-Vietnamese contacts would certainly give attention to many decades – even full centuries – when all was peaceful and the benefits to the Vietnamese were quite considerable in such areas as commerce, tributary exchange, and educational, administrative, and technological acculturation."[4] Marr adds that Chinese influence was much stronger among the Vietnamese elite than among the peasant masses and that the Vietnamese elite made use of Chinese traditions and institutions to control the masses over whom they ruled. This included Confucianism, and as in China, the Vietnamese governing elite, or scholar-gentry, was chosen almost exclusively from members of the landlord class who had passed rigorous examinations based on Confucian texts. Marr thus finds it "no surprise" that during times of political turmoil and fragmentation some of those struggling for power would turn to the Chinese for help.[5]

Keith Weller Taylor is the revisionist scholar who has done the most to provide a corrective to the conventional account of a heroic and united Vietnamese people forging and preserving their identity and ultimately establishing their independence in the face of centuries of Chinese pressure and aggression. A Vietnam veteran, Taylor has served as chair of the Department of Asian Studies at Cornell University and is one of the world's preeminent scholars of early Vietnamese history. His monograph *The Birth of Vietnam* (1983), which covers that history from the third century BC to the tenth century AD, is widely regarded as the standard work on the formative period in the history of the Vietnamese

---

[4] David G. Marr, *Vietnamese Anticolonialism, 1885–1925* (Berkeley: University of California Press, 1971), 17.
[5] Ibid., 20.

people, and his more recent *A History of the Vietnamese* (2013) likewise has been highly praised, with one reviewer calling it "by a wide margin, the finest general survey of Vietnamese history ever produced in any language."[6]

In Taylor's view, a fundamental point about Vietnamese history is that the modern Vietnamese people exist not in spite of centuries of pressure from China but in part because of their lengthy interaction with China. Far from the Vietnamese forming their national identity in the process of resisting the Chinese, "Vietnamese history as we know it today could not exist without Chinese history." The Vietnamese traditionally trace their roots to people who lived in and around the Red River plain before the arrival of the Chinese from the north. While that may be true to some extent in a strictly genetic sense, what Taylor calls "the distinctive features of Vietnamese culture," and therefore what may be considered the modern Vietnamese people, do not date from that early period. Taylor stresses that the people who lived on the Red River plain before the arrival of the Chinese and the people who lived there 1,000 years later "would surely have been unrecognizable and unintelligible to each other." During that millennium the local culture was transformed by the influence and presence of the Chinese. Art, literature, philosophy, music, technology, political thought, techniques of government, and even things such as cuisine "were derived from, inspired by, or modeled upon the ideas and practices" of Chinese civilization, among them Confucianism and Daoism. Even Buddhism, which originated in India and was destined to become the most widespread religion in Vietnam, reached the Vietnamese in the second century AD via China when Chinese monks arrived seeking refuge from troubles in their native land. The Vietnamese language, which belongs to the Mon-Khmer branch of the Austroasiatic language family as opposed to the Chinese language family, absorbed many Chinese words to emerge as what is recognizable today as Vietnamese by about the tenth century; about

---

[6] This section relies heavily on Taylor's work. See *The Birth of Vietnam* (Berkeley: University of California Press, 1983) and *A History of the Vietnamese* (Cambridge and New York: Cambridge University Press, 2013). For the review mentioned, see Bruce M. Lockart, Review of *A History of the Vietnamese*, by K. W. Taylor, *Sojourn: Journal of Social Issues in Southeast Asia* 29, no. 1 (2014): 743. Readers might also be interested in "How I began to teach about the Vietnam War" (*Michigan Quarterly Review*, Fall 2004), in which Taylor traces his personal intellectual journey while outlining the basic reasons he dissents from the conventional orthodox narrative of the Vietnam War.

three-quarters of modern Vietnamese vocabulary comes from Chinese. Meanwhile, waves of immigration produced a new elite ruling class of mixed Chinese-Vietnamese ancestry.[7] This, in fact, was true for the local population as a whole. As Taylor puts it: "In the tenth century, the people of what is now northern Vietnam were an amalgam of settlers from the north and indigenous peoples; for centuries they had lived together, intermarried, developed bilingual habits of speech, and formed a regional perspective on imperial civilization."[8]

Overall, life within the southernmost borders of various Chinese states brought the Tonkin people peace and relative prosperity. They absorbed aspects of Chinese culture and developed a new identity. In short, the people living in the Red River delta region between one and two thousand years ago quite literally needed the Chinese to become the people who today are known as the Vietnamese.

During that formative millennium, there were, to be sure, periodic rebellions by inhabitants of the Red River plain against the rulers from the north. But, Taylor maintains, that does not support the popular narrative of constant and heroic Vietnamese resistance to Chinese rule. Even the iconic first-century rebellion by the Trung sisters against the Han dynasty, so often touted as an example of Vietnamese national resistance to Chinese rule, was rather less than meets the eye, at least when looking through a nationalist prism. While records are sparse, those that exist suggest that high taxation was the primary cause of that rebellion. Other rebellions generally occurred during times of weakened dynastic rule from the north that left the frontier regions in the south unprotected or during times of political turmoil. Some of them did involve indigenous peoples, such as an obscure rebellion by Lao tribesmen at the end of the seventh century or an uprising by a mysterious figure known as the Black Emperor in the early eighth century. Generally, however, those who led the rebellions – such as Ly Bi, a descendent of Chinese immigrants who briefly set himself up as king of a county he called Can Xuan in the mid-sixth century – were disappointed office seekers and/or ambitious local

---

[7] Taylor, *A History of the Vietnamese*, 3, 9–10, 24. This volume is the source of the first and third quotation in this paragraph. See also Keith W. Taylor, "The Vietnamese Civil War of 1955–1975 in Historical Perspective," in *Triumph Revisited*, 18–19. It is the source of the second and fourth quotations. For the ethnic composition of the evolving Vietnamese ruling class, see Keith Weller Taylor, *The Birth of Vietnam*, xix. The point about Buddhism is from Moss, *Vietnam: An American Ordeal*, 6.

[8] Taylor, *A History of the Vietnamese*, 50.

commanders rather than leaders of the indigenous people of the region. They were not Vietnamese nationalists in the modern sense of that term.[9]

Independent Vietnam and China

Vietnam's independence officially dates from a military victory over Chinese forces, the Battle of the Bach Dang River, in the year 939. While the battle itself featured considerable drama and brilliant strategy on the Vietnamese side, in a larger context the people of the Red River valley were not doing anything unusual given the situation at the time. In 907 the once-mighty Tang dynasty, after decades of decline, had finally collapsed, to be succeeded by a number of smaller kingdoms that had emerged to fill a huge power vacuum. In the general reordering of political power in the region, the Vietnamese won their independence from one of those successor states, which controlled two provinces in southern China. As for the area the Vietnamese controlled, it was only about the northern third of today's Vietnam along the Gulf of Tonkin. While gradual southward expansion followed, it took until the fifteenth century for the Vietnamese to reach the 17th parallel.

What followed the Battle of Bach Dang River was not, as one often reads, a millennium in which the now-independent Vietnamese were forced to repel continued Chinese attempts to reincorporate them into their empire. The Song dynasty (960–1279), having reunited much of China under its banner by 960, did invade Vietnam in 980, only to be repelled and confronted with the realization that it lacked the strength to restore the more extensive frontiers that had existed under both the Tang and, previously, the Han. For their part, the Vietnamese hastened to follow the example of other East Asian states by assuming tributary status to the Middle Kingdom. The popular narrative of constant Chinese efforts to reassert their rule over the next thousand years simply did not occur. A second Song invasion of Vietnam in the eleventh century occurred in response to a Vietnamese incursion across a disputed border. During the thirteenth century there were three wars with the Mongol rulers of China. Those wars, however, do not mean the Vietnamese were at war with the Chinese. The Mongols were nomads from northern Asia beyond China's Great Wall who had conquered China and destroyed the Song dynasty before turning their sights on Vietnam. To the Chinese they were detested

---

[9] Taylor, ibid., 35–36; Taylor, "The Vietnamese Civil War of 1955–1975 in Historical Perspective," 19; Taylor, *The Birth of Vietnam*, 190–92.

"barbarians," alien conquerors they finally overthrew and drove out of their country in the mid-fourteenth century. The Chinese were hardly alone in being victims of the Mongols, whose conquests, destruction, and terror extended westward deep into Europe, southward into the Middle East, and eastward to the shores of Japan, where it took a huge typhoon – what the Japanese called their "divine wind" or *kamikaze* – to save that island nation. Since Chinese refugees fleeing that conquest actually joined the Vietnamese in their successful struggle to repel the Mongols, it does not make sense to view this particular episode in the history of Vietnam's struggle to maintain its independence as one in which the antagonist was China. Instead, in this case one finds a short-term alliance of sorts between the Vietnamese and refugee Song Chinese against a mutual enemy, the Mongols. Early in the fifteenth century the Chinese were back, this time in the form of the Ming dynasty (1368–1644) that had driven the Mongols from China. In this case Chinese imperial dreams were encouraged by Vietnamese who were seeking outside help after their dynasty, known as the Tran, was overthrown. However, like the Song, the Ming who invaded Vietnam were reaching beyond the limits of their strength, and determined resistance by those Vietnamese who had overthrown the Tran dynasty drove them from Vietnam after about two decades. Their leader then founded the Le dynasty, the longest lasting in Vietnamese history. Vietnam once again became a tributary to China, and more than three centuries of peace between the two countries followed.[10]

Prior to the French conquest of Vietnam in the nineteenth century, the Chinese Empire would return to Vietnam only one more time, in the late eighteenth century under the Qing dynasty (1644–1911). Once more it was by invitation, again from supporters of a Vietnamese dynasty – this time the Le – that had just been overthrown by peasant rebels known as the Tay Son. It bears mentioning that the Qing dynasty that sent Chinese troops to Vietnam was itself foreign to China. It had been founded in the mid-seventeenth century by the Manchus, who like the Mongols were nomads from beyond the Great Wall who had conquered China. Taylor argues that the Qing had limited aims – restore their client, the Le dynasty, to the Vietnamese throne and then depart – although some scholars

---

[10] Taylor, "Author's Response," *Sojourn: Journal of Social Issues in Southeast Asia* 29, no. 3 (2014): 748–49; Taylor, "The Vietnamese Civil War of 1955–1975 in Historical Perspective," 19–21; Taylor, *A History of the Vietnamese*, 177, 188. For a harsher assessment of Ming policies see David G. Marr, *Vietnamese Anticolonialism*, 14–15.

believe that the Qing intended to stay in Vietnam. In any event, the Tay Son did not wait to find out whether or not the Qing intended to leave. In January 1789 they launched a surprise attack against the occupying Chinese troops and routed them. The attack was completely unexpected because it came during the Tet lunar new year, the most important holiday of the Vietnamese calendar. The victorious Vietnamese, this time acting as expected, quickly made peace with the Qing, and Vietnam resumed its traditional tributary status vis-à-vis the Middle Kingdom. The Chinese would not intervene again in Vietnam for more than a century, and when they did in the 1880s it was because the Vietnamese again asked them for help, this time against the French, who were completing the process of turning Vietnam into their colony. As Taylor points out, "Altogether, these episodes do not account for much in the context of a millennium."[11]

Vietnam's tributary relationship with China obviously was onerous in many ways. At the same time, it often had its benefits. Historian D. R. SarDesai has pointed out that Vietnam's vassalage to China could at times serve as a deterrent to smaller but nonetheless dangerous enemies in Southeast Asia. Not the least of them, directly to the south, was the kingdom of Champa, for several centuries "the perpetual thorn in the Vietnamese side." In addition, Chinese intervention on two occasions ended long periods of civil war, once in 1540 and again in 1673. An interesting fact is that the first intervention was less significant for establishing a lasting peace than it was for bringing about an agreement establishing the division of Vietnam and thereby foreshadowing China's role in the Geneva Conference of 1954 that produced North and South Vietnam. The second intervention likewise ended with a divided Vietnam, although this time it also produced a peace that lasted for almost one hundred years.[12]

A NEW WAY OF BEING VIETNAMESE AND DIFFERENT VISIONS OF VIETNAM

If the Vietnamese generally got along better with the Chinese than is commonly believed, how did they get along with each other? Beyond

---

[11] Taylor, "Author's Response," 748–49; Taylor, "The Vietnamese Civil War of 1955–1975 in Historical Perspective," 21. Taylor, *A History of the Vietnamese*, 378. The quotation is from "Author's Response." For a different assessment of Qing intentions see "The First Tet Offensive of 1789," *Vietnam Magazine*, June 12, 2006. Available online at www.historynet.com/the-first-tet-offensive-of-1789.htm

[12] D. R. SarDesai, *Vietnam Past and Present* (Cambridge, MA: Westview Press, 2005), 20, 27–28.

that, how over time did people living in different parts of the country come to view what it meant to be Vietnamese?[13] We already know that the Vietnamese were not, as is often claimed, fiercely united in fending off the Chinese. In fact, as previously noted, two Chinese interventions, by the Ming in the fourteenth century and by the Qing in the eighteenth century, were by invitation from one of the factions fighting for the Vietnamese throne at the time. In the 1370s one family competing for the throne went so far as to seek help, and thereby invite military intervention, from the king of Champa, Vietnam's bitter enemy to the south that controlled territory that today constitutes central Vietnam.[14] Ironically, given their ultimate role as colonizers, during the early nineteenth century even the French would be invited to interfere in a struggle for the throne by a Vietnamese faction. Nor were the Vietnamese any more unified than most other peoples in governing themselves. There certainly were strong dynasties and able rulers. But internal conflicts during the first seventy years of independence caused three dynasties to rise and fall, and other eras of Vietnamese history are pockmarked by internal rebellions. The Vietnamese have also committed their share of aggression against minorities within their borders and neighbors to the south. In Taylor's view, "There is abundant evidence that, in quantitative terms, Vietnamese suffered much more from the misgovernment and oppression of their own rulers than they ever suffered from 'foreign aggression.'"[15]

In making his case about Vietnamese self-inflicted wounds, Taylor refers to more than 170 years of war since the fifteenth century between competing Vietnamese political entities. This reality in turn raises a fundamental point about Vietnamese history often overlooked or mentioned only in passing in textbooks that introduce students to the Vietnam War: that Vietnam was divided de facto between two states for about two centuries beginning in the sixteenth century.[16] Nor is it irrelevant that the dividing line was approximately at the 17th parallel, the same line that divided North and South Vietnam between 1954 and 1975. Perhaps more

---

[13] The term "a new way of being Vietnamese" comes from Li Tana (see note 18); the notion of different "visions," or more precisely "two Vietnamese visions of the future of the country," comes from Taylor (see note 29). For a good overview of the literature on this issue and on Vietnam's relationship with China, see Martin Loicano, "Vietnam Divided: Regional History and the Vietnam Wars, 1598–1975," in *America and the Vietnam Wars: Re-examining the Culture and History of a Generation*, eds. Andrew Wiest, Mary Kathryn Barbier, and Glenn Robins (New York and London: Routledge, 2010), 15–33.

[14] Taylor, *A History of the Vietnamese*, 154–57.   [15] Taylor, "Author's Response," 748.

[16] See Herring, *America's Longest War*, 4; Moss, *Vietnam: An American Ordeal*, 7; Turley, *The Second Indochina War*, 10.

important, during those two centuries Vietnam was not just divided politically; it increasingly became divided in terms of lifestyle and outlook. Ultimately this produced what Taylor calls "a new version of being Vietnamese," and that in turn, the passage of several centuries notwithstanding, bears on how one should evaluate the bitter division and war that rent Vietnam in the second half of the twentieth century.[17]

Southward Expansion and Vietnamese Identity

The "new way of being Vietnamese" was the product of Vietnamese southward expansion from their base in Tonkin. This process began as early as the eleventh century, albeit very slowly; it took until the early fifteenth century for the Vietnamese to get approximately to the 17th parallel. At that point the way south was blocked by the kingdom of Champa, a state more than a thousand years old. The Chams had arrived in Southeast Asia from the islands of Indonesia, and their civilization was based on Hinduism imported from India. As late as the end of the fourteenth century, Champa had been strong enough to invade Vietnam on several occasions. But weakened by incessant warfare with its neighbors, it was virtually destroyed by the Vietnamese in 1471. Thereafter Champa was a defenseless remnant unable to stop Vietnamese southward migration and occupation. Most of the indigenous population of the south was either killed, absorbed, or driven eastward into Cambodia. By 1500 the Vietnamese were about three-quarters of the way down the coast, and by the 1757 they controlled the Mekong River Delta, giving Vietnam its current geographic configuration.

Vietnam's first era of political division dates from the mid-sixteenth century. At that time instability and civil war in Tonkin contributed to the first big wave of Vietnamese migration south of the 17th parallel.[18] At the same time, an aristocratic family usually referred to as the Nguyen lords was consolidating its control in what then was the southern part of Vietnam, with the city of Hue, just south of the 17th parallel, serving as its capital. Civil war between two other families – the Trinh and the

---

[17] Taylor, "Author's Response," 748–49; Taylor, "The Vietnamese Civil War of 1955–1975 in Historical Perspective," 24.

[18] Li Tana, *Nguyen Cochinchina: Southern Vietnam in the Seventeenth and Eighteenth Centuries* (Ithaca: Southeast Asia Program Publications, 1998), 27, 99. Also see Li Tana's article "An Alternative Vietnam? The Nguyen Kingdom of the Seventeenth and Eighteenth Centuries," *Journal of Southeast Asian Studies* 29, no.1 (March 1998): 111–21.

Mac – continued in Tonkin until almost the end of the century until the Trinh, who ruled in the name of the puppet Le dynasty, emerged victorious. It was not long before the Trinh attempted to conquer the south, an effort that led to a half century of war beginning in 1620. As part of their defense the Nguyen lords built a system of walls from the highlands in the west to the sea in the east – sometimes called the "Small Wall of Vietnam" – on which they placed artillery and garrisoned thousands of soldiers, a formidable defense the Trinh were never able to penetrate. Not until 1673 did the fighting stop, a peace mediated by the Chinese. This de facto division of Vietnam continued for another century.[19] While in theory Vietnam remained united under the Le dynasty, in practice the Le had no power: Vietnam north of the 17th parallel was ruled by the Trinh family while south of that line the Nguyen family ruled.

Vietnamese southward expansion does get mentioned in orthodox textbook accounts of the war the United States fought in Vietnam, which sometimes add that one result was Vietnam's division into separate rival states, divided at the 17th parallel, for about two centuries. A small population and many natural resources in the south, including fertile soil that provided abundant crops, helped the Vietnamese who moved there live more prosperously than those they left behind in the north. A consequence of this, likewise sometimes noted by orthodox commentators, is that over time the lifestyle in the south diverged from that in the north, with the southerners tending to be more easygoing, individualistic, materialistic, and less rigid or disciplined.[20] However, when any implications about this phenomenon with regard to America's effort in Vietnam are mentioned, and they rarely are, it is to point out, as Frances Fitzgerald does in *Fire in the Lake*, that by backing South Vietnam "the United States

---

[19] Taylor, "The Vietnamese Civil War in Historical Perspective," 24–25; SarDesai, *Vietnam Past and Present*, 27–28; Olga Dror and K. W. Taylor, "Introduction," in *Views of Seventeenth-Century Vietnam: Christoforo Borri on Cochinchina and Samuel Barron on Tonkin*, eds. Olga Dror and K. W. Taylor (Ithaca: Southeast Asian Program Publications, 2006), 20.

[20] For example, see David L. Anderson, *The Vietnam War* (Basingstoke: Palgrave MacMillan, 2005), 4–5 and Mitchell K. Hall, *The Vietnam War* 2nd ed. (Edinburgh Gate: Pearson Longman, 2007), 1; William S. Turley, *The Second Indochina War: A Concise Political and Military History* 2nd ed. (Lanham: Rowman and Littlefield, 2009), 9–10. Herring, who provides just a few paragraphs of historical background before beginning his narrative in 1945, mentions only what he calls the "fragile" nature of Vietnamese national unity (*America's Longest War*, 4). Moss provides several pages of background and also mentions the division of Vietnam and some differences between northerners and southerners (Moss, *Vietnam: An American Ordeal*, 6–7). Turley focuses on geography.

was taking on what had historically been the weakest part of Vietnam."[21] In other words, Vietnam's history of being divided and the resultant differences between North and South provide yet another reason the United States should not have supported South Vietnam's military struggle to remain independent of North Vietnam, this time because of South Vietnam's weakness.

From Taylor's perspective, the implications of Vietnamese southward expansion and its consequent division into two political entities are entirely different and suggest a correspondingly different conclusion regarding South Vietnam versus North Vietnam. For him, the key point is that during Vietnam's two centuries of division, a "new version of being Vietnamese" emerged from the evolving lifestyle in the south. Taylor therefore has more to say about how people lived in the south than do orthodox commentators. He begins with the established observation that southern Vietnamese enjoyed the benefit of abundant natural resources, which helped them build a significantly more prosperous society than that in the north. But then he goes further. Taking advantage of their natural resources, the southerners engaged in much more foreign trade than did the northerners, an activity encouraged by their Nguyen rulers, and therefore were exposed to foreign influences.[22] Southern society, with its vibrant economy and extensive trade contacts with foreigners, provided more opportunity to exercise personal freedom than did northern society. There was more social mobility in the south than in the north. Over time, Taylor notes, southern Vietnamese became "less disciplined by poverty and oppression than were northerners, less awed by authority, less constrained by notions of fate and cyclic passivity, more self-reliant, and more susceptible to opportunity." Even peasant villages were different. Taylor notes that while northern peasant villages typically were closed and encircled by bamboo hedges, southern villages generally were built without such barriers along the shores of rivers and canals. Taylor's point

---

[21] Fitzgerald, *Fire in the Lake*, 66. She then leaps to the ahistoric and untenable generalization that the "south represented anarchy in contrast to the order of the north." For her assessment of Vietnamese personality types, Fitzgerald quotes a RAND Corporation study based on interviews with Communist guerrillas. *Fire in the Lake* won a Pulitzer Prize in 1973.

[22] Taylor, "The Vietnamese Civil War of 1955-1975 in Historical Perspective," 24. For an overview of an account written by a northern official who came to the south and found a trading society far different from what existed in the north, see Alexander Woodside, "Central Viet Nam's Trading World in the Eighteenth Century as Seen in Le Quy Don's 'Frontier Chronicles,'" in *Essays into the Vietnamese Pasts*, eds. K. W. Taylor and John K. Whitmore (Ithaca: Studies in Southeast Asia, 1995), 157-72.

about villages in southern Vietnam is important not because he is stating something new – Frances Fitzgerald notes the same phenomenon, citing studies from the 1960s – but because of the implications he draws. To Fitzgerald, once again, what happened is a sign of weakness: along with losing the "fortress aspect" of northern villages, southern villages lost the "disciplined social organization that gave the northern villages their political strength." To Taylor, what matters is that, unlike enclosed and fortified villages in the north, those in the south were "open to the outside world."[23]

Taylor's assessment of southern Vietnamese society and culture is solidly grounded in his own extensive research and that of other scholars. Perhaps the most comprehensive overview in English of what was in effect an independent southern Vietnam is Li Tana's *Nguyen Cochinchina: Southern Vietnam in the Seventeenth and Eighteenth Centuries*. Li Tana stresses how Vietnamese immigrants to the south adopted important aspects of other cultures they encountered, most notably, but not only, that of the Chams. Foreign trade further exposed the southern Vietnamese to influences from outsiders such as Japanese Christians, European Christian missionaries, and Chinese Buddhist monks. Not incidentally, it also provided the Nguyen rulers with the financial resources they needed to acquire modern weaponry, a crucial asset in their long conflict with the Trinh, who had a far larger population to draw on in building their military. Meanwhile, exposure to other cultures combined with Nguyen political interests to lessen Chinese influence in the south. Because the Nguyen lords needed to establish their own legitimacy in opposition to the Trinh in the north, they deemphasized Confucianism so that over time it "played a political and social role that was relatively minor compared to its role in the north."[24]

As an alternative the Nguyen lords turned to Mahayana Buddhism, which had the advantage of reaffirming Vietnamese ethnic identity in the south. At the same time, the Nguyen lords, with their Buddhist-based authority, distinguished themselves from the Trinh, whose authority was Confucian based. All of these factors combined to the point where, as Li Tana puts it, "from the early seventeenth century we find developing a sense of separateness, and with it the beginnings of local identity."[25] What Li Tana calls "this successful experiment" did not stop there. As the

[23] Taylor, "The Vietnamese Civil War of 1955–1975 in Historical Perspective," 24; Fitzgerald, *Fire in the Lake*, 64.
[24] Li Tana, *Nguyen Cochinchina*, 103.   [25] Ibid., 102–4.

southern Vietnamese interacted with new neighbors, they created a "Southeast Asian" pattern and in turn a "new social space" that led them to develop in ways different from their Vietnamese contemporaries to the north. This enabled the southern Vietnamese society to develop outside the Sino-Vietnamese framework that for centuries had determined northern politics and culture.[26] For two centuries there were "two separate Vietnamese states and two distinctive Vietnamese economic systems." That said, the southern Vietnamese did not lose their original identity and become "non-Vietnamese." Instead, as they adjusted to their new environment, demonstrated their willingness to experiment, and took advantage of new opportunities, they "developed another way of being Vietnamese."[27]

To orthodox commentators like Fitzgerald, the characteristics that differentiated southern Vietnamese from their northern brethren were the result of a "cultural washout," a loss of "disciplined social organization," and this cultural loss allegedly led to weakness. Li Tana, in contrast, sees the two centuries of de facto independence as having given southerners traits such as "their curiosity and tolerance towards new things and new ideas, their more open and spontaneous nature, [and] their unwillingness to be fettered by history and tradition."[28] Thus Taylor, pointing to the southern effort to preserve its freedoms against the north's efforts at conquest that began the early seventeenth century, argues that in the twentieth century South Vietnam's cause had a "genealogy" going back to that time. Far from seeing what existed in South Vietnam as a "cultural washout," he stresses:

The war of 1955–1975 was a war between two different Vietnamese visions of the future of the country. These visions primarily came from contrasting northern and southern perspectives on ideology, economics, society, and politics. They have existed for over four centuries, ever since southern Vietnamese began to form their own structure of authority.[29]

This long-standing bifurcation that has characterized Vietnam makes it fair to say that there was nothing "predestined," to use Mark Moyar's term, about the country's unification under a Communist dictatorship that took place in 1975. As Moyar observes, geographic contiguity and a shared language did not produce the unification of the United States and

---

[26] Ibid., 109–10.   [27] Ibid., 156–57.
[28] Fitzgerald, *Fire in the Lake*, 64–65; Li Tana, *Nguyen Cochinchina*, 156.
[29] Taylor, "The Vietnamese Civil War of 1955–1975 in Historical Perspective," 18.

Canada or Germany and Austria.[30] Other examples could be cited, from Central and South America to North Africa and the Middle East and, perhaps most interesting, to East Asia itself, where today there are two dramatically contrasting visions of what it respectively means to be Chinese and Korean. Nor should it be overlooked that in the end, military force was decisive in both the unification of Vietnam and the imposition of the vision under which it was unified. Since that vision led, as many observers from Taylor to Stanley Karnow[31] have pointed out, to decades of misgovernment and oppression, one can reasonably say that how Vietnam was unified says nothing about the merits of the victor's vision as opposed to that of the vanquished. It thus should not be difficult to understand how differing interpretations of the contrasts between northern and southern Vietnam might influence how one views the manner in which the United States should have responded to the North Vietnamese effort to take over South Vietnam.

VIETNAMESE NATIONALISM

Vietnamese nationalism in the modern sense of that term arose out of the French colonial occupation of Vietnam, a process that began in the far south (Chochinchina) in the late 1850s but was not completed until 1884. Ironically, that conquest began barely a half century after Vietnam was first united in its current configuration from north to south by the emperor Gia Long, who had completed that task, with French aid, in 1802. The French had to confirm their conquest with a short war against China when the Vietnamese emperor, following a well-established tradition, appealed to Beijing for help against the new intruders. The Chinese, who themselves were unsuccessfully battling Western encroachment, did intervene militarily in 1884 on behalf of their tributary, but they were decisively defeated by 1885. The French then divided Vietnam into three entities – Chochinchina in the south, Annam in the center, and Tonkin in the north – which they ruled as part of what they called the Indochinese Union, an entity that included Cambodia and, from 1893, Laos. In Vietnam itself, only Chochinchina was technically governed directly

---

[30] Moyar, *Triumph Forsaken*, 6.
[31] Karnow, *Vietnam: A History*. This volume, published in 1983, is one of the standard orthodox histories of the Vietnam War. Karnow's first chapter is called "The War Nobody Won." It includes the following observation: "The rest of Asia is booming but Vietnam is an island of poverty" (31).

as a colony; the rest of the country was officially a French protectorate under a puppet emperor, with its capital in the old Nguyen capital of Hue. Vietnam's de facto political capital was Hanoi, where the French governor-general was based. The country's economic center, however, was far to the south in Saigon, a city whose history officially goes back to 1698 when the Vietnamese were first settling in the Mekong River Delta. By the middle of the eighteenth century Saigon was a major town and base for Nguyen rule in the south and also a thriving commercial center, a development due in part to the presence of Chinese refugees fleeing the Manchu conquest of their country. Under the French, Saigon was designated the capital of Chochinchina; because of the economic potential of the south, it attracted French capital and became the economic and commercial center of Vietnam.

French colonial rule contributed to the modernization of Vietnam via the building of roads, bridges, irrigation works, and other infrastructure. The French also fostered the spread of an alphabetical system, first developed by Portuguese Catholic missionaries, of writing Vietnamese, which previously had been written with Chinese characters. That said, French rule was at once economically exploitative and politically repressive, as was European colonial rule elsewhere in Asia and Africa during the nineteenth and twentieth centuries. The introduction of rubber plantations, which were French owned and produced for export, exacerbated the problem of peasant landlessness in the south. So too did the commercial production of rice, also for export, which increasingly was grown on large estates. A few Vietnamese managed to become large land owners and share in the spoils, but many more were dragged into the French capitalist economy as laborers on the countryside or in mines and factories and suffered greatly.

Two points merit mentioning in this regard, neither of which is intended to minimize the negative impact of French colonial rule on Vietnam. First, the problem of peasant landlessness in the south did not begin with the French; the pattern of large landownership and a majority of landless peasants, often working as virtual slaves, dated from the early eighteenth century and the Vietnamese development of the Mekong River region.[32] What French policies did was make the land situation much worse. Second, French colonialism in some ways increased the differences between northern and southern Vietnam. More economic development took place in the south, with the result, as Taylor puts it, that

---

[32] Taylor, *A History of the Vietnamese*, 463.

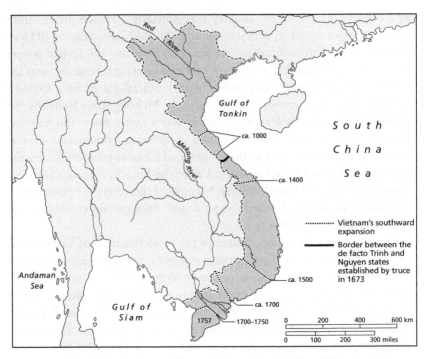

MAP 1 Vietnam's Southward Expansion and the Trinh and Nguyen States

Chochinchina region became "more integrated into the modern world than other parts of Vietnam."[33] But if Saigon, which earned the sobriquet "Paris of the Orient," provided a desirable modern lifestyle for its French residents and the small minority of Vietnamese who were able to position themselves to benefit from colonial rule, the great majority of Vietnamese endured poverty and repression. Out of this situation, among certain elements of the local elite, emerged Vietnamese anti-colonialism and nationalism.

Protonationalists, Scholar-Patriots, and Modern Nationalists

Vietnamese nationalism developed in several stages. Initial resistance to French rule originated among the country's traditional elite and was based on traditional values. Active opposition, led by low-level officials, military officers, and sometimes by peasants, began in the towns and villages of

[33] Taylor, "The Vietnamese Civil War in Historical Perspective," 26.

Chochinchina during the early 1860s but was poorly organized and had little success. What William J. Duiker calls "a relatively organized campaign of violence against French rule" began in 1885. It was inspired by an edict issued on behalf of the emperor – the so-called loyalty to the king edict – but was crushed by the French after about a decade. Duiker notes that the traditional elites who led this early resistance actually are best understood as "protonationalists." They knew little of the Western concept of the nation-state and in their efforts against the French did not distinguish between Vietnam as a nation and its monarchy.[34]

With the new century and the maturing of a new generation, the crafting of Vietnamese nationalism passed from people with a strictly traditional perspective to those with a broader outlook. As Duiker observes, "This new generation represented the transition between traditional and modern Vietnam."[35] While generally members of scholar-gentry families – Duiker calls them "scholar-patriots" – Vietnam's new generation of nationalists had been exposed to Western thinking and institutions, and they based key aspects of their political outlook on what they had learned about the world outside their country. They were influenced by Chinese reformers and nationalists and deeply impressed by the success of Japan, which after 1868 had not only undertaken a successful modernization campaign but had demonstrated its resultant strength by decisively defeating a European great power, the Russian Empire, in the Russo-Japanese war of 1904–1905.

The most important member of this generation was Phan Boi Chau (1867–1940), who was active from just after the turn of the century until he was arrested by French security forces in 1925, after which he spent the last fifteen years of his life under house arrest. A prolific writer, Phan Boi Chau advocated Vietnamese independence to a growing audience in the cities and was involved in an unsuccessful uprising in 1908. He did not, however, believe that Vietnam was ready for democracy, which is why he argued that an independent Vietnam should be ruled by a monarchy. On this point he disagreed with his country's other leading contemporary nationalist, Phan Chu Trinh (1871–1926), a proponent of democracy and constitutional government. The two men also disagreed about the use of violence, which Phan Boi Chau supported and Phan Chu Trinh opposed. Foreshadowing what would happen to future Vietnamese

---

[34] William J. Duiker, *The Rise of Nationalism in Vietnam, 1900–1941* (Ithaca and London: Cornell University Press, 1976), 25–30. The term "protonationalist" appears on page 30.
[35] Ibid., 31.

nationalists – that is, the activists on behalf of independence who were not Communists – the disagreements between the two men prevented them from working together.

In any event, by the late 1920s the era of the scholar-patriots was over: Phan Boi Chau was no longer active politically and Phan Chu Trinh had died. A new era in the history of Vietnamese nationalism was beginning. Dominated by the first generation of Vietnamese with a French rather than a traditional Vietnamese education, it would see the emergence of modern nationalist groups. It would also see the arrival on the scene of the first Vietnamese Communists. The Communists were very different from their countrymen whose first and foremost concern was Vietnamese independence from French colonial rule. To be sure, the Vietnamese Communists would become participants in their country's nationalist movement and, in the end, come to dominate it, but as revisionist historians stress, their primary loyalty was to international Marxism-Leninism, an ideology that viewed the nationalism in colonial regions as a means to be used to promote world revolution rather than an end it itself. And that would change the history of Vietnam.

Modern Vietnamese nationalism developed along several tracks. The moderate track was most notably represented by the Constitutionalist Party, a group made up of prominent businesspeople, landlords, civil servants, and other Vietnamese who had become beneficiaries of French rule. Based in Saigon, the Constitutionalist Party's demands were limited to reforms as opposed to independence, and it never acquired a mass base. Far more militant, and the most important non-Marxist organization in Vietnam, was the Vietnam Nationalist Party (VNQDD). Formed in Hanoi in 1927, the VNQDD took a militant stand against French colonialism and was prepared to use violence to achieve its aim of Vietnamese independence. The VNQDD soon had about 1,500 members divided into twenty cells in and around Hanoi, although it quickly was thoroughly infiltrated by French agents. Most of its members were students, small merchants, soldiers, and low-level bureaucrats. Nguyen Thai Hoc, its leader, drew his "three principles" of national unity, democracy, and social welfare from Sun Yatsen, founder of the Chinese Nationalist Party. Then, in 1929, a party member acting against instructions assassinated a Frenchman in charge of recruiting Vietnamese laborers to work on Chochinchina rubber plantations, where conditions were deplorable. This act provoked a wave of arrests of party activists that virtually crippled the VNQDD. The party leadership concluded that survival depended on a nationwide insurrection, and in February 1930 this assessment resulted in what is known as the Yen Bay uprising. The French effectively and brutally suppressed the uprising, actually a sporadic series of violent incidents lasting several days, capturing and executing most of the remaining VNQDD leadership. A second wave of repression during 1931 and 1932, following an unsuccessful attempt to assassinate the French governor-general, drove the remnants of the VNQDD leadership into exile in China where, joined by the remnants of other groups and rent by factionalism, it ineffectually remained until the end of World War II.[36]

The virtual destruction of the VNQDD was paralleled by the fate of the non-Communist nationalist movement as a whole. The nationalists suffered from several critical weaknesses. Their movement was primarily urban with a small membership, with leaders who did not understand the need to develop support in the countryside, where most Vietnamese lived. Those leaders lacked the skills to build clandestine organizations able to thwart infiltration by French agents. They were divided into factions that proved unable to cooperate. Unlike the Communists, they did not receive outside help to overcome their weaknesses or to recover from their defeats. As a result, during the 1930s the French colonial authorities were able to cripple Vietnam's nationalist organizations. Ironically, by repressing these nationalists so effectively, the French cleared the way for the rise of the Communists. The latter, with the main nationalist groups in disarray and with crucial help from outside Vietnam, were able to tap into Vietnamese nationalist sentiments and exploit them to build the movement, albeit with a very different set of goals, that eventually drove France from Vietnam.

WORLD WAR II, THE AUGUST COUP, AND 1946

World War II drastically weakened the French hold on Vietnam and Indochina. After Nazi Germany defeated France in June 1940, a puppet regime was set up in the town of Vichy to govern the part of France the Germans did not directly occupy. The Vichy regime was in no position to resist Japanese demands regarding Indochina, and in late 1940 the Japanese occupied northern Vietnam. They took over the rest of Vietnam and Indochina the next year. Until March 1945, when Japan

---

[36] For details see Duiker, *The Rise of Nationalism in Vietnam*, 156–65 and Taylor, *A History of the Vietnamese*, 504–7.

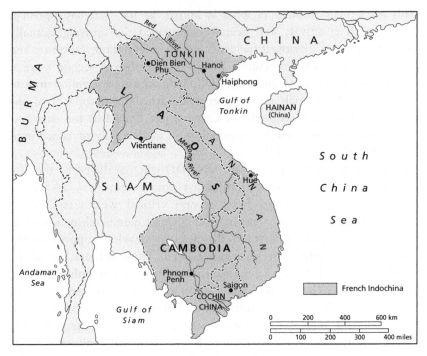

MAP 2 French Indochina

finally took direct military control of Vietnam to better protect its home islands against advancing Allied forces, Tokyo left the collaborationist French colonial administration in place. However, it answered to the Japanese army that directly controlled Vietnam's main cities and strategic assets such as ports, airfields, and railways.

France's defeat by Nazi Germany, followed by the Japanese occupation of Vietnam, should have been a golden opportunity for the Vietnamese nationalists to break free of French control and foreign occupation. But none of the nationalist parties had managed to recover from the decimation they had suffered in the early 1930s. The remnants of the VNQDD, still the most important non-Communist Vietnamese party, were in southern China, but the party did not have a functioning organization inside Vietnam. Meanwhile, some groups in the nationalist camp adopted pro-Japanese attitudes under the assumption that the Japanese represented the most powerful Asian force opposed to European colonialism and therefore a potential source of help to the cause of Vietnamese independence. They included two religious sects with large followings in Vietnam: the Cao Dai, founded in 1926, and the Hoa Hao, founded in 1939. Four other groups organized during the late 1930s that hoped to use the Japanese to end the French hold on Vietnam drew on both the Vietnam's past triumphs and on nineteenth- and twentieth-century nondemocratic European ideas to formulate their ideologies. These groups all incorporated the term Dai Viet (Great Viet) into their names, and in 1944 they united in the Dai Viet National Alliance. It bears mentioning that in this rejection of Western democracy, these groups were in step with their countrymen in the Indochinese Communist Party (ICP), which as a Leninist organization had no use for democracy in any form, and, significantly, for the authoritarian political tradition of Vietnam itself, which had always been ruled by aristocrats and emperors.[37] Meanwhile, in 1942 a French Catholic intellectual from a prominent family named Ngo Dinh Diem organized a group he called the Dai Viet Restoration Society.[38] During the 1930s Diem had briefly served as interior minister under Emperor Bao Dai, but he resigned when he realized the French were unwilling to make genuine reforms that would allow Bao Dai to function as more than a puppet ruler. The group Diem formed in 1942 was ineffectual, but after 1954, and the partition of Vietnam, he would emerge as the surprisingly effective leader of the anti-Communist regime in South Vietnam.

During World War II the VNQDD's deficiencies left it unable to make effective use of support it received from the anti-Communist Chinese government led by Chiang Kaishek. That support, to be sure, was mini- mal and consisted mainly in promoting the VNQDD as the core and leading party in a coalition of several Vietnamese non-Communist nationalist groups, all of which were small and weak.[39] The coalition itself was called the Vietnam Revolutionary League, or Dong Minh Hoi. In return for their organizational assistance and a monthly subsidy, the Chinese expected help in gathering intelligence on Japanese activities inside Vietnam, a job the groups that originally made up the Dong Minh Hoi were unable to do. The Chinese therefore turned to Ho Chi Minh – that name was a new alias adopted to hide his Comintern past – whom

---

[37] Taylor, *A History of the Vietnamese*, 528. On the absence of a democratic tradition in Vietnam see Mark Moyar, *Triumph Forsaken*, 35–38, 55–56.

[38] Taylor, *A History of the Vietnamese*, 528–29.

[39] Arthur J. Dommen, *The Indochinese Experience of the French and the Americans: Nationalism and Communism in Cambodia, Laos, and Vietnam* (Bloomington and Indianapolis: University of Indiana Press, 2001), 73–74.

they had arrested when he entered China in 1942. In 1943 Ho was
released from prison; the Vietminh, the Communist-front group he had
established in 1941, was brought into the supposedly non-Communist
Dong Minh Hoi, and in early 1944 Ho took on a leadership role in that
organization. That awkward arrangement lasted only several months, at
which point Ho, with a bodyguard provided by the Chinese, returned to
Vietnam.[40] Not incidentally, by then Ho had gotten his hands on something far more valuable: weapons the United States provided in return
for help against the Japanese. Those weapons were funneled to the
Vietminh by the Office of Strategic Services (OSS), the wartime precursor
to the CIA.

After years of struggle in which there was virtually no movement
toward independence, the year 1945 witnessed a sudden surge forward
toward the brink of achieving that goal. By the early months of 1945, the
Japanese, while still militantly unwilling to surrender, were on the verge
of military defeat at the hands of the United States and its allies.
Concerned that the French in Vietnam, who heretofore had collaborated
with them, might now change sides, the Japanese in March 1945 staged
a coup and took direct control over Vietnam. With French rule suddenly
terminated and Japanese rule clearly tenuous as the United States closed
in on the Japan's home islands, Ho Chi Minh recognized that an opening
had developed for the Vietminh to seize power. To be sure, the VNQDD
and other nationalist groups saw the same opening, but they lacked the
skills and resources to exploit it. As events would soon demonstrate, they
also lacked the ruthlessness, a quality not lacking in Ho and the
Vietminh. By the summer of 1945 Japan stood entirely alone, as the
war in Europe had ended with Germany's surrender in May. Still, the
expectation was that it would take an invasion of Japan to end the war,
which meant the fighting would continue at least into 1946. Then
on August 6, 1945, the United States revealed to the world its most
closely guarded wartime military secret when it dropped an atomic
bomb on the city of Hiroshima, destroying most of the city;
on August 9, a second atomic bomb obliterated most of the city of
Nagasaki. Japan surrendered on August 14, with the news reaching
Hanoi the next day. Suddenly the war was over, and control of
Vietnam, it seemed, was up for grabs.

---

[40] Robert F. Turner, *Vietnamese Communism: Its Origins and Development* (Stanford:
Hoover Institution Press: 1975), 33; Taylor, *A History of the Vietnamese*, 521–23,
528–29; Dommen, *The Indochinese Experience of the French and the Americans*, 74.

The Vietminh were prepared to seize the moment; the non-Communist nationalist groups were far less ready, some military preparations by certain groups notwithstanding. For example, the Dai Viet National Alliance began to prepare for military activity in March 1945, and by the summer the VNQDD had some military forces near Hanoi.[41] But all the nationalist groups were badly overmatched by the Vietminh. During the five months since the Japanese coup, the Vietminh had dramatically expanded its influence in the countryside, especially in the mountain areas north of Hanoi. In urban areas, where it was weakest, it had focused on infiltrating nationalist groups, either to take them over or lure away their members.[42] On August 19, in a bloodless coup but a coup nonetheless, Vietminh forces seized control of Hanoi. In doing so the Vietminh goal was not independence; had it been, the Vietminh would not have immediately turned to neutralizing the nationalist parties with all available means, including murder and other acts of violence. After all, while strengthening the Vietminh relative to non-Communist nationalist groups, the assault against non-Communist nationalists simultaneously weakened the overall strength of those Vietnamese prepared to resist any French attempt to reassert control over Vietnam. Instead, the goal on August 19 was to preempt rival Vietnamese groups to make sure that independence would result in a Vietminh dictatorship or, more accurately, an ICP dictatorship, since the ICP controlled the Vietminh. As historian Arthur J. Dommen has put it, "The seizure of power pitted Vietnamese against Vietnamese, not Vietnamese against any foreigner."[43]

During the evening of August 19, as the Vietminh consolidated its control over Hanoi, representatives of the Da Viet National Alliance and the VNQDD met to discuss their options. One VNQDD leader stressed that to accept the Vietminh coup was political suicide and argued for a counter coup, but he received no support. By default, most nationalists adopted a wait-and-see approach.[44] They did not have long to wait, nor would most of them like what they saw. On August 29 Ho presented the country with a government that

[41] Taylor, *A History of the Vietnamese*, 534–35.

[42] On this point see Huynh Kim Khanh, *Vietnamese Communism, 1925–1945* (Ithaca and London: Cornell University Press, 1982), 336–37. Khanh is highly sympathetic to Ho Chi Minh and Vietnamese Communism, which he views as a fusion between nationalism and Leninism.

[43] Dommen, *The Indochinese Experience of the French and the Americans*, 114–15.

[44] David G. Marr, *Vietnam 1945: The Quest for Power* (Berkeley: University of California Press, 1995), 400–401.

included token representatives from several political groups to give the appearance of inclusiveness but which in fact was dominated by the Vietminh; on September 2 Ho declared the independence of the state he called the Democratic Republic of Vietnam (DVN). Meanwhile, the initial coup in Hanoi was extended to the rest of the country, accompanied by a campaign of assassination of actual and potential opponents of Vietminh rule that claimed thousands of victims. Dommen aptly calls it "The First Liquidation." It is true that some victims of the Vietminh assassination squads had been collaborators with the French or Japanese, and severe post–World War II vigilante justice was not unique to Vietnam or the Vietminh. But it is also true that many Vietminh targets were genuine nationalists from across the political spectrum. They included Ngo Dinh Khoi, the older brother of Ngo Dinh Diem, who was buried alive. Some of the victims were Marxists, as the Stalinists who controlled the Vietminh turned their guns on Vietnamese Trotskyists in the latest episode of the deadly intra-Marxist feud that had started two decades earlier thousands of miles from Vietnam in the Soviet Union.[45]

All of this was dwarfed by the wave of terror, arrests, and murder the Vietminh waged against nationalist groups during 1946. That campaign, it should be noted, was conducted in de facto collaboration with French forces, as Paris was maneuvering to restore its control of Vietnam and saw the Vietminh campaign as a handy tool to destroy as many nationalist organizations as possible.[46] It was facilitated by the withdrawal of Chinese troops from northern Vietnam, where they had supported and protected the VNQDD. It was less successful in the south, where French troops, which had entered the country in September 1945 after Japan's surrender, were largely in control.[47] Still, the death toll reached into the tens of thousands, and the number arrested was much higher. Systematic Vietminh repression during 1946 severely weakened the VNQDD and other non-Communist organizations and strengthened the Vietminh. As a result, when the war for independence began at the end of 1946, it

---

[45] Duiker, *The Communist Road to Power in Vietnam*, 115; Dommen, *The Indochinese Experience of the French and the Americans*, 120–21; Moyar, *Triumph Forsaken*, 16–17; Marr, *Vietnam 1945*, 519.

[46] Turner, *Vietnamese Communism*, 58–59.

[47] The Vichy government that had governed unoccupied France during most of World War II had been replaced in August 1944 by what was known as the provisional government of the French Republic, led by General Charles de Gaulle. It was succeeded by the Fourth French Republic in 1946.

was a struggle between the Vietnamese Communists on the one hand and French colonialists on the other. The non-Communist Vietnamese organizations had been relegated to the sidelines. They would remain there until the war ended with a total French defeat and a partial Vietminh victory in 1954.

3

Vietnamese Communism, 1920–1959

The revisionist critique of Vietnamese Communism is grounded on three major points. First and most important, Vietnamese Communists were not authentic nationalists. Instead, they were committed to an ideology, Marxism-Leninism, under which nationalism in colonial areas was nothing more than a means to the end of a world socialist revolution. This ideology was alien to other Vietnamese nationalists and virtually all ordinary, nonactivist Vietnamese. Second, the Vietnamese Communists had a critical advantage over their traditional nationalist rivals, especially when it came to surviving French repression, because they received vital and continuous outside aid. That aid came from an organization called the Communist International, or Comintern, which served the foreign policy interests of the Soviet Union. Conventional Vietnamese nationalist groups, in contrast, had to fend for themselves. Third, a key reason that Vietnamese Marxist-Leninists were able to attract widespread outside support, especially among the peasantry, is that they deliberately and successfully masked their true ultimate aims. Strong evidence exists to support all these claims.

HO CHI MINH AND THE ORIGINS OF VIETNAMESE COMMUNISM

The man most responsible for the spread and influence of Marxism in Vietnam was Ho Chi Minh. That name, as with many Marxist revolutionaries, was an alias, the last of a series he used during his long career. Ho was born in 1890 into an educated but poor family in central Vietnam. After receiving a traditional Confucian education as a young boy, he attended Vietnam's most prestigious modern secondary school in the city of Hue, the same school that Ngo Dinh Diem, Ho's most important nationalist rival, would later attend. The young Ho became a militant nationalist but left Vietnam in 1911, not to return for three decades. He eventually found his way to France, where like many Vietnamese intellectuals he was drawn to Marxism. In Ho's case this occurred after the Allies at the Versailles Peace Conference of 1919 that drew up the treaty ending World War I failed to grant Vietnam its independence.

In 1920 Ho read "Theses on the National and Colonial Questions" by Vladimir Lenin, the founder and leader of Russia's Bolshevik Party. The Bolsheviks had seized power in Russia in November 1917, crushed all opposition to their one-party rule, and established a Marxist dictatorship in that country, which after 1922 was officially known as the Union of Soviet Socialist Republics (USSR), or the Soviet Union. Lenin's basic argument was that the nationalist struggles for independence against European colonial rule could contribute to the international effort to overthrow capitalism and establish a socialist world. Lenin's "Theses" deeply impressed Ho, and in 1920, under the alias of Nguyen Ai Quoc, he became a founding member of the French Communist Party. In 1923 he moved to Moscow and became an agent of the Comintern. Tasked by the Soviet regime that had established it in 1919 with promoting Communism throughout the world, the Comintern directed and financed Communist parties from North America to Europe to the Far East. It also had agents in its service such as the man then known as Nguyen Ai Quoc who moved from country to country. All Communist parties associated with the Comintern, aside from building local movements, were required to support Soviet foreign policy without question. For the next two decades Ho served that organization, and Soviet dictator Joseph Stalin, effectively and loyally in a variety of Asian countries, most notably China but also in Southeast Asia. Aside from organizing and building a Communist movement in Vietnam for the Comintern, Ho did the same in Siam (today: Thailand), Malaya, and Singapore. As the Comintern official in charge of the Indochinese Communist Party, he controlled Communist activities in Laos and Cambodia as well as in Vietnam.

It is a staple of orthodox historiography, one that gained popularity with best-selling books by journalists David Halberstam, Neil Sheehan, and Stanley Karnow, that Ho Chi Minh and his fellow Vietnamese Communists were also authentic nationalists, with the latter commitment not infrequently being placed ahead of the former in importance. Typical of this viewpoint is Sheehan's contention that the "motivating force within him [Ho Chi Minh] and those who became his disciples has always been nationalism."[1] William J. Duiker, author of the most authoritative biography of Ho (*Ho Chi Minh: A Life*, 2000), essentially takes the same position. However, that volume and Duiker's other works also provide considerable documentation supporting a different view of Ho. Sometimes the presumed non-Marxist aspects of Ho's outlook have had what can reasonably be called a halo effect on how he is viewed. Thus a ruthless politician who ordered the mass murder of political opponents, small landowners, and even peasants resisting the confiscation of their land has received encomiums such as "half Gandhi, half Lenin" and "Confucian humanist."[2] Whatever one thinks about Gandhi, Lenin, or Confucius, the notion that nationalism shared primacy of place with Marxism and its goal of a world communist revolution in Ho's short list of commitments is belied by his actions and political stands. Being Vietnamese did have meaning to Ho, notwithstanding that his priority was international Marxism. However, as Philippe Papin, a French specialist on Vietnam, argues, Ho Chi Minh's actions demonstrate "without any ambiguity – or with ambiguities that are entirely tactical – that he was an orthodox Marxist, an internationalist, a man caught up in the Comintern game."[3] Mark Moyar has summed up this nationalist/ Marxist dichotomy well:

Ho Chi Minh was a nationalist in the sense that he had a special affection for Vietnam's people and favored Vietnamese unification and independence, but, from his reading of Lenin's theses onward, he firmly adhered to the Leninist principle that Communist nations should subordinate their interests to those of the Communist international movement.[4]

---

[1] Cited in Stephen J. Morris, "The Internationalist Outlook of Vietnamese Communism," in *The Real Lessons of the Vietnam War*, 72–73. This section relies heavily on Morris's article.

[2] For "Half Gandhi" see William J. Duiker, *The Communist Road to Power in Vietnam*, 329; for "Confucian humanist" see Frances Fitzgerald, "Half Lenin, Half Gandhi," review of *Ho Chi Minh: A Life*, by William S. Duiker, *New York Times*, October 15, 2000, Sunday Book Review, 14. Actually, in his biography of Ho, Duiker tones down his description by noting that "Ho Chi Minh's *image* [italics added] was part Lenin and part Gandhi, with perhaps a dash of Confucius." Of course, Duiker himself, a distinguished and influential historian, helped create that image. Lest there be any confusion, this author considers only the "half Gandhi" part of the first phrase to be an encomium.

[3] Philippe Papin, Review of *Vietnam: Un État need la Guerre 1945–1954*, by Christopher Goscha, in *H-Diplo Roundtable Review* XIV, no. 1 (2012): 24. Available online at https:// issforum.org/roundtables/PDF/Roundtable-XIV-1.pdf

[4] Moyar, *Triumph Forsaken*, 9.

Two anecdotes taken from widely separated periods in his political life provide a useful introduction to Ho Chi Minh's political priorities. In 1941, when he set foot in his homeland for the first time in three decades, Ho established his headquarters in a cave near the mountain village of Pac Bo, about a half mile from the Chinese border. Overlooking the cave was a massive stone outcropping; 140 feet below the cave ran a stream. To mark what he apparently considered a historic event, his return to Vietnam, Ho decided to give them names. The stone outcropping henceforth would pay homage to the prophet of communism as "Karl Marx Peak"; the stream below would do the same for the founder of the world's first Communist state as "Lenin Stream." Heroes from the venerable pantheon of Vietnamese nationalism went unrecognized. Decades later an elderly and apparently somewhat spiritual Ho issued a series of final testaments. He did this three times, so he certainly had the opportunity to refer to Vietnamese nationalist figures he might have initially overlooked. Instead, he accurately framed how his commitments should be understood and his legacy crafted by writing about "when I shall go and join Karl Marx, Lenin, and other revolutionary leaders."[5]

Ho Chi Minh's fidelity to Marxism might be viewed as compatible with a genuine commitment to nationalism had Marxism not consistently dominated policy once he was in power. To be sure, when the Vietnamese Communists were struggling for power and had to garner public support, they understood that proclaiming devotion to nationalism was far more effective in winning the support of most Vietnamese than doing the same to Communism. Their propaganda therefore stressed nationalism rather than Marxist socialism, both when they were appealing to fellow Vietnamese and, significantly, when they were trying to garner foreign support. The latter was particularly true and important when the object of those appeals, as was the case in the waning days of World War II and the months immediately after the war's end, was the United States. However, as Stephen J. Morris aptly notes, "when we consider what happened *after* the seizure of power in North Vietnam in 1954 and South Vietnam in 1975, we find that the domestic policies instituted by the Vietnamese Communists indicate values that are not explained by the 'Communism is nationalism' assumption." Rather, each seizure of power was followed by the establishment of a one-party Marxist dictatorship, the nationalization of industry, collectivization of

---

[5] Duiker, *Ho Chi Minh: A Life* (New York: Hyperion, 2000), 250; Stephen J. Morris, "The Internationalist Outlook of Vietnamese Communism," 76.

agriculture (which failed in the south after 1975, but not from lack of commitment by the Hanoi regime), the establishment of a massive secret police apparatus to monitor the people, and other oppressive staples of Communism that have absolutely nothing to do with traditional nationalism. Stalin became a hero in Communist Vietnam and his birthday a cause for celebration. In contrast, when Joseph Broz Tito, leader of the Marxist dictatorship in Yugoslavia, first attempted to infuse elements of genuine nationalism into his country's Communist system, Ho's government, in 1950, called Tito "a spy for American imperialism." In 1963, in a joint statement with the president of the People's Republic of China, Ho Chi Minh denounced "the Yugoslav revisionist clique," saying it had "betrayed" Marxism-Leninism and engaged in "sabotage against the socialist camp." Ho's unwavering devotion to the international Communist movement as his first and foremost priority also was demonstrated by his efforts to mediate the Sino-Soviet split when it emerged during the 1960s.[6]

By the time Ho became a Comintern functionary in the 1920s, Marxism had evolved along various competing lines, some of them bitterly hostile to others. The dominant version, by virtue of the Bolshevik regime that ruled the Soviet Union, is known as Marxism-Leninism or, simply, Leninism. (The terms will be used interchangeably here.) The beauty of Leninism for Ho, in William Duiker's apt phrase, is that it offered Ho exactly what other political organizations in Vietnam lacked: "organization, cohesion, external support, and a plan."[7]

While there are some important differences between Marxism as originally conceived and Leninism, neither had any use for genuine nationalism, or the idea of people identifying with and being loyal to a larger entity based on a common language, culture, history, and geographic living space. Marxism as formulated by Karl Marx in the mid-nineteenth century, categorically opposed nationalism as a reactionary tool of the bourgeoisie in capitalist countries to mislead and oppress the working class and thereby keep it in thrall. As such, it was destructive and had to be combated in all its forms. The workers, *The Communist Manifesto* proclaimed, had no country, only their class identity. Lenin,

---

[6] Stephen J. Morris, "The Internationalist Outlook of Vietnamese Communism," 73–79. Tito's nationalist gambit failed since Yugoslavia was a conglomeration of feuding nationalities, and the country disintegrated in 1991.

[7] Duiker, *The Communist Road to Power in Vietnam*, 20.

writing during World War I as the leader of the Bolshevik Party and after the war as the leader of Soviet Russia, took a more nuanced but still rejectionist approach to nationalism. As he saw it, world capitalism, or what he called imperialism, depended on the exploitation of European colonial empires in Asia and Africa. Nationalism among colonial peoples, or "revolutionary" nationalism, was a force that could undermine those empires, and as a result world capitalism. Revolutionary nationalism therefore was a useful tool and temporary expedient Marxists could use in their struggle to build a socialist world. But the revolutionary nationalism of colonial peoples in no way was an end it itself: it was simply a means to the end of socialism, a useful tactic during the early stage of the struggle for socialism to be discarded when it had served its purpose.

From 1920 until the end of his life, Ho's main loyalty – or the "main motivating force within him," as Sheehan puts it – was to the grand international vision of Leninism and a worldwide socialist revolution, not to parochial Vietnamese nationalism and local independence. This becomes clear when one examines how Ho and his fellow Leninists dealt with other nationalist groups. Vietnamese nationalists were not countrymen with a common concern that took precedence over their differences, or even rivals within a common political process. They were instead enemies to be exploited when possible and/or necessary and then discarded and, as was brutally demonstrated when Ho and his comrades were in a position to do so, destroyed.

There is a revealing debate in this regard about how Ho dealt with one political figure in particular. Phan Boi Chau was the most revered Vietnamese patriot of his generation (see Chapter 2). His career ended when he was betrayed to French security forces and arrested in 1925. A number of scholars have argued that it was Ho who betrayed Phan Boi Chau in return for a large sum of money. The evidence is not conclusive, and Ho has his defenders. William Duiker is among them, but it is interesting what he has to say about this controversial incident in the history of Vietnamese nationalism. Duiker doubts that Ho would have seen any advantage to having Phan Boi Chau arrested, but he does not put such an act of betrayal past Ho. In his book on Vietnamese nationalism published in 1976, Duiker comments that if Ho betrayed Phan Boi Chau "for a few pieces of silver, it was one of the few truly shortsighted decisions of his long career." Twenty-four years later in his biography of Ho, after stating that "it is unlikely" that Ho wanted Phan Boi Chau arrested, Duiker added: "This is not to deny that he [Ho] was capable of betraying the old patriot if he believed it would serve the interests of the revolutionary cause." In short, even when it came to the revered Phan

Boi Chau, to Ho it was not Vietnamese nationalism but revolutionary socialism and the world socialist movement that mattered.[8]

THE VIETNAMESE REVOLUTIONARY YOUTH LEAGUE

The historical record on revolutionary socialism versus nationalism is clear and goes back to the very beginning of Ho's service to the Comintern in Vietnam. In 1925, working beyond the reach of the French in China, on Comintern orders Ho formed an organization called the Vietnamese Revolutionary Youth League. The league promoted itself by stressing nationalist and anti-imperialist goals and muting, although not hiding, its actual Marxist ones. In reality it was not what it claimed to be but instead a classic Communist front, run by Ho's secret inner circle of six or seven Marxist-Leninists. The league's purpose was to lay the basis for a Marxist movement that one day would take over Vietnam by attracting nationalist Vietnamese with radical inclinations who subsequently would provide the nucleus for a Vietnamese Communist party. At this early stage the league also tried to spread its influence by establishing alliances with existing nationalist groups while attempting to undermine them. A favored technique was to poach the membership of nationalist organizations, in particular by inviting selected individuals to the league's training school in Canton, China, where their training included orders not to associate with their former colleagues upon returning to Vietnam. Some of the most promising recruits were dispatched to Moscow, where they received intensive indoctrination in Marxism-Leninism and instruction in how to be professional revolutionaries at an institution called the University of the Toilers of the East, also soon known as the Stalin School. Nationalists who rejected the league's advances often became the object of what Bernard B. Fall calls a "simple but effective cure": their photographs and travel plans were leaked to French security officials, and they were arrested upon arrival home. These activities for good reason were resented by non-Communist nationalist leaders, who understood, as Duiker has written, that Ho and his comrades were "more interested in domination than collaboration." This awareness prevented Ho from building an alliance of groups he could control. However, his poaching did enable him to bring many future Communist leaders into the Marxist-Leninist fold, while his betrayal of those unwilling to embrace

---

[8] Duiker, *The Rise of Nationalism in Vietnam, 1900–1941*, 87; Duiker, *Ho Chi Minh: A Life*, 127.

Marxism-Leninism weakened non-Communist nationalist groups. Ho's successful operation of recruitment and deceit was facilitated by a regular subsidy from the Comintern.[9]

THE INDOCHINESE COMMUNIST PARTY (ICP)

Marxism-Leninism nonetheless had its share of problems in Vietnam. The Vietnamese Revolutionary Youth League, with Ho absent from the scene while on other Comintern assignments, lasted only until 1929. By that point three feuding Communist factions in Vietnam were competing with one another for members, and in early 1930 the Comintern sent Ho from Siam to Hong Kong to restore order in the movement. He did so in February of that year by melding his fractious comrades into the Vietnamese Communist Party, whose name was then changed in October, on Comintern orders, to the Indochinese Communist Party (ICP) so as to include Cambodia and Laos within its purview of operations. Economic hard times resulting from the worldwide Great Depression meanwhile presented what looked like a golden opportunity for the ICP in Vietnam, ironically just months after the Yen Bay uprising (February 1930) that led to the decimation of the Vietnam Nationalist Party (VNQDD). The ICP became active in a rash of strikes in factories and on plantations, and organizations, called soviets, were established in several rural regions to instigate peasant uprisings. The French response to this so-called Nghe-Tinh revolt of 1930–1931 was brutal and effective; an estimated 10,000 Vietnamese were killed and 50,000 arrested and deported. Many ICP members were among the victims; of those arrested, 80 were executed and 400 sentenced to long prison terms. Overall, about 90 percent of the party leadership was eliminated. Like the VNQDD before it, the ICP was virtually destroyed. Ho, in Hong Kong during the turmoil, survived physically but ended up sidelined politically for eight years. Arrested by the British in 1931, he had the good fortune to be released in December 1932. But the Comintern seems to have lost confidence in Ho, as he subsequently remained in the

---

[9] Duiker, *The Communist Road to Power in Vietnam*, 18–25; Duiker, *Ho Chi Minh*, 122; Duiker, *The Rise of Nationalism in Vietnam*, 204. Duiker, of course, is an orthodox historian and credits Ho with genuine nationalist sentiments. The quotation is on page 24 of *The Communist Road to Power in Vietnam*. On Ho's betrayal of Vietnamese nationalists, see Turner, *Vietnamese Communism*, 11 and Bernard B. Fall, *The Two Vietnams: A Political and Military Analysis*, 2nd rev. ed. (New York: Praeger, 1967), 93–94.

Soviet Union for five years before the Comintern finally sent him to China as a military advisor in 1938.

While Ho was on the shelf in Moscow, his comrades in Vietnam carried on and over time enjoyed some success in reviving the ICP. As with all Vietnamese political groups, the ICP benefited when the French relaxed their repression beginning in 1936. Many activists of all political persuasions arrested at the beginning of the decade were released. The change in French policy occurred after the parliamentary election of 1936 brought the so-called Popular Front – an alliance of leftist parties led by the French Socialist Party – to power in Paris. The Popular Front included the French Communist Party, as in Moscow Stalin had decided that Soviet interests required a common front against the growing threat presented by Nazi Germany.[10]

The Popular Front policy did not heal the internal divisions in the international Marxist camp; in Vietnam, Marxists, as elsewhere, remained split into factions with various ideological differences. The most prominent rift, part of a fracture that extended across the Marxist world, was that between the Stalinists, who owed allegiance to Soviet dictator Joseph Stalin, and the Trotskyists, the followers of Stalin's exiled rival Leon Trotsky. The ICP was controlled by Stalinists, and during the 1930s it enjoyed more success than any other Vietnamese political group. A key reason was the help it received from the Soviet Union via the Comintern. As William Duiker notes,

the ICP had one incalculable advantage of all other nationalist groups in Vietnam – the support of the world communist movement, headed by the Comintern. During the four years from the fall of the soviet movement [the Nghe-Tinh revolt] until ... March of 1935, the Comintern provided ideological, financial, and educational support, by means of which the ICP was able to busy itself with reestablishing its base in Vietnam ... the Comintern was able to bring to Moscow for training in Marxist-Leninist doctrine and revolutionary techniques several dozen recruits for one to three years. Graduates of the Stalin School were returned by circuitous routes to East Asia, from whence they were directed to rebuild the shattered apparatus of the party.[11]

---

[10] Stalin's Comintern policy between 1928 and 1935, under which Communist parties throughout Europe had viciously attacked socialist parties as "social fascists" had divided the political left and contributed to the rise of Nazism in Germany. The Popular Front directive was a belated effort to correct this error. After the signing of the Nazi-Soviet nonaggression pact in August 1939, Communist parties affiliated with the Comintern were ordered to stop criticizing Nazi Germany and turn their ideological guns on Europe's few remaining democracies.

[11] Duiker, *The Rise of Nationalism in Vietnam*, 234–35.

By 1939 the ICP had an estimated 10,000 members. With the nationalist parties badly divided or dysfunctional, the ICP by default had become the leading party resisting French colonial rule, although at times the Trotskyists bested their Stalinist rivals in local elections permitted by the French. The ICP was even making progress in overcoming the one serious disadvantage of Comintern membership: the ideological straitjacket Stalin imposed on the organization. During the early 1930s Stalin had ordered the Comintern to follow classic Marxist principles and focus on organizing the proletariat, even in unindustrialized countries such as Vietnam where that social class was tiny. Both promoting local nationalism and working with the peasantry – a reactionary and backward class according to classic Marxist theory – were regarded with suspicion. Even with the shift to the Popular Front, this outlook persisted among many ICP members during the second half of the 1930s. However, by the late 1930s the Comintern was paying less attention to Vietnam and Indochina, and this allowed local activists more freedom to formulate their ideas. Their experience during the Popular Front era intensified interest in making use of nationalism in the quest for a social revolution. Ho Chi Minh, from his vantage point in China, agreed with that assessment, and in July 1939 he wrote a report to the Comintern advocating that the ICP cooperate with nationalist groups to build a broad front against the French. In addition, party leaders in Vietnam were increasingly conscious of the potential role the peasantry could play in that effort. One of them was a history teacher named Vo Nguyen Giap, who soon would become a student of military science and then the brilliant commander first of the Vietminh's and later of North Vietnam's military forces. Thus the two key ideological components of the strategy the Communists needed to come to power in Vietnam – the need to place nationalism in the forefront and the importance of the peasantry as a mass base – were taking shape. Meanwhile, the man with the extraordinary skills needed to pull things together, Ho Chi Minh, was in China, right next door to Vietnam.[12]

What the Communists in Vietnam needed in 1939 was a break, some kind of event that would decisively weaken France and thereby its grip on Vietnam. World War II, about to erupt in September of that year, while bringing catastrophe to so many, would give it to them.

---

[12] Turner, *Vietnamese Communism*, 26; Taylor, *A History of the Vietnamese*, 516–17; Duiker, *The Rise of Nationalism in Vietnam*, 235–37, 250–51, 254–55, 291–92; Duiker, *Ho Chi Minh*, 234–36.

THE VIETMINH

Two events early in World War II, the defeat of the French in Europe in 1940 and the Japanese occupation of Indochina during 1940–1941, created unprecedented opportunity for opponents of French rule in Vietnam. For the ICP, however, these developments initially led to two costly defeats at the hands of French colonial authorities. Both occurred in late 1940: the first a failed uprising in the mountains north of Hanoi in late September and October, and the second a failed uprising far to the south in Cochinchina during November and December. Meanwhile, Ho Chi Minh, who had been serving the Comintern with Chinese Communist forces in northern China, arrived in southern China and turned his attention to Vietnam. In February 1941 Ho returned to his native country for the first time in thirty years, and he immediately focused on the task of reviving the fortunes of the ICP. In May, as the representative of the Comintern, Ho presided over a seminal ten-day meeting of the ICP central committee in Pac Bo, its so-called Eighth Plenum. The main agenda item, in light of the new circumstances and opportunities, was to develop a strategy for taking power in Vietnam. The key to doing that, the ICP resolved, was to subordinate its ultimate goal of a socialist revolution, which had little popular support, to the traditional nationalist goal of independence, which had wide popular support. The task at hand, according to official resolutions of the plenum, was to "employ an especially stirring . . . method of appeal to awaken the traditional nationalism of the people." This presumably would enable the ICP to win broad popular support and boost its effort to come to power. Socialist revolution unquestionably remained the party's goal; however, it would not be publicized for fear of alienating those who supported independence but opposed Communism. It was time "to take a shorter step in order [later] to try to take a longer one." Publicizing the ICP's real objectives, the Eighth Plenum's resolutions warned, would be counterproductive: "not only will we lose an allied force who would support us in the revolution to overthrow the French and Japanese, but we would also push that force to the side of our enemy, as the rear guard of our enemy."[13] In short, the ICP

---

[13] Cited in Khanh, *Vietnamese Communism*, 260–61. Khanh generally is sympathetic to Ho Chi Minh and the Vietnamese communist movement but does not cover up the ICP's manipulation of Vietnamese nationalism, or, as he calls it, Vietnamese "patriotism." On the last page of his book he raises the question of whether Marxism-Leninism has been "a vehicle for Vietnamese patriotism" or if that patriotism has been "exploited for the sake of expanding Communist ideology" (p. 341).

had decided to perpetrate a fraud on the Vietnamese population. This tactic worked, and it would be used repeatedly.

The vehicle for implementing the ICP's policy was a new organization called the Vietnam Independence League, or Vietminh. The Vietminh was a front for the ICP; its purpose was to enlist the backing of nationalist groups and individual supporters of independence while remaining under complete ICP control. Given the task at hand, every effort was made to camouflage the Vietminh's puppet status. This included Nguyen Ai Quoc hiding his Comintern association by taking on a new alias, Ho Chi Minh, and naming a real non-Communist – ironically, with the family name Ho (Ho Ngoc Lam) – as the Vietminh's chairman. Even the Vietminh's name did that, as the word "Indochina," which appeared in the name of ICP, was replaced by what Duiker calls the "more emotive" word "Vietnam."[14] The central committee of the ICP explained the name change at greater length. It noted that the "current tactic of our party is to use a method of great appeal." Therefore, the name used for a previous front organization set up back in November 1939 – the National Anti-Imperialist Front of Indochina – would not do. A name "with a greater nationalistic nature and a greater appeal" that was "more consistent with the present situation" was needed. From that necessity "our party's political front in Vietnam today shall be designated the *Vietnam Doc Lap Dong Minh* [League for the Independence of Vietnam] or Viet Minh, in short."[15]

Consistent with its new name and goal of broadening its support beyond the Communist faithful, the new front's fifteen-page program stressed three points: expulsion of the French and Japanese to establish Vietnamese independence; alliance with the United States, China, and other countries fighting Germany and Japan; and the eventual establishment of a Democratic Republic of Vietnam, which, the Vietminh promised, would guarantee a wide range of civil liberties including freedom of the press, freedom to organize, and universal suffrage. Not mentioned were earlier ICP policies such as confiscation of land from "counterrevolutionary landlords" and its distribution to poor peasants. As Ho himself admitted later, this was done to attract "all the patriotic forces" to the Vietminh, including "patriotic landlords,"[16] a group, it bears mentioning, Ho and his comrades no longer recognized as existing once the Vietminh came to power.

---

[14] Duiker, *Ho Chi Minh*, 252. [15] Cited in Turner, *Vietnamese Communism*, 30.
[16] Ibid., 31.

Meanwhile, during the early 1940s and the upheavals of World War II, the Vietminh's main source of outside help changed. The Comintern – which Stalin abolished in 1943 as a goodwill gesture to his Western allies fighting Nazi Germany – was not providing Ho and the Vietminh with significant help, as all Soviet resources were devoted to the war effort. The Chinese Communist Party (CCP) filled that void in an important way. In 1940 both the future People's Army of Vietnam (PAVN) commander Vo Nguyen Giap and future Democratic Republic of Vietnam (DRV) prime minister Pham Van Dong went to China to receive military and political training from the CCP. During the early 1940s the CCP also helped the Vietminh with military advisors and training. As a result, Communist Chinese principles were integrated into the Vietminh's approach to guerrilla war, albeit in combination with the operational experience and views of Ho and Giap. In 1942, a future People's Republic of China (PRC) defense minister came to Vietnam to instruct the Vietminh on military matters. This and other help from CCP military specialists contributed to the creation of a force of several thousand organized into small guerrilla units that by 1944 enabled the Vietminh to control much of the mountainous countryside north of the Red River delta.[17]

When in late 1944 Ho Chi Minh entrusted Giap with organizing a more formidable force that would become the basis of the PAVN, the former history teacher could count on more than his experience as a guerrilla fighter in the field and what he had learned from his own self-study efforts. Thanks to the CCP, while in China he had benefited from studying Mao Zedong's writings on guerrilla warfare and learning about tactics, strategy, equipment, training, and recruitment while observing the CCP's army as it fought Japanese forces in that World War II arena. Giap had to begin small when he returned to Vietnam: the first unit of what eventually grew into the PAVN had only thirty-four men and very few guns, some of them antiquated weapons that dated from the Russo-Japanese War of 1905. Still, within days, Giap's troops had won their first victory and captured valuable arms and ammunition in the process when they overran two isolated French outposts.[18] During its war of 1946–1954 against the French, the Vietminh would get much more Chinese Communist military

[17] Khanh, *Vietnamese Communism*, 282–83.
[18] Cecil B. Curry, *Victory at Any Cost: The Genius of Vietnam's Vo Nguyen Giap* (Dulles, VA: Brassey's, 1997), 51–53, 80–84.

help, and it would prove crucial in the much larger-scale battles Giap's forces would fight in that conflict.

Before that, however, the Japanese coup of March 1945, by breaking French power in Vietnam and opening the door to political and military activity to all Vietnamese groups, opened it farthest to the Vietminh, the best organized of those groups thanks to its puppet master, the ICP. Two factors were central to the Vietminh's success. First, the Vietminh were able to take advantage of a national crisis. The poor harvest of 1944 had combined with the confiscation of rice by the Japanese and French and wartime conditions to cause a famine in northern Vietnam, and by early 1945 the death toll had reached an estimated million people. No effort at amelioration came from either the French or the Japanese. The Vietminh responded by sending armed units to seize grain from landlords and, more importantly, from Japanese rice transports and granaries, where it was being held for export to Japan. This significantly increased public support for the Vietminh, perhaps most critically among peasants in several of the hardest hit rural areas, and that in turn helped Vietminh expand its area of control in those areas. Second, the Vietminh made effective use of brute force. In rural areas, the overall Vietminh approach was to move into a village or hamlet and dispense what historian David Marr has called "rough revolutionary justice." The targets of this "justice" often were those who had collaborated with the French or Japanese, sometimes by betraying ICP or Vietminh operatives to the occupiers. But, as Marr points out, "the overriding purpose of the killings was to cow opponents and perhaps garner support from ordinary citizens angry at the way they had been treated" by the French authorities. One important target was the Dai Viet National Alliance, which like several other nationalist groups had cooperated with the Japanese because it saw the Japanese as a vehicle for ending French control of Vietnam and thereby achieving national independence. People associated with the Dai Viet National Alliance were assassinated and terrorized, as Marr notes, not only because the Vietminh and ICP considered them Japanese lackeys but also because they were "potential rivals for political power."[19]

These tactics worked, and by the time Japan surrendered to the United States and its allies in August 1945 the Vietminh had established what they called a "liberated area" in several provinces north of Hanoi that contained more than one million people. In Hanoi itself, as well as in other

---

[19] Khanh, 313–14; David G. Marr, *Vietnam 1945: The Quest for Power* (Berkeley: University of California Press, 1995), 234–37.

urban areas where gaining control was impossible, the Vietminh engaged in what historian Huynh Kim Khanh calls "selective terrorism" in an effort to spread fear and demonstrate Vietminh power. These killings, Khanh adds, "were not numerous, but sufficient to cow adversaries and to advertise the Vietminh presence."[20]

One reason for the Vietminh's growing power between Japan's March coup in Vietnam and its ultimate surrender in mid-August was that its armed forces had modern weapons supplied by the United States. The United States agreed to provide these and other supplies in return for Vietminh intelligence on Japanese activities in Indochina, help in rescuing downed US airmen flying missions over Vietnam into southern China, and attacks on Japanese forces. This collaboration was arranged by the US Office of Strategic Services (OSS), the wartime precursor to the CIA. American supplies included weapons, communications equipment, medical supplies, and other material, with the first arms deliveries beginning in 1942. Aid and cooperation were upgraded significantly in July 1945 when a six-man team of advisors parachuted into northern Vietnam to equip and train Vietminh fighters. The Americans were totally taken in by Ho and his comrades, who successfully portrayed themselves as pro-American nationalists. The OSS reports, as journalist and historian Arthur Dommen has observed, "reveal with unequaled clarity the astounding naiveté of its authors." One early report informs Washington to "Forget the Communist Bogy [sic]. VML is *not* Communist. Stands for freedom and reforms from French harshness." Dommen notes the following: "This snap judgment, which conveniently ignores 15 years of party history and Ho's 22 years in the service of the Comintern, heads a bulky file of many such judgments made by American military men, diplomats, and journalists regarding Vietnam."[21] The Vietminh/US deal certainly did not benefit each side equally. Ho and the Vietminh did provide some intelligence and help with downed fliers, but Vietminh military forces avoided any serious combat against the Japanese. There is in fact only one recorded Vietminh attack against Japanese troops; a total of eight Japanese troops were killed.[22] Prior to the Japanese surrender, and immediately thereafter during late 1945 and 1946, the American weapons and training the Vietminh received found their main use against Vietnamese opponents of the Vietminh; subsequently they would be used against the French.

[20] Khanh, *Vietnamese Communism*, 320.
[21] Dommen, *The Indochinese Experience of the French and the Americans*, 94–97.
[22] Turner, *Vietnamese Communism*, 34–35; Hammer, *The Struggle for Indochina*, 97.

THE COUP OF AUGUST 1945 AND THE EVENTS OF 1946

On August 19, 1945, the Vietminh seized control of Hanoi. However, the Vietminh did not seize power from the Japanese, who had surrendered to the Allies on August 14, nor from the French, who had been deposed by the Japanese five months earlier. The Vietminh seized power from the government of the Vietnamese emperor Bao Dai, who had served as a puppet ruler from the old imperial city of Hue under both the French and, after they took control of the country, the Japanese. Whatever his many shortcomings, Bao Dai actually had beaten Ho Chi Minh to the punch on one point: in the wake of the Japanese coup, on March 11, 1945, Bao Dai had declared Vietnam independent of France, albeit with somewhat ambiguous language to avoid a military reaction from Tokyo, whose troops, after all, controlled the country.[23]

The well-orchestrated Vietminh seizure of power took place almost without opposition from either supporters of Bao Dai or Japanese troops still in Hanoi awaiting disarmament by the Allies and repatriation home. The Vietminh also had either tacit or active support of various other groups, a result of successful organizing and propaganda that gave it what Duiker calls an "image of moderation."[24] This helped them take control of large parts of Vietnam during the next ten days. Bao Dai abdicated on August 25, a provisional government was formed on August 29, and on September 2, 1945, Ho Chi Minh declared the independence of what he called the Democratic Republic of Vietnam at a mass rally of half a million people in the center of Hanoi. He famously quoted the first sentence of the US Declaration of Independence in his speech, a gesture that impressed American officials present at the ceremony but, as events would quickly demonstrate, was meaningless since it did not reflect an intent on Ho's part to establish democracy, or anything close to it, in Vietnam.

It turned out that in 1945 independence was no more in the cards for Vietnam than was democracy, albeit in the former case because of the Allies. In the wake of Japan's defeat and ongoing departure from

---

[23] For details see Dommer, *The Indochinese Experience of the French and the Americans*, 84–85. Bao Dai declared that "the Government of Vietnam publicly proclaims that from today the protectorate treaty with France is abrogated and that the country resumes its rights to independence." He made no reference to the territorial unity of Vietnam, which the French had divided into three units. Bao Dai, with the approval of the Japanese military, chose as his prime minister a respected scholar and educator named Tran Trong Kim.

[24] Duiker, *The Communist Road to Power in Vietnam*, 104.

territories it still occupied, the British and Americans had agreed to allow the French to return to Vietnam as the governing colonial power. The arrival of British troops during September in the south began that process as the British immediately released and armed French troops who had been interned by the Japanese earlier in the year. That same month the Chinese Nationalist government of Chiang Kaishek sent a large army into northern Vietnam. These developments enormously complicated matters for Ho Chi Minh but did not stop him from attempting to control Vietnam. During late 1945 and early 1946, Ho and the Vietminh skillfully acted on several fronts. Ho dealt with the Chinese occupation army by bribing its commanding generals, and they in turn did not interfere with the newly proclaimed Vietminh government. To get the Chinese out of Vietnam, Ho worked out an arrangement with the French regarding their presence in Vietnam (while the French in turn negotiated with the Chinese on the issues dividing them). This triangular set of negotiations brought about the withdrawal of Chinese troops from northern Vietnam and permitted France to position 25,000 troops there for six years.[25]

Covering every flank, the Vietminh, in secret, even sought Japanese help. It came from hundreds of officers and enlisted men in Vietnam who were among the thousands of personnel interned and awaiting repatriation to their homeland. One estimate is that during 1945 General Giap recruited 1,500 soldiers; they were led by a colonel, 230 noncommissioned officers, and 47 officers of the dreaded Japanese military police wanted by the Allies for questioning about war crimes. All recruits were given Vietnamese names, identity papers, and citizenship to hide who they really were. Their most important service to the Vietminh was as weapons instructors and in maintaining equipment.[26] In other words, as he had done in the late 1920s with the French colonial authorities when he provided them with travel information about nationalists who refused

---

[25] For details regarding these complicated negotiations see Moss, *Vietnam: An American Ordeal*, 37–39.

[26] Marr, *Vietnam 1945*, 543; Curry, *Victory at Any Cost*, 125–26. Curry's estimate of 1,500 is based on a US Defense Intelligence document he obtained through the Freedom of Information Act. The Japanese military police, or Kempetai, for good reason has been compared to the German Gestapo. For a detailed account of this episode, see Christopher E. Goscha, "Belated Asian Allies: The Technical and Military Contributions of Japanese Deserters (1945–1950)," in *A Companion to the Vietnam War*, ed. Marilyn B. Young and Robert Buzzanco (Malden, MA: Blackwell, 2002), 37–64, especially 44–47. Most of these Japanese joined the Vietminh; however, some were recruited by the Cao Dai and Hoa Hao religious sects.

Communist indoctrination, in 1945 and 1946 Ho did not hesitate to collaborate with the French, Chinese, or Japanese when it suited his purposes. Meanwhile, as punishment for this presumed crime, he had Vietminh hit squads assassinate thousands of members of various nationalist groups, often for far lesser acts of collaboration.

When it came to the Vietnamese people, after the August 1945 coup and into 1946 the Vietminh followed a two-pronged policy of outward moderation combined with systematic repression of non-Communist nationalists. Outward moderation began with the composition of the provisional government. Several non-Communists were given ministries, and every effort was made to hide the real affiliation of the majority of ministers, including Ho himself, who were in fact Communists. In November the ICP, so troublesome to the Vietminh's moderate public relations image, conveniently disappeared when Ho announced its dissolution. In fact the ICP did not dissolve; as Ho himself put it, the ICP "went underground ... And though underground, the Party continued to lead the administration and the people."[27] While the decision to hide the ICP was taken to appease the Chinese and the Western powers, whose combined military forces controlled most of the country, the main audience for this act of political theater was the Vietnamese people. As one important ICP official, who later defected, explained:

They [the Vietminh] were not able to mobilize all of the people to fight the French so long as the Communist doctrine and the Communist Party were present. Therefore, as a tactical move, as a temporary measure, they had to put an end to the Indochinese Communist Party ... If the Communists were there, then the people would not join the [Vietminh] movement. People dared not unite with the Communists – especially the South Vietnamese people, who did not have any liking for the Communists ... In fact, the Party just went underground.[28]

Another act of political theater was the election of a national assembly, which took place on January 6, 1946. The term political theater is used here because at no point in his political career was Ho Chi Minh, a Marxist-Leninist to the core, ever prepared to allow elections to determine the fate of Vietnam. Elections, when held, were a tool to be used, with the results guaranteed in advance by whatever means necessary, to achieve dictatorial power. In any event, the Vietminh, as Bernard Fall notes, had a great advantage over its nationalist rivals in the January 1946

[27] Quoted in Turner, *Vietnamese Communism*, 35. See also 69–70 on efforts to hide Ho's Communist past.
[28] Ibid., 35–36.

elections because it had used the previous six months "to implant its power through policy, army, and control of communications and ... [because it] represented 'the Government' to the inexperienced and largely illiterate average Vietnamese voter."[29] The VNQDD and Dong Minh Hoi, aware of their weaknesses, therefore accepted an offer of 70 seats in a legislative body of about 300. The elections were a sham and yielded the required overwhelming Vietminh majority. According to official claims, Giap won his seat with 97 percent of the vote, second only to Ho himself, who according to the official record garnered 98.4 percent of the vote in his Hanoi constituency. Vietnam's National Assembly held its inaugural meeting to do the Vietminh's bidding in March, its first task being to replace Ho's provisional government with one called the Coalition Government of National Union and Resistance. Like the government it replaced – the entire process took only half an hour – the new one featured Ho as president, included some ministers from non-Communist parties who were in practice rendered powerless by a variety of methods, and was dominated by Communists from the Vietminh.[30]

This pose of moderation was a cover for a systematic and ruthless policy of repression, similar to what was done after the Japanese coup in March, designed to silence all opponents to Communist rule. Precise figures on what happened in the months immediately after the coup of August 1945 cannot be ascertained, but the number of assassinations of Vietminh opponents clearly reached into the thousands. Tens of thousands more were arrested and often held for many months. This was a well-organized campaign. The lists of "traitors" and "reactionaries," to be sure, included Vietnamese who had collaborated with the French and/or Japanese but was hardly limited to them. Members of the VNQDD, moderate political parties such as the Dai Viet Nationalist Alliance and Constitutionalist Party, and the Cao Dai and Hoa Hao sects were assassinated, as were Trotskyites. The victims ranged from Bui Quang Chieu, a longtime Constitutionalist Party leader and advocate of peaceful struggle for independence (murdered along with his four sons), to Ngo Dinh Diem's brother Ngo Dinh Khoi (buried alive), to Ta Thu

---

[29] Cited in ibid., 45–46.

[30] Ibid., 50. For example, a Communist deputy minister was attached to every non-Communist minister to countermand in one way or another any decision the minister made that was contrary to Ho's policies. Ministerial responsibilities also were shifted so that non-Communist ministers lost their key powers. See Curry, *Victory at Any Cost*, 110–11.

Thau, the country's most talented Trotskyite writer and speaker (shot on a beach after a mock trial). The assassination of Ta Thu Thau shocked intellectuals of most political viewpoints and caused many to believe, correctly it turned out, that the Vietminh hit list included genuine nationalists and anti-colonialists as well as collaborators.[31] The scope and organization of this campaign across the spectrum of the non-Marxist nationalist camp and from there into the non-Stalinist Marxist camp effectively debunks any claim that it was conducted by people to whom nationalism was the first or even a primary political goal. This was a Stalinist political purge designed to destroy anyone opposed to a Marxist Vietminh dictatorship in Vietnam. As Dommen notes, "As the liquidations began, it became obvious that the Viet Minh had no intention of heeding appeals from many quarters for a conciliation of all Vietnamese nationalists in order to 'consolidate independence.'"[32]

What followed during the spring and summer of 1946 was even more violent and emphatic in demonstrating the dictatorial Communist as opposed to nationalist agenda of Ho and the Vietminh. In March 1946, Ho negotiated an ambiguous agreement with the French regarding Vietnamese independence. It called for the Democratic Republic of Vietnam to be a "free state" within the so-called French Union. How free the DRV would actually be was unclear, especially since the agreement called for thousands of French troops to be stationed in northern Vietnam. There was, however, an immediate upside for Ho and the Vietminh since the arrival French troops facilitated the withdrawal of Chinese troops, and the latter were providing the main protection for the VNQDD and other nationalist groups in northern Vietnam. The first French troops landed in Hanoi within days, a development greeted with dismay and anger by many Vietnamese nationalists. Meanwhile, subsequent discussions to clarify the agreement revealed that the French in fact had no intention of granting Vietnam real independence. In June, Ho therefore left for France to negotiate directly with the French government. While he tried to deal with the French, the external and most powerful threat Vietminh rule, he left General Giap to deal with local nationalists, the domestic and far weaker challenge to that rule.

As he had done before and would do again, Giap carried out his task with ruthless efficiency. Ho as usual attempted to hide his latest campaign

---

[31] Dommen, *The Indochinese Experience of the French and Americans*, 120–21; Marr, *Vietnam 1945*, 435, 519.

[32] Ibid., 121.

against Vietnamese nationalists behind what Dommen calls a "mask of reconciliation," this one a new front group formed in May called the National Popular Front of Vietnam (*Hoi Lien Hiep Quoc Dan Viet Nam*). When the last Chinese troops departed in mid-June, Giap launched his campaign against the now largely defenseless nationalists. He began by demanding that all nationalist groups join the newly minted National Popular Front of Vietnam. Those that refused were branded reactionaries and traitors or, according to the official Vietminh newspaper, "reactionary saboteurs."[33] Along with the Dong Minh Hoi, the VNQDD, and the Dai Viet National Alliance, other alleged reactionary saboteurs included anti-French nationalists who had opposed the March agreement as well as Trotskyists and Roman Catholics. Newspapers were shut down, people were arrested, and hundreds executed. Giap's police and newly formed army were assisted not only by his Japanese recruits but also by the French, who wanted all nationalist opponents of the March 1946 agreement, especially the VNQDD, eliminated. The French therefore released Vietminh leaders from jail and provided Giap's troops with artillery to attack Dai Viet National Alliance strong points. French troops helped Vietminh forces eliminate VNQDD positions in Hanoi and the Dong Minh Hoi positions in a coastal town east of the city. As Giap biographer Cecil B. Curry observes, "Hundreds of nationalists who might in the future provide guidance for a rival anti-French resistance movement were executed during this campaign."[34] Giap's methods included binding people together and throwing them into rivers to drown as they floated out to sea, a technique of execution the general dubbed "crab fishing."[35]

Another technique was to slander opponents with false accusations of atrocities. Thus in mid-July 1946, Giap's forces seized the VNQDD headquarters in Hanoi, an action accomplished with French help in the form of armored cars that sealed off the area to prevent VNQDD activists from reaching the building to help their colleagues on the scene. Giap then ordered what Curry calls a "chamber of horrors" be built and that bodies be exhumed from graves and placed outside the building. People who visited the grisly site were shown evidence of this presumed VNQDD atrocity. Adding insult to injury, many of the bodies Giap placed at the scene were those of murdered VNQDD members. In the end, thousands of Vietminh opponents, perhaps as many as 15,000, were assassinated. Late in July, as Gaip's campaign was nearing its end, the head of the newly

[33] Ibid., 153.   [34] Curry, *Victory at Any Cost*, 125–26. The quotation is on page 126.
[35] Ibid.

reopened US consulate in Hanoi, apparently less naïve than the OSS operatives Ho had so impressed, reported to Washington, "the Vietminh League seems steadily to be eliminating all organized organization."[36] Some years later Nguyen Duy Thanh, who before defecting served the Vietminh for four years, including in an important diplomatic post, offered a more in-depth analysis, one that explains why he ultimately rejected the Vietminh:

Though we all knew that Ho Chi Minh and his Party were all Communists of long standing, still, we thought that they would put first and foremost the cause of their country over party interests. Our expectations were sadly belied. Day after day the communists showed up their fascist tendency and adopted a hostile attitude towards the nationalists who did not brook communist ideals.[37]

By the end of 1946 the non-Communist nationalist political parties had been severely weakened or virtually destroyed. By then the death toll among Vietminh opponents probably reached into the tens of thousands.[38] No domestic nationalist force was capable of resisting the rule of the Vietminh. But France, the foreign colonial power determined to restore its control over Vietnam, had that capability. The destruction of the nationalist parties therefore turned out to be a two-edged sword, as in achieving that goal Ho and the Vietminh had unavoidably weakened the overall Vietnamese ability to oppose French ambitions. During 1946 Ho worked feverishly to delay a showdown with the French, but in this he did not succeed. The French effort to nip Vietnamese independence in the bud would begin with a vengeance before the year was out.

THE FIRST INDOCHINA WAR, 1946–1954

The so-called First Indochina War began during December 1946 when the French launched attacks, including massive artillery bombardments, on Vietminh strongholds in and around Hanoi. The first phase of the war, through 1949, was essentially a military stalemate. During that time, along with fighting the French on the battlefield, Ho had to focus on a second front, the Vietnamese people. The situation was in some ways paradoxical. On the one hand, the vast majority of the Vietnamese people did not want or support Communism; on the other, as Dommen points

---

[36] Dommen, *The Indochinese Experience of the French and the Americans*, 154.

[37] Quoted in Curry, *Victory at Any Cost*, 109. Thanh's twenty-eight-page memoir, published in 1950, is titled *My Four Years With the Vietminh*.

[38] Moyar, *Triumph Forsaken*, 19.

out, "in the interests of preserving their independence they supported a government under the control of the communists that was carefully camouflaged by an alliance with other political parties that were largely phantoms ... and by a front organization, the Lien Viet [National Popular Front of Vietnam], that claimed to represent all strata of society."[39] But the Lien Viet veil could not conceal the real nature of Ho's regime, and the desire for independence notwithstanding, opposition to the Vietminh was growing. Robert Turner points out that ruthless repression of nationalists and what looked like collaboration with the French were taking a toll on Vietminh credibility. So too were Vietminh policies in areas they controlled, the so-called liberated zone. According to Philippe Devillers, a prominent French historian based in Vietnam during those days:

> The Vietminh had subjected the people to an extremely painful strain, practically a permanent mobilization ... with its control of thoughts and acts, with its atmosphere of suspicion and its informers ... and with the arrests, the abduction or assassination of its opponents and even of those considered lukewarm or suspect. If the Vietminh still seemed to be the only movement capable of bringing about ... national independence and ... social justice, it nevertheless ruled with the aid of physical terror and moral constraint. As under the old regime, the political police ... was the main buttress of the regime.[40]

In southern Vietnam, especially the Mekong River delta area, where the Vietminh were weakest, efforts to work out some kind of cooperative relationship with Hoa Hao and Cao Dai religious sects ran afoul of Vietminh attacks on those groups, which included the capture and murder of the founder of the Hoa Hao sect. Both groups in the end chose an alliance with the French as the lesser evil compared to the treatment they received from the Vietminh.[41]

As these problems mounted, the Vietminh received a huge boost at the end of 1949. And as had happened before, that boost to the Communist cause in Vietnam came from outside the country. In October 1949, the Chinese Communist Party completed its defeat of the Nationalist regime of Chiang Kaishek and proclaimed the establishment of the People's Republic of China. Soon PRC military forces reached the China-Vietnam border, and in December Ho Chi Minh began a trip on foot that took him to China in January 1950. That same month both the PRC and the Soviet Union officially recognized the Democratic Republic of

---

[39] Dommen, *The Indochinese Experience of the French and the Americans*, 169.
[40] Quoted in Turner, *Vietnamese Communism*, 68.
[41] Duiker, *The Communist Road to Power in Vietnam*, 132.

Vietnam as the government of Vietnam, notwithstanding that Ho's regime was now based in the countryside with its authority restricted to scattered areas it called liberated zones. Within days, the Soviet Union's puppet regimes in Eastern Europe followed suit. More helpful to the Vietminh was the arrival of military weapons and equipment, most from the PRC but some from the Soviet Union. During the first nine months of 1950, these deliveries included 14,000 rifles, 1,700 machine guns and recoilless rifles, 60 artillery pieces, and 300 bazookas. Significantly, both Stalin and Mao made their commitments to provide military aid to the Vietminh several months before the United States did the same for the French. Stalin insisted that the PRC would have to provide the bulk of the aid but added, "What China lacks, we will provide." By April 1950 Chinese military advisors in the form of the Chinese Military Advisory Group (CMAC) were in Vietnam assisting the Vietminh, and by the summer a force of 20,000 troops had been trained and equipped in China. The Communist victory in China also gave the Vietminh a sanctuary just across the Vietnam-China border where its forces could get away from the French and regroup to fight another day.[42]

Strengthened by its newfound support from the CCP and Soviet Union, the Vietminh concluded it could shed part of its nationalist mask and reveal more of its Communist agenda. It did this in a series of announcements and policies during 1950 and 1951. For example, Ho no longer spoke of the DRV as being neutral in the emerging Cold War struggle "like Switzerland," as he had told a journalist while in Paris in 1946. Instead, as Duiker puts it, "the DRV openly advertised its new 'lean to one side' policy toward its socialist allies."[43] When the DRV officially recognized the Communist states of Eastern Europe that had extended it recognition, it emphasized its position by ignoring Yugoslavia, the one Communist state that had asserted its national independence and broken with that bloc. Inside Vietnam the dominant influence was the neighboring PRC rather than the distant Soviet Union. Throughout areas under its control, using

---

[42] Turner, *Vietnamese Communism*, 72–73; Duiker, *The Communist Road to Power in Vietnam*, 140–41; Moyar, *Triumph Forsaken*, 22–23; Taylor, *A History of the Vietnamese*, 550–51; Duiker, *Ho Chi Minh*, 422–37. The Stalin quote is on page 422. President Truman authorized the first US military aid to help the French in Vietnam in July 1950, after the Korean War began with the North Korea's invasion of South Korea. An American military mission to help the French army arrived in Vietnam in late September.

[43] Turner, *Vietnamese Communism*, 70; Duiker, *The Communist Road to Power in Vietnam*, 141.

materials translated from Chinese into Vietnamese, the Vietminh carried out a major campaign to indoctrinate Vietminh cadres in CCP doctrine and methods. The step that most clearly revealed the Vietminh's Communist agenda was taken in 1951 when Ho officially revived the ICP, albeit under a new name. The party reemerged at a congress held in northern Vietnam in February 1951 as the Vietnamese Workers' Party (VWP). Ho naturally occupied the top post of party chairman. In the keynote speech by party general secretary Troung Chinh, the party now openly proclaimed its Marxist-Leninist agenda for Vietnam. Interestingly, while the cloak covering the existence of the party and its agenda was off, a significant fig leaf remained in place. The word "Communist" was not included in the party's name because, as a party circular put it, "if we keep the name of 'Communist Party' a certain number of landowners, progressive intellectuals and members of religious sects would not want to follow us."[44]

The party briefly also continued to pull its punches when it came to land reform by limiting land confiscations in the areas it controlled. The ground began to shift in 1952 as the training activity and hence the influence of Chinese advisors on the Vietminh increased. By the fall of 1952, Ho had a land reform plan. It had been worked out with the top CCP leadership and submitted to Stalin for his approval. In January 1953 Vietminh announced it was accelerating land reform efforts, and, more importantly, in December of that year Ho announced a new radical land redistribution policy. Following the model used by the CCP during its victorious civil war, the Vietminh increased not only the pace and extent of confiscations but the violence it used to accomplish them.[45]

Another way the name "Vietnam Workers' Party" was misleading involved the organization's agenda for Indochina. The first word in its name and the creation of supposedly independent parties for Laos and Cambodia notwithstanding, the VWP party program spoke of

---

[44] Quoted in Turner, *Vietnamese Communism*, 78. See also Duiker, *The Communist Road to Power in Vietnam*, 140–43.

[45] Duiker, *The Communist Road to Power in Vietnam*, 153–54. Taylor, *A History of the Vietnamese*, 566–67. For additional information on the violence by which the Vietminh carried out land reform before 1954, see Hoang Van Chi, *From Colonialism to Communism: A Case History of North Vietnam* (New York: Praeger, 1964). Hoang Van Chi, although not a Communist, supported the Vietminh in its war against the French until 1954. However, he was repelled by North Vietnamese repression and moved to South Vietnam, where he served in the government of Ngo Dinh Diem until 1960. He eventually settled in the United States. There have been attempts to discredit Hoang's work, in particular his estimates of deaths that resulted from land reform in North Vietnam after 1954, but overall his work his withstood that criticism.

establishing a "federation of the states of Viet-Nam, Laos, and Cambodia" with the meaningless caveat "if the three peoples so desire." A memorandum circulated at the time was quite clear about any inappropriate "desires" on the part of the Laotians and Cambodians: "The Vietnamese Party reserves the right to supervise the activities of its brother parties in Cambodia and Laos." In November 1951 a top secret document noted that "when conditions permit" the three Communist parties of Indochina would be reunited. That made perfect sense, since some months earlier Ho Chi Minh, not having consulted any of the peoples involved, had told his comrades that he looked forward to the "great union of Vietnam-Laos-Cambodia."[46] In short, the VWP saw itself first and foremost as a participant in the world Communist revolution, not a nationalist group focused on the country in which it was based and whose name it carried.

The biggest payoff of the Vietminh's close relationship with the CCP was its victory over the French at the battle of Dien Bien Phu in 1954. By then Chinese aid to the Vietminh had reached 4,000 tons of supplies per month, ten times the quantity of 1951. The French had turned this remote village in northern Vietnam into a fortress, one of whose purposes was to lure the Vietminh into a set piece battle that the French, with their superior firepower, were sure they would win. But the French did not anticipate the massive military aid the Vietminh received from China. It included vital advice from top Chinese commanders in planning and fighting the battle, artillery and antiaircraft weapons, 1,000 trucks (made in the Soviet Union), advanced rocket launchers manned by Chinese experts, and thousands of Chinese porters to carry disassembled weapons into position in the mountains surrounding Dien Bien Phu. The Vietminh siege lasted almost two months, with both sides suffering heavy casualties. The fortress fell on May 7, ending the war and setting the stage for the French withdrawal from Vietnam.

It is important to understand the pattern underlying the sequence of events that began in the 1920s and eventually produced the Vietminh's 1954 triumph. Vietnam's Communists always needed, and regularly received, help from outside their country. In the 1920s and 1930s, they received vital help from the Soviet Union, first to get organized and then to survive French repression. In those days that help arrived via the Comintern and its agent Ho Chi Minh. In the 1940s aid came primarily

[46] Turner, *Vietnamese Communism*, 78–79; Duiker, *The Communist Road to Power in Vietnam*, 143.

from the Chinese Communist Party. Between 1950 and 1954, aid from Communist China was essential first to get the upper hand against the French on the battlefield and then defeat and drive them from Vietnam. Some aid also came from the Soviet Union. It was the Vietminh's good standing in the world Communist movement, not its Vietnamese nationalist credentials, that was decisive in its victory at Dien Bien Phu. For all the military skill of General Giap, the Vietminh could not have planned the battle much less fought and won it without massive Communist Chinese, and some Soviet, help. The decisive events of 1954 in Vietnam reaffirmed the importance of the aid lifeline Vietnam's Marxists had to Communist powers abroad and thereby the pattern for their success established in the 1920s. That pattern, this time involving a massive aid lifeline that ran from the Soviet Union and PRC to North Vietnam, would be repeated in the 1960s and 1970s.

COMMUNISM IN NORTH VIETNAM, 1954–1959

Shortly after Dien Bien Phu, an independent Democratic Republic of Vietnam, or North Vietnam, emerged from the Geneva Conference of 1954 (April 26 to July 20). The Geneva Accords produced by that conference also led to the establishment of the Republic of Vietnam, or South Vietnam. The two rival states were divided at the 17th parallel, approximately where Vietnam had been divided for about 200 years from the sixteenth to eighteenth centuries.

In North Vietnam, it was a commitment to Communism rather than nationalism that guided Ho Chi Minh and his comrades. The VWP set up a Marxist totalitarian state modeled largely on that of the People's Republic of China and, to a lesser extent, the Soviet Union. The North Vietnamese state was a one-party dictatorship backed by a ubiquitous secret police that quashed any dissent. The state controlled the media, education, and all cultural and artistic life. Traditional forms of cultural expression, something that presumably would be encouraged by nationalists, were discouraged or suppressed as part of the effort to indoctrinate the people in Marxist values. Traditional village festivals were forbidden and many temples and shrines were shut down. An effort was made to control religion by limiting the number of Buddhist monks and Catholic priests and carefully regulating their activity. Confucianism was denounced, although some of its precepts were recycled to encourage the people to obey the Communist authorities. By the early 1960s the economy had been largely transformed into a classic Communist planned economy based on state control of all industry and collectivized agriculture. In K. W. Taylor's apt description, "The Democratic Republic of Vietnam became a local version of the type of modern totalitarian state that emerged in the twentieth century under the banners of communism and fascism."[47]

The nature of the North Vietnamese regime is largely beyond debate, other than within a few sectarian Marxist-Leninist circles. More controversial is the land reform program of the mid-1950s, during which the regime seized the land of the landlords and distributed it to the peasantry. The objective, however, was not to create a class of prosperous independent peasants, as the subsequent collectivization of the land demonstrates. The primary goal of this campaign was to destroy once and for all the authority of the landlords and replace it with the power of the state, or, as Pham Van Dong put it at the time, "to abolish the political influence of the landlords and former officials and to establish the political supremacy of the working peasants."[48] Of course, the "supremacy of the working peasants" was to be exercised by the VWP. Ironically, in contrast to the situation south of the 17th parallel, even before land reform more than 90 percent of peasants in North Vietnam farmed their own land. The burning question is how many people died as a result of land reform. One orthodox scholar who tends to be favorable to the North Vietnamese regime has estimated the figure to be between 3,000 and 15,000, with the most likely number being 5,000; that estimate, however, is based on statistics provided by the North Vietnamese, who had every reason to minimize the actual toll. More credible are Bernard Fall's estimate of 50,000 executions and at least double that number sent to forced labor camps and an estimate of 32,000 executions based on the report of a cadre who witnessed the campaign and later defected, a figure cited by both Dommen and Moyar. The French scholar Jean-Louis Margolin believes 50,000 executions took place. He points out that some of the victims were party members swept up in the wave of paranoia and fear that raged across the country. Either way, as Robert Turner points out, the total death toll is much larger than the number of executions since many people committed suicide or starved to death when their families were dispossessed of their property. To that must be added the unknown

---

[47] Taylor, *A History of the Vietnamese*, 571–72.
[48] Quoted in Turner, *Vietnamese Communism*, 130.

number of people who died when they were imprisoned or sent to forced labor camps.[49]

The situation became so bad that in the summer of 1956 the campaign was halted and the party began a "Rectification of Errors." Both Troung Chinh, the party general secretary, and the vice-minister in charge of land reform lost their positions.[50] A brief time of relaxation followed when intellectuals were allowed to criticize what had happened, a development that, not coincidentally, paralleled events taking place in both the Soviet Union and the PRC.

However, "rectification" and the right to criticize the party were halted at the end of 1956. Although a proposed three-year economic plan was now the most important item on the regime's agenda, by 1957 Hanoi was turning its attention to South Vietnam. Some top party leaders, most notably Le Duan, were arguing for the DRV to intervene forcefully against the Saigon government of Ngo Dinh Diem. After personally inspecting the situation south of the 17th parallel, Le Duan warned the party in 1959 that Diem was on the brink of successfully crushing the Communist movement there. This led to direct Northern intervention in the South to overthrow Diem, resulting in a crisis for the Diem regime, the US decision to upgrade its role in preserving South Vietnam, and to what we know as the Vietnam War.

An additional word on Communism in Vietnam seems in order here. After 1959, along with embarking on a conquest of South Vietnam, the Vietnamese Workers' Party established a centrally planned socialist economic system in North Vietnam. This was done dictatorially according to the principles of Marxism-Leninism and included the forced collectivization of agriculture and the nationalization and state control of all industry. The goal was to modernize Vietnam according to the model pioneered in the Soviet Union in the 1930s and largely replicated in China during the 1950s. From 1954 until 1963, there was a competing modernization model in Vietnam: Ngo Dinh Diem's doctrine known as Personalism, which drew on Catholic philosophy for many of its basic ideas (see Chapter 4). Personalism had its problems and quirks, and certainly its critics, from the America officials who had to work with Diem to

---

[49] Moyar, *Triumph Forsaken*, 62, 431, n.7; Turner, *Vietnamese Communism*, 130–31, 142–46; Jean-Louis Margolin, "Vietnam and Laos," in *The Black Book of Communism: Crimes, Terror, Repression*, Stéphane Courtois et al. (Cambridge and London: Cambridge University Press, 1999), 568–70; Dommen, *The Indochinese Experience of the French and the Americans*, 339–41; Fall, *The Two Vietnams*, 156.

[50] Hoang Van Chi, *From Colonialism to Communism*, 209.

orthodox journalists and scholars who have evaluated him. These commentators have consistently compared Personalism unfavorably to Marxism-Leninism as an ideology providing a blueprint for modernization. This is true whether the author in question is discussing Personalism in particular or, without specifically mentioning Personalism, Diem's program for South Vietnam in general. Thus Herring notes that Diem had "no blueprint for building a modern nation" and Moss lists among Diem's flaws his "obsolete ideology." Even Philip E. Catton, a historian whose book on Diem demonstrates convincingly that these assessments are inaccurate, writes that Diem's "chosen formula ... paled in comparison to the theoretical rigor of Marxism-Leninism."[51]

What one does not read in these assessments is that Marxism-Leninism, which was imposed on Vietnam under the leadership of Ho Chi Minh, has everywhere been a catastrophic failure as a blueprint for modernization. Its "theoretical rigor" notwithstanding, Marxism-Leninism as an economic system failed completely in the Soviet Union. In China Marxist-Leninist economics was discarded in the 1980s by the Chinese Communist Party and replaced by a form of state capitalism. Marxist-Leninist economics also failed in Eastern Europe and everywhere else it was tried. In Vietnam, in the 1980s, following the example set in China by the CCP, the Vietnam Communist Party (the VWP's name after 1976), while preserving its one-party dictatorship, junked its moribund Marxist-Leninist economic system in favor of its own version of state capitalism, at which point the country began to develop and prosper. All of this raises a basic question: if one is going to be critical of Ngo Dinh Diem for lacking a realistic program to modernize, what should be said – in fairness, at the same time – of Ho Chi Minh?

---

[51] Herring, *America's Longest War*, 59; Moss, *Vietnam: An American Ordeal*, 110; Catton, *Diem's Final Failure*, 48. For an overview of collectivization of agriculture in North Vietnam see Alec Gordon, "Class Struggle, Production, and the Middle Peasant," *Economic and Political Weekly* 16, no. 10/12: 459–64.

4

America Comes to Vietnam, 1954–1963

Direct American involvement in Vietnam began in 1954 with the Geneva Accords and the subsequent partition of the country into two states, the Democratic Republic of Vietnam (North Vietnam) and the Republic of Vietnam (South Vietnam). Elsewhere in Indochina, Laos and Cambodia became independent states pledged to neutrality in international affairs. American policy to support South Vietnam was part of Washington's overall Cold War policy of containment, which was put in place beginning in 1947 to limit Soviet expansion in Europe. Containment was extended to Asia when in June 1950, less than a year after the Communist victory in the Chinese civil war, North Korea invaded South Korea and thereby began the Korean War. The imperative to defend South Vietnam from a Communist takeover was reinforced by acceptance of the domino theory. As detailed in Chapter 1, revisionist historians have marshaled compelling evidence to defend the policy of containment, its application to South Vietnam, and the validity, at least in certain cases, of the domino theory.

THE GENEVA ACCORDS

In *The War Everyone Lost – and Won*, political scientist Timothy Lomperis introduces the agreements reached at Geneva in July 1954 with a heading that has the word "Accords" in quotation marks. His point is that beyond ending the war between the French and Vietminh, the Geneva Accords settled nothing; rather, they left critical matters ranging from the legal status of the demilitarized zone (DMZ) at the 17th parallel to an election to unify the country "in

94

limbo."[1] In other words, the Geneva Accords did not provide a legal framework for the future of Vietnam. This perspective contrasts with the generally accepted position among orthodox commentators, which holds that the Accords provided for a temporary division of Vietnam and for national elections in 1956 to unify the country under a single regime.[2] Occasionally orthodox historians acknowledge, as does George Herring, that the Accords "were vague in certain places, and different people viewed their meaning quite differently."[3] However, this does not prevent most orthodox commentators from labeling the subsequent American decision to defend South Vietnam as an independent state a violation of the Accords, as well as a disastrous mistake.[4]

In fact, both the terms in the Accords and the context from which they emerged refute the orthodox interpretation. Guenther Lewy was one of the first commentators to make this point. The Geneva Accords, Lewy writes in *America in Vietnam*, have "been the subject of much misunderstanding."[5] They consisted of a variety of documents, eleven in total, most of which cannot be considered formally binding accords. The only binding accords were the three cease-fire agreements, which are signed by the appropriate military commands. The cease-fire agreement that applied to Vietnam (the other two applied to Laos and Cambodia), signed by the French and Vietminh military commands, provided for the separation of the French and Vietminh forces at the 17th parallel, with the French withdrawing to what the agreement called its "regrouping zone" south of that line and the Vietminh to its north.

The documents that cannot be considered binding are the six unilateral declarations; the minutes of the last plenary session of the conference; and, most importantly, the final declaration. The final declaration is problematic for a variety of reasons. As Lewy notes, it was not signed by any of the nine delegations that attended the conference or adopted by a formal vote. Beyond that, while the final declaration called for a political settlement to be determined by free elections by secret ballot

[1] Timothy J. Lomperis, *The War Everyone Lost – and Won: America's Intervention in Vietnam's Twin Struggles*, rev. ed. (Washington, DC: Congressional Quarterly Inc., 1993), 46, 48.

[2] For example, see Herring, *America's Longest War*, 49; Moss, *Vietnam*, 65–67; Prados, *Vietnam: The History of an Unwinnable War*, 35–36.

[3] Herring, *America's Longest War*, 49.

[4] For a recent example, see Prados, *Vietnam*, 37, who complains about a nonexistent "solemn vow" not to disturb the Geneva agreements that "would be broken by U.S. subversion of reunification elections."

[5] Lewy, *America in Vietnam*, 7.

in 1956, it also mandated that all people in Vietnam be permitted to decide whether they wanted to live north or south of the 17th parallel. Lewy therefore asks, "Why have a massive exchange of population if the two zones were to be unified within 700 days or so?" He answers this crucial question by quoting the noted political scientist Hans J. Morgenthau, who commented that the free elections provision "was a device to disguise the fact that the line of military demarcation was bound to be a line of political division as well."[6] With specific regard to the elections, the government of South Vietnam objected to the proposed date and reserved for itself "complete freedom of action" to guarantee the freedom and independence of the Vietnamese people. The United States added that the elections had to be "free and fair" and, significantly, supervised by the United Nations. This "American Plan," which had the support of South Vietnam and Great Britain, was rejected by Soviet foreign minister Vyacheslav Molotov, the head of the Soviet delegation, with the backing of the other Communist delegations. The United States, along with supporting the South Vietnam's declaration, then reaffirmed that it would not enter into an agreement that would deny the Vietnamese people the right to determine their own future.[7] Both the US and South Vietnamese delegations thus refused to accept key parts of the final declaration, a document that was not legally binding on them in the first place.

Looking more broadly at all the conference participants, Lewy points out that in the absence of "either written or verbal consent of all of the nine participants" in the 1954 Geneva Conference, "the final declaration created no *collective* conference obligations." He cites one of the most comprehensive and respected works on the conference, Robert F. Randle's *Geneva 1954: The Settlement of the Indochinese* War (1969), to the effect that "the operative terms of the declaration were not binding on *all* of the participants of the Geneva Conference." Lewy adds that while in certain cases oral statements may create obligations under international law, both the United States and South Vietnam "stated their opposition in no

---

[6] Ibid., 8.
[7] Ibid., 8–9. On the "American Plan" and Molotov's reaction, see Robert F. Turner, "Myths and Realities of the Vietnam Debate," 4. Available online at www.viet-myths.net/turner .htm. This article originally was published in the *Cambell Law Review*, 9, no. 3 (Summer 1987). For the texts of the Final Declaration and the US statement see the website of the Avalon Project: http://avalon.law.yale.edu/20th_century/inch005.asp and http://avalon .law.yale.edu/20th_century/inch006.asp

uncertain terms. Neither of them, therefore, could be considered bound by the provision for elections in 1956."[8]

There is some irony here, mainly the divergence between the attitudes of the major powers on both sides of the Cold War divide on the one hand and the attitude of the Vietnamese in the Communist and non-Communist camps on the other. With regard to the former, both the Soviet Union and the PRC as well as the United States supported a permanent partition to prevent Vietnam from causing another Cold War crisis that these powers did not want. In sharp contrast, both the Communist and non-Communist Vietnamese delegations wanted to unify Vietnam under a single regime, although they obviously disagreed about who should control the country. The crucial point, however, is that Ho Chi Minh and his colleagues, who without question would not have accepted the US standard for genuine free elections, clearly did not expect any national elections. Thus, just after the conference ended, Pham Van Dong, the head of the Vietminh delegation, responded to a question about the elections as follows: "You know as well as I do that there won't be any elections." Later Le Duan told his party's central committee, "Everyone clearly understood that there was no way elections would ever be held."[9]

It is reasonable to conclude that neither the wording of the Geneva Accords nor the manner in which they were interpreted by the key players at the time support the orthodox contention that the Geneva Conference of 1954 provided for a united Vietnam to be created by elections held in 1956. Therefore there was nothing illegal according to international law in American support for the new government of South Vietnam or in that government's refusal to participate in national elections in 1956, elections that in territory controlled by North Vietnam would have been neither free nor fair. Meanwhile, as Robert Turner points out in *Vietnamese Communism*, from the start North Vietnam violated several binding articles of the Accords. Article I of the cease-fire agreement between the French and Vietminh called for all Vietminh forces to regroup north of the 17th parallel, yet an estimated 10,000 to 15,000 guerrillas and other operatives remained behind for future operations. The North Vietnamese violated Article 14 of the cease-fire agreement by preventing several hundred thousand civilians and possibly many more, the majority of whom were Catholics, from moving to the South. Hanoi also violated Articles 16 and 17 of the agreement by strengthening and resupplying its

---

[8] Lewy, *America in Vietnam*, 8–9. The quotation from Randle is on page 9.
[9] Quoted in Moyar, *Triumph Forsaken*, 430, n.65, 58.

army with aid from the PRC, aid that included hundreds of artillery pieces.[10] What the Geneva Accords did was end the Franco-Vietminh war and give the French an exit route from Vietnam. They also de facto divided Vietnam into two states. In the absence of any mechanism to regulate the relationship between those two states, their fates depended on what they and their respective outside backers did next, not on the assorted and ambiguous documents known as the Geneva Accords.

SOUTH VIETNAM AND NGO DINH DIEM

Between 1954 and 1963, the American effort to prevent a Communist takeover of Vietnam south of the 17th parallel rested on support of the regime headed by Ngo Dinh Diem. There is relatively little debate about some aspects of Diem's first years in power. In June 1954 Diem was appointed prime minister of what was then called the State of Vietnam by the Emperor Bao Dai. His chances of survival, and those of the regime he served, were slim. As General Phillip B. Davidson has aptly put it, "Diem had inherited chaos – a mishmash of conflicting political cliques and religious factions, an ineffective and almost nonexistent governmental apparatus, and a farce for a police force and army."[11] Diem's ramshackle government was opposed by the Cao Dai and Hoa Hao religious sects, both of which had armies, the former's numbering about 20,000 and the latter's about 15,000, and by a formidable criminal gang known as the Binh Xuyen, which controlled much of the gambling, prostitution, and other vice in Saigon and fielded an armed force of 25,000. The French also still had 160,000 troops in South Vietnam, and Paris was not friendly to Diem, viewing him as a tool America was using to push France completely out of Vietnam. All this was in addition to the thousands of cadres (and their hidden weapons) the Vietminh, in violation of the Geneva Accords, had left behind in 1954 to maintain its presence in rural areas.

It was under these daunting circumstances that in 1954 the United States began providing the Diem regime with limited aid and military advice. Washington also saw to it that the Southeast Asia Treaty Organization (SEATO), formed in the fall of 1954 to combat Communism in Asia, took South Vietnam under its protective wing.

---

[10] *Vietnamese Communism*, 100–104. The estimate for the number of Vietminh who remained in the South is from Herring, *America's Longest War*, 56.

[11] Davidson, *Vietnam at War*, 288.

MAP 3 Indochina from the Geneva Accords of 1954 to Black April of 1975

American support was forthcoming despite the fact many policy makers working for US President Dwight Eisenhower, including important figures on the scene in Vietnam, had little faith in Diem personally or in his ability to survive politically. But between 1954 and 1956 Diem did precisely that, and considerably more. During 1955, with American help, he defeated the Cao Dai and Hoa Hao and destroyed the Binh Xuyen. Diem benefited greatly from advice and technical assistance on many vital matters provided by Lt. Colonel Edward G. Lansdale, who was sent with a small team of assistants to South Vietnam in mid-1954. Meanwhile, the French withdrew their forces from the country, removing another anti-Diem player from the scene. In October 1955 Diem held an election, albeit one that was rigged, according to which the people of southern Vietnam replaced the monarchy with a republic and, with 98 percent in favor, voted for Diem as their leader. Diem then proclaimed himself president of the Republic of Vietnam and in 1956 had a constitution written that gave the country the powerful presidency he wanted. By then Diem's political base had been reinforced by about 700,000 Catholic refugees (out of a total of about 900,000 Vietnamese) who had fled Ho Chi Minh's Communist dictatorship and, in the process, doubled the Catholic population of South Vietnam. Meanwhile, Diem's highly successful, if often brutal, "Denounce the Communists" campaign during 1955 and 1956 in rural areas dramatically weakened the position of the cadres Ho had left behind in South Vietnam; by 1957 that campaign had reduced Communist membership in the villages to what Herring calls "precarious levels."[12] The restoration of order in the countryside enabled rice production to double between 1955 and 1960, despite the limitations and inadequacies of Diem's land reform program, a situation that stood in stark contrast to the shortages in North Vietnam. Orthodox commentators have stressed that Diem's regime received more than $1 billion in US military and economic aid between 1955 and 1961 and that his anti-Communist campaign included arbitrary arrests of non-Communists as well as Communists and led to several thousand executions. Revisionist scholar Mark Moyar, citing orthodox scholarship, responds that "Diem's crackdowns of the 1950s were not as bloody or cruel as the North Vietnamese land reform or the 'Destruction of Oppression' in 1960." Moyar also correctly points

---

[12] Herring, *America's Longest War*, 81.

out that after 1954 North Vietnam received substantial military and economic aid from both the Soviet Union and the PRC.[13]

Many commentators on the Vietnam War have treated Diem harshly. This negative image dates from the reporting by a number of American journalists who covered the Vietnam War beginning in the early 1960s and over time reached wide audiences. Some American journalists reporting from Vietnam did defend Diem while he was in office, but by 1963 the negative picture was the one that predominated in news reports Americans read or saw on television. That picture prevailed among important officials of the Kennedy administration as well. The mainstream US media generally portrayed Diem as a repressive reactionary without a plan for modernizing his country. Making matters worse, that narrative continued, Diem had built an autocratic regime, with most power closely held by members of his family, that was based on Vietnam's Catholic minority and therefore lacking in public support. He also had ignored US advice to make reforms that might have broadened his base of support.

That general assessment of Diem became, and has remained, a staple of orthodox historiography. For example, in 1994 William Duiker wrote that Diem "had no political party and no mass popular base." He was a member of a privileged religious minority (Vietnam's Catholic community) that "had aroused suspicion and resentment among most of the local population." And unlike a number of other Asian leaders – Duiker lists Indonesia's Sukarno, India's Nehru, and Burma's U Nu, none of whom were Communists, along with Ho Chi Minh – Diem lacked the "charismatic appeal" needed to "symbolize in his person the aspirations and ideals of his people."[14] In 2002 George Herring explained that Diem "was an elitist who had little sensitivity to the needs and problems of the Vietnamese people." He "looked backward to a Vietnam that no longer existed" and "had no blueprint for building a modern nation or mobilizing his people." Diem in addition "lacked the qualities necessary for the formidable challenge of nation building," a failing made worse because by 1960 he faced internal opposition, supported by North Vietnam, "that he, like the French before him, seemed increasingly incapable of handling."[15]

---

[13] Mark Moyar, "Section III Response," 207; *Triumph Forsaken*, 56. On the problems with Diem's land reform see Joseph Buttinger, *Vietnam: A Political History* (New York and Washington, DC: Praeger, 1968), 434–35.

[14] William J. Duiker, *U.S. Containment Policy and the Conflict in Indochina* (Stanford: Stanford University Press, 1994), 146.

[15] Herring, *America's Longest War*, 59, 87.

According to historian David L. Anderson, writing in 2005, Diem not only "lacked the charisma and political skills usually associated with a political leader," he also "projected a mandarin's reserve toward the common people, and he had no political following."[16] And in 2009 John Prados provided his readers with a relentless account of Diem's unsuitability to lead South Vietnam.[17]

Another staple of orthodox historiography is that the Diem regime was a failure on most fronts. Orthodox commentators acknowledge that Diem's efforts against the Communists during the mid and late 1950s were highly successful, but they counter that in the end his repressive policies alienated many non-Communists throughout South Vietnamese society. Urban intellectuals resented restrictions on political activity, Buddhists were antagonized by favoritism shown toward Catholics, and peasants were alienated by the failure to implement land reform and Diem's reversal of land distribution the Vietminh had undertaken in areas it controlled before 1954. Herring thus is repeating a widely held viewpoint when he argues that because of Diem's "misguided policies," Communist insurgents found a "receptive audience" when North Vietnam began promoting a rebellion in South Vietnam in 1959. The orthodox narrative maintains that the signature part of Diem's effort to counter the spreading insurgency, his strategic hamlet program, under which peasants were placed in fortified villages to separate and protect them from the Vietcong, also was a failure.[18] As a result by 1963 the Diem regime had made so many enemies in South Vietnam that it was unable to cope with the Communist insurgency and was on the verge of collapse. Some revisionist commentators, perhaps most notably Guenter Lewy, while far more sympathetic to Diem because of the challenges he faced, also paint a generally negative portrait of him.[19]

Diem did have defenders while he was in office, including historian and specialist on Vietnam Ellen Hammer and journalists Joseph Alsop and Marguerite Higgins. To them and other American scholars and journalists must be added the Vietminh, who, as Arthur Dommen points out, ranked Diem as "the only nationalist Vietnamese the Communists were worried about."[20] Among the prominent revisionist commentators who later challenged the orthodox view of Diem was William Colby, who spent years in

---

[16] Anderson, *The Vietnam War*, 28.
[17] Prados, *Vietnam: The History of an Unwinnable War*, 57–81.
[18] Herring, *America's Longest War*, 82, 106–7.   [19] Lewy, *America in Vietnam*, 18–28.
[20] Dommen, *The Indochinese Experience of the French and the Americans*, 263.

Vietnam in key posts and later became head of the CIA. Colby rose to Diem's defense in 1989 with the publication of *Lost Victory*. While not overlooking what he saw as Diem's weaknesses, Colby argues that Diem understood Vietnam and its problems better than most Americans on the scene and was committed to his country's modernization. He praises Diem's "strength and leadership" and maintains that, contra Diem's orthodox critics, the strategic hamlet program was a success and in fact "seized the initiative in the contest with the Communists for the first time."[21]

A few orthodox historians also have challenged the conventional orthodox assessment of Diem, most comprehensively Philip E. Catton. To be sure, the title of Catton's monograph, *Diem's Final Failure*, reflects his overall judgment that Diem's shortcomings outweighed his attributes and his general agreement with the orthodox case. Still, Catton rejects the standard orthodox view of Diem as a "dyed-in-the-wool reactionary, who stymied U.S. attempts to reform his regime in order to preserve an old-fashioned autocracy." According to Catton, Diem was a "modern nationalist" who had his own strategy for modernization and nation building. As he put it in an article written after his book's publication, "Diem was a conservative modernizer rather than a traditional autocrat; he was looking forward, not backward." Diem's approach to modernizing Vietnam was a doctrine known as Personalism, an ideology developed in France during the 1930s by the Catholic philosopher Emmanuel Mounier that drew on Catholic humanism and concerns with social reform. The idea of applying Personalism to Vietnam came from Ngo Dinh Nhu, Diem's younger brother and closest advisor. One problem with Personalism, which had authoritarian political characteristics, was that the US approach for moving forward in South Vietnam was based on American democratic principles. That led to serious tensions between Washington and Saigon when Diem and Nhu, convinced that US policy proposals were unsuited to Vietnamese realities, resisted or ignored those proposals. Catton acknowledges that he is questioning a fundamental orthodox tenet by asserting that Diem had a "coherent nation-building program" and that his regime and non-Communist Vietnamese nationalism in general "had some real ideological substance to them." That said, Catton affirms his orthodox credentials by asserting that there were "enormous obstacles to the creation of a viable South Vietnam" and that to call Diem a modern

---

[21] Colby, *Lost Victory*, 34–36, 102–3, 158. The quotation on the strategic hamlets is on page 102.

nationalist is not to reject the fundamental orthodox tenet that for the United States the war in Vietnam "was ultimately unwinnable."[22]

Another orthodox historian who has dissented from part of the conventional assessment of Diem is Edward Miller. In *Misalliance: Ngo Dinh Diem, the United States and the Fate of South Vietnam*, Miller characterizes Diem's program to modernize as "an ambitious attempt to synthesize certain contemporary ideas and discourses about Catholic Christianity, Confucianism, and Vietnamese national identity." Miller goes beyond Catton when he acknowledges that by 1962 Diem's strategic hamlet program significantly increased the percentage of South Vietnam's rural population under the government's control. That achievement was part of a broader pattern of success at the time that Miller calls "significant and impressive."[23]

THE DIEM REGIME, 1956–1963

Diem's partial rehabilitation by some revisionist and a few orthodox commentators has not gone nearly far enough for Mark Moyar. Moyar's more comprehensive rehabilitation of Diem is a central part of the case he makes for the American defense of South Vietnam in *Triumph Forsaken*. To Moyar, "Diem was one of the finest national leaders of the Cold War and ... many of his alleged faults were not faults at all."[24] He understood his country better than did his American critics. Moyar rejects the notion held by many critics of Diem's dictatorial behavior that Vietnam's authoritarian political culture and institutions could be quickly replaced by a political system based on American democratic traditions and principles. He approvingly quotes what Diem said on this point to Marguerite Higgins: "Procedures applicable to one culture cannot be transplanted wholly to another culture." Diem added that Vietnam did have some democratic traditions at the village level, but they could not be extended to the national level in South Vietnam in the middle of a war; in the present crisis only authoritarian methods could hold his country together. Moyar further maintains that those Americans on the scene "who treated Vietnam on its own terms" usually respected and supported

---

[22] Catton, *Diem's Final Failure*, 2–3, 41, 209–12; Catton, "Ngo Dinh Diem and South Vietnam Reconsidered," in *Triumph Revisited*, 32–36. The first two quotations are from Catton's book; the others are from his article.

[23] Miller, *Misalliance*, 21, 248–49.

[24] Moyar, "Section I Response," in *Triumph Revisited*, 62.

MAP 4 South Vietnam, 1954–1975

Diem.[25] Moyar's staunchly positive view of Diem as presented in *Triumph Forsaken* and subsequent publications has been challenged by orthodox historians, but he has directly and vigorously engaged his critics in debate, including in several published forums.[26] In this commentator's judgment, Moyar has fared exceedingly well in these debates. His main arguments therefore will be the basis of the overview of the Diem regime between 1956 and 1963 that constitutes the remainder of this chapter.

The defense of Diem logically begins with Personalism, his program for the modernization of Vietnam. Diem and Nhu wanted to modernize Vietnam while still retaining fundamental elements of its culture. It therefore was important that despite its Catholic origins, Personalism had a lot in common with Confucianism, which the Ngo brothers greatly admired. They were convinced that Personalism provided a system for modernizing Vietnam that balanced the needs of the individual, society, and the state. They believed the state should implement programs to promote the well-being of the people, and while in power they attempted to do that. The object was to enable people to develop as individuals but also understand and carry out their responsibility to the group. Diem and Nhu saw Personalism as an alternative to both Marxism, which crushed individual liberty and initiative, and liberalism, which to them was excessively individualistic and overlooked the needs of the community. The Ngo brothers despised Marxism, considering it an alien, oppressive, and inhumane ideology. They considered Western liberalism and democracy unsuited to Vietnam because of its authoritarian traditions and because those doctrines would not make it possible to implement the drastic changes the country urgently needed. Diem further argued that the Vietnamese wanted leaders with military power who could provide good leadership and inspire them with the force of their personalities.[27] Moyar sympathetically notes that "Diem adopted some of the traditional practices of the mandarins and the emperors because of both reverence for the past and confidence that these methods would still work."[28] Diem himself told Australian journalist Denis Warner that "our political system

---

[25] Moyar, *Triumph Forsaken*, 38, 229–30.

[26] See "Triumph Forsaken Roundtable Review," H-Diplo, July 2, 2007. Available online at http://h-diplo.org/roundtables/PDF/TriumphForsaken-Roundtable.pdf;   "Triumph Forsaken? A Forum on Mark Moray's Revisionist History of the Vietnam War, 1954–1965," *Historically Speaking*, November/December 2007: 29–41; "A Roundtable on Mark Moyar's *Triumph Forsaken: The Vietnam War, 1954–1965*," *Passport*, December 2007; and *Triumph Revisited*.

[27] Moyar, *Triumph Forsaken*, 35–37, 158.   [28] Ibid., 34.

has been based not on the concept of management of the public affairs by the people or their representatives, but rather by an enlightened sovereign and an enlightened government." However, as he stressed to Marguerite Higgins, "We are not going back to a sterile copy of the mandarin past. But we are going to adapt the best of our heritage to the modern situation."[29]

Diem's view about how he should govern and lead Vietnam quickly got him into trouble with the United States. Ironically, Diem's genuine credentials as a nationalist, which enabled him to win US backing in the first place, actually exacerbated his problems with Washington. Both the Eisenhower and Kennedy administrations viewed US-South Vietnam relations as a patron-client relationship and expected that as the patron the United States would dictate South Vietnamese policy on crucial issues. One sees this assumption axiomatically expressed by officials from John Foster Dulles, Eisenhower's secretary of state; to Averill Harriman, who negotiated an agreement on the neutralization of Laos that Diem bitterly opposed; to Henry Cabot Lodge, Kennedy's ambassador to Saigon during Diem's last years in office.[30] As a nationalist determined to see his country independent not only of the French but also of the Americans, Diem rejected that relationship. As he rhetorically asked journalist Marguerite Higgins in August 1963, in the face of the threat that the United States would cut off aid if he did not follow Washington's dictates, "If you order Vietnam around like a puppet on a string, how will you be different – except in degree – from the French?"[31]

Moyar backs up his positive evaluation of Diem by presenting evidence that, far from being a failure and despite setbacks and errors, Diem on the whole and despite the odds was successful in combating Communism and North Vietnamese aggression during his time in office. His disputes with the American government notwithstanding, Diem enjoyed considerable success during the second half of the 1950s. Beginning in 1957, under direction from Hanoi, the Communist cadres who had remained in South Vietnam after the Geneva Accords began a campaign of assassination and terror against government officials in the countryside. Diem's military response was remarkably successful to the point where by the end of the year the Communist rural infrastructure was severely damaged in many areas and party membership in South Vietnam as a whole had fallen

[29] Denis Warner, *The Last Confucian: Vietnam, Southeast Asia, and the West* (Harmonsworth: Penguin, 1963), 91; Higgins, *Our Vietnam Nightmare*, 166.
[30] Catton, *Diem's Final Failure*, 11–12.   [31] Higgins, *Our Vietnam Nightmare*, 168.

by two-thirds. Moyar quotes a Communist source to make the point that during 1958 and 1959, "with a number of wicked agents already trained, with an espionage system already established in hamlets and some reactionary organizations set up in rural areas," a Diem regime offensive "succeeded in dismembering 80–90 percent of our organization in many base areas." Although these victories masked some serious weaknesses and policy errors of the Diem regime, Moyar is on solid ground when he stresses Diem's successes during this period. This includes Diem's oft-maligned land reform program, which reduced the percentage of landless peasants in the Mekong Delta from an overwhelming majority to a minority, albeit one that was still too large.[32] Indeed, it was precisely those successes that in 1959 forced North Vietnam, aware that the Communist cause south of the 17th parallel was on the verge of collapse, to abandon its effort to undermine the Diem regime by pulling strings from afar and intervene directly in that struggle with its own troops and military equipment.

Moyar acknowledges that Diem initially did not have a response to North Vietnam's direct intervention in South Vietnam. Whereas at the end of 1959 Vietcong guerrillas had little influence or power in the countryside, by the end of 1960 they were mounting a strong insurgency. Several factors accounted for this, including widespread resentment against government abuses, the Vietcong's use of assassination and terrorism against South Vietnamese officials and civilians, and the infiltration of soldiers and party cadres into the South via the Ho Chi Minh Trail, a network of jungle pathways extending from the North into the South the North Vietnamese began building in 1959.[33] The third factor makes it clear that what Diem faced was not an "indigenous" rebellion being carried on by local guerrillas, as many orthodox commentators have claimed.[34] By 1961 the number of infiltrators from North Vietnam exceeded 10,000, and while the great majority of them were so-called regroupees – that is Vietminh originally from the South who had moved to the North after 1954 – these infiltrators were not South Vietnamese by any standard. When Vietnam was divided, they became North Vietnamese by choice and conviction, just like Le Duan and other top leaders of the Hanoi

---

[32] Moyar, *Triumph Forsaken*, 73–83. The Communists in their official documents call this period their "darkest hour." Duiker, *The Communist Road to Power in Vietnam*, 183–84, 359, n.29.

[33] See Moyar, *Triumph Forsaken*, 84–85, 91, 115–16, "Section III Response," 62.

[34] For example, see Prados, *Vietnam: The History of an Unwinnable War*, 66.

regime who had been born south of the 17th parallel. All of them had undergone training and indoctrination in North Vietnam. The soldiers were drawn from People's Army of Vietnam (PAVN) combat units. Warren Wilkins, author of *Grab Their Belts to Fight Them*, a well-received volume that focuses on Vietcong warfare against US troops, reports that these soldiers had received "expert instruction in guerrilla warfare, ambush tactics, and the building of fortifications." They mastered these skills at special training facilities.[35] And the role of these North Vietnamese soldiers and party cadres was critical, even greater than their numbers suggest. Thus the official history of the People's Army of Vietnam, published in Hanoi in 1988, reports that by 1963 these infiltrators from the North "represented 50 percent of the full-time armed forces in the South and 80 percent of the cadre and technical personnel assigned to the command and staff organizations in South Vietnam." Between 1961 and 1963 they had trekked down the Ho Chi Minh Trail accompanied by 165,000 weapons – including artillery pieces, antiaircraft weapons, and mortars – as well as hundreds of tons of other military equipment.[36]

This infusion of soldiers, cadres, and weapons from the North saved the faltering Communist rebellion in the South. Whereas at the beginning of the rebellion the North Vietnamese leadership limited itself to exploiting discontent in the South without resorting to direct intervention, the new infiltration turned the situation into straightforward aggression from the outside. Hanoi's effort to mask this change included setting up the National Liberation Front (NLF) in South Vietnam in December 1960. Supposedly an indigenous organization uniting a broad range of opponents of the Diem regime, including non-Communists, a claim accepted and trumpeted for years by many orthodox commentators, in fact the NLF was controlled by the Communist leadership in Hanoi from the start. The effectiveness of North Vietnam's direct intervention, as opposed to its remote-control effort before 1959, in turn led President John F. Kennedy, who took office in 1961, to dramatically increase American aid to South Vietnam, including raising the number of advisors assisting its army (the Army of the Republic of Vietnam, or ARVN) from less than 1,000 in 1961 to about 16,000 in 1963.

[35] Warren Wilkins, *Grab Their Belts and Fight Them: The Viet Cong's Big-Unit War Against the U.S., 1965–1966* (Annapolis: Naval Institute Press, 2011), 8; Turley, *The Second Indochina War*, 64–66.
[36] *Victory in Vietnam: The Official History of the People's Army of Vietnam, 1954–1975*, trans. Merle L. Pribbenow (Lawrence: University Press of Kansas, 2002), 115.

There is no dispute about the serious decline in the fortunes of the Diem regime between 1959 and 1961. The disagreement is over what happened during the next two years. Moyar argues that the Diem regime recovered and that by 1963 it again held the upper hand in the military struggle against the Communist forces in the South. He credits large-scale American military assistance, which came in the form of aircraft, armored vehicles, radios, and other modern equipment as well as thousands of military advisors, whose numbers quadrupled during 1962. Moyar also credits the considerable improvement in South Vietnamese military and civilian leadership as personnel trained since 1954 replaced those from the colonial era. All of this strengthened not only South Vietnam's regular army but also local militia forces. He notes that during 1963 South Vietnamese forces "aggressively sought battle and inflicted many defeats" on Communist forces.[37] This assessment has received strong support, albeit with some caveats, from military historian Andrew J. Birtle, a leading specialist on the history of the US Army's experience in counter-guerrilla warfare. Birtle asserts that claims that South Vietnam was losing the war in 1962 "do not bear up against the weight of the evidence" and adds that progress continued into 1963. He cites Communist sources and reports from those years to back up this assessment.[38]

Moyar has particular praise for the strategic hamlet program, which he argues "revolutionize[d] the war effort."[39] Established by the Diem government in 1961, the strategic hamlet program was a counterinsurgency effort designed to protect Vietnamese peasants from the Vietcong by moving them into fortified villages. Orthodox commentators have consistently portrayed it as a failure.[40] Moyar vigorously argues the opposite. He maintains that the program was working and gaining strength during 1962 and 1963, until Diem was overthrown and murdered in the coup of November 1, 1963. His claim is based not only on assessments by Western participants and observers on the scene at the time but also,

---

[37] Moyar, *Triumph Forsaken*, 154–60.

[38] Andrew J. Birtle, "*Triumph Forsaken* as Military History," in *Triumph Revisited*, 127–29. Birtle, while disagreeing with Moyar on some points, provides evidence of his own to demonstrate the improvement of South Vietnam's military situation during 1962 and 1963.

[39] Moyar, *Triumph Forsaken*, 155–56. Moyar points out the differences between the strategic hamlet program and Diem's earlier and unsuccessful agroville program, under which entire hamlets were often forced to relocate. See *Triumph Forsaken*, 158.

[40] See Herring, *America's Longest War*, 108; Moss, *Vietnam: An American Ordeal*, 133; Duiker, *The Communist Road to Power in Vietnam*, 215, 228; Catton, *Diem's Final Failure*, 192, 198, 211.

significantly, on Communist sources. The former group includes Australian guerrilla war expert Colonel Ted Serong; British expert Sir Robert Thompson, whose efforts against Communist guerrillas in Malaya provided a model for the program in Vietnam; Rufus Philips, the chief American advisor to the program, who wrote a highly positive report in May 1963; and Marine Major General Victor H. Krulak, who toured all of South Vietnam to report on the war in June 1963. There certainly were problems with the program, particularly in several provinces in the Mekong Delta, but the overall picture was decidedly upbeat.[41] Contemporary Communist sources reinforce this conclusion, as the following report demonstrates:

The enemy has been able to grab control of population and land from us, and he has drawn away for his own use our sources of resources and manpower. We have not yet been able to stop them. On the contrary, from an overall perspective, the enemy is still pushing his program forward into our areas.[42]

Birtle provides interesting nonmilitary evidence regarding the success of the strategic hamlets when he points out that after 1960 the area under rice cultivation in South Vietnam increased so that by 1962 more land was producing rice than in 1959, when North Vietnam began infiltrating troops into the South.[43] When answering critics in *Triumph Revisited*, Moyar himself observes that in critiquing *Triumph Forsaken*, Philip Catton does not dispute his (Moyar's) contention that the strategic hamlet program and war effort as a whole were going well, "a contention that runs contrary to what he [Catton] had written in his book." Moyar then adds, "It appears to be an example of a disproven falsehood disappearing quietly."[44] In the end the strategic hamlet program did collapse under Vietcong pressure, but Moyar cites both contemporary US and Communist sources to demonstrate this happened only after the coup against Diem.[45]

THE BUDDHIST REVOLT AND THE END OF THE DIEM REGIME

Another essential aspect of Moyar's defense of the Diem regime concerns the so-called Buddhist revolt of 1963. This event was decisive in undermining the Kennedy administration's support for Diem and led to

[41] Moyar, *Triumph Forsaken*, 207–8, 247–48.   [42] Ibid., 248.
[43] Britle, "*Triumph Forsaken* as Military History," 128–29.
[44] Moyar, "Section I Response," 62.   [45] Moyar, *Triumph Forsaken*, 283–84.

the US-sponsored coup by a group of South Vietnamese generals that overthrew his government on November 1, 1963. The trouble began in May 1963 when Buddhist monks in Hue demonstrated to protest what they claimed was discrimination against the country's Buddhist community by the Diem regime. This action led to mass demonstrations in several cities after troops in Hue fired into the crowd, killing nine people. The crisis intensified further when a monk committed suicide by self-immolation on a Saigon street in June, the first of several such incidents. After unsuccessful attempts to negotiate an end to the protests, in August the Diem regime carried out a series of raids on Buddhist monasteries in Hue (the epicenter of the demonstrations), Saigon, and other cities during which more than 1,400 monks were arrested. The raids quelled the revolt, but they also contributed directly to Washington's decision to support a group of generals who were seeking to overthrow Diem.

Moyar does not dispute this narrative. What he disputes is the orthodox view that the Buddhist monks had legitimate grievances and widespread public support, that all of them were sincere nationalists, and that the entire series of events demonstrated the isolation of the Catholic-dominated Diem regime from the predominantly Buddhist population of South Vietnam. He also accuses US journalists on the scene of misleading and inflammatory reporting and certain American officials of recklessly pushing for Diem's removal from office.

With regard to alleged discrimination against Buddhists, Moyar points out that Diem actually had helped his country's Buddhists, a fact that stands "in stark contrast to Ho Chi Minh," who after 1954 had acted brutally to end any independent activities by Buddhists in North Vietnam. Diem permitted Buddhist activities forbidden by the French. By 1963 about a quarter of South Vietnam's 4,766 Buddhist pagodas had been built during Diem's tenure, often with government help.[46] To be sure, as K. W. Taylor notes, Diem was not without fault in dealing with Vietnam's Buddhist community. While he had no intention of discriminating against non-Catholics, there was what Taylor has called an "undercurrent of incipient favoritism toward Catholics" associated with his government. This was mainly due to Diem's elder brother, Ngo Dinh Thuc, a Catholic priest who was appointed archbishop of Hue in late 1960. Thuc's efforts to promote Catholicism combined with his influence on government policy undermined the good relations that had prevailed between the

[46] Ibid., 215–16.

government and local Buddhist monks and thereby contributed to the crisis that erupted in May 1963. Diem's fault in this case, Taylor notes, was that he could not admit that the elder brother he had always respected and deferred to was causing a serious problem.[47]

It is against this background that the refusal of the protesting Buddhist monks' militant leadership to come to terms with the Diem government must be understood. The key issue here is the matter of Communist influence among these monks. There is no doubt that Communist operatives infiltrated the lower and middle levels of the Buddhist movement, although their presence at the top levels remains uncertain. Moyar quotes Communist sources published in Hanoi during the 1990s, by which time the need to cover up such subversive activities had dissipated, to demonstrate that Communist agents influenced the course of events. For example, one Hanoi source reports "our Party provincial and city committees stayed close to *and directed* [italics added] the movement from the inside through the use of our agents in the mass organizations and in the Buddhist Church." Another cites the role of the National Liberation Front's central committee in directing people to cooperate with the Buddhist monks and nuns. Other sources describe how Communists in the South infiltrated the Buddhist movement in Saigon. Moyar also notes that the Buddhist movement, which was an urban phenomenon, actually was a minority movement as far as South Vietnam's Buddhists were concerned since most of them were peasants living in the countryside who were neither informed about nor involved in what was happening in Saigon or Hue.[48]

At the center of this discussion is the role of the monk Thich Tri Quang, the most important leader of the protest movement. Tri Quang, who consistently rejected any accommodation with the Diem regime, is controversial because he was accused of being a Communist agent. Moyar acknowledges that Hanoi has never admitted to this but adds that substantial evidence points in that direction. For example, Tri Quang stated in his sermons that Buddhism was compatible with Communism; his methods for rallying crowds were similar to those used by Communists and different from what Buddhists normally did; and "over and over again, Tri Quang would refuse generous concessions from the government." Other Buddhist leaders later accused Tri Quang of working with the Vietcong. Moyar concludes by arguing that the "sum of the evidence

[47] Taylor, *A History of the Vietnamese*, 585–86.
[48] Moyar, *Triumph Forsaken*, 214–17, 458, n.58. The quotation is on page 217.

strongly suggests that Tri Quang was a Communist operative" and that, at a minimum, he "caused enormous harm to every South Vietnamese regime from 1963 to 1966."[49]

The nature of the Diem government – that is, whether it was a Catholic regime ruling over a Buddhist population – is important when one considers the Buddhist crisis of 1963. Moyar points out that although Catholics were overrepresented in Diem's government compared to their percentage of the South Vietnam's population, this was largely because they had a higher percentage of educated people than the population as a whole. But Diem's government was far from a Catholic regime. His cabinet had five Catholics, five Confucians, and eight Buddhists, with the last group including the country's vice-president and foreign minister. Twelve of Diem's provincial chiefs were Catholics along with twenty-six who were Buddhists or Confucians, while only three of the country's nineteen top military leaders were Catholics.[50] At least half of the ten generals who in August 1963 urged Diem to quell the Buddhist revolt were themselves Buddhists, and when that was done on August 21 both the general in charge in Saigon and the overall supervisor of the operation were Buddhists.[51]

Finally there is the matter of the coup itself, which emerged directly out of the Buddhist crisis in general and the August 1963 raids on the pagodas in particular. Moyar is critical of inaccurate reporting on the Buddhist crisis by American journalists, who "were ready to publish unsubstantiated gossip that supported their views." He is especially scathing regarding *New York Times* correspondent David Halberstam, who, among other inaccuracies, "wrote a string of fallacious front-page articles on the pagoda raids." The inaccuracies of Halberstam and other Western journalists are not surprising since two of their most important Vietnamese sources were Hanoi's agents. This reporting influenced American officials and US public opinion and contributed to Kennedy's decision to encourage the generals' coup against Diem. Moyar is equally tough on several American officials who pushed hard for the coup, among them Henry Cabot Lodge, the newly appointed US ambassador to Saigon, State Department undersecretaries Averell Harriman and Roger Hilsman, and National Security Council member

---

[49] Ibid., 217–18. "Thich" is a surname taken by all Vietnamese Buddhist monks. Moyar does not use it, referring simply to "Tri Quang."

[50] Ibid., 215–16.

[51] Ibid., 231–32. The general in charge in Saigon was the son of a Buddhist nun.

Michael Forrestal.[52] They prevailed in spite of strong opposition to the coup from Vice-president Johnson, Secretary of Defense McNamara, the CIA, the Joint Chiefs of Staff, and others, all of whom believed Diem was the best bet the United States had in Vietnam and that his removal would make things much worse.

More than half a century after the event there is widespread agreement among revisionists that the decision to overthrow of Diem, which also resulted in the murder of both Diem and Nhu, was a disastrous error. R. B. Smith writes that the coup "opened a Pandora's box" of trouble the United States could not control. Ellen Hammer, a strong supporter of Diem, makes the same point in *A Death in November*, as do a number of other scholars.[53] As Moyar has convincingly demonstrated, it was only after the coup that the strategic hamlet program fell apart and the 1962–1963 successes against Communist forces on the battlefield were reversed. Diem provided far more effective leadership than any of his successors was able to do for years, and that in turn had pivotal implications for what the United States would have to do. One this point at least, Moyar and Catton are not that far apart. Thus according to Catton:

The Diem government looked like a model of order and stability compared with the floundering, revolving-door regimes that followed in the period 1964–1965. In the absence of a functioning South Vietnamese government, President Johnson was forced to confront the eventuality that his predecessor had not: the prospect of the south's collapse without a dramatic increase in the U.S. commitment. Johnson's response was to send five hundred thousand U.S. troops to South Vietnam, in an attempt to overcome Saigon's weaknesses by overwhelming the enemy militarily.[54]

Moyar puts it as follows:

Because of Diem's accomplishments in 1962 and 1963, the Viet Cong lacked the ability to defeat the government at the time of Diem's death, and for a considerable period thereafter. Had Diem lived, the Viet Cong could have kept the war going as long as they continued to receive new manpower from North Vietnam and maintained sanctuaries in Cambodia and Laos, but it is highly doubtful that the war would have reached the point where the United States needed to introduce several hundred thousand of its own troops to avert defeat, as it would under Diem's successors.[55]

[52] Ibid., 233–36.
[53] Smith *An International History of the Vietnam War*: vol. 2, 190; Hammer, *A Death in November*, passim.
[54] Catton, *Diem's Final Failure*, 211.   [55] Moyar, *Triumph Forsaken*, 286.

William Colby perhaps summed the consequences of the coup most succinctly when he wrote that the Kennedy administration's 1963 decision to support the coup against Diem "must be assigned the stigma of America's primary (and perhaps worst) error in Vietnam."[56]

Interestingly, that consensus extends, at least in part, into the orthodox camp. For example, Moss writes that the coup "weakened rather than strengthened the security of South Vietnam."[57] More significantly, it extends all the way to Hanoi, where Ho Chi Minh had the following to say when he heard about the coup and Diem's murder: "I can scarcely believe that the Americans would be so stupid." The North Vietnamese Politburo as a whole agreed, officially resolving that "Diem was one of the strongest individuals resisting the people and Communism. Everything that could be done in an attempt to crush the revolution was carried out by Diem." And pro-Communist Australian journalist Wilfred Burchett reported that Vietnamese Communist leaders told him that "the Americans have done something that we haven't been able to do for nine years and that was to get rid of Diem."[58]

Diem, on nationalist grounds, had always opposed American efforts to manage the war against the Communists in South Vietnam. In doing so, he was not only asserting his country's independence but doing the United States a favor by keeping it out of the war. By sponsoring Diem's overthrow, Washington opened the door to the Americanization of the Vietnam War. It would prove to be a frustrating and painful experience.

---

[56] Colby, *Lost Victory*, 366.   [57] Moss, *Vietnam: An American Ordeal*, 144.
[58] All three quotations are cited by Moyar. See *Triumph Forsaken*, 286.

5

The Americanization of the Vietnam War, 1963–1968

The overthrow and murder of Ngo Dinh Diem and assassination of President John F. Kennedy in November 1963 set in motion a sequence of events that by early 1965 resulted in the beginning what is generally called the Americanization of the Vietnam War. Between late 1963 and early 1965, chaos reigned in the South under Diem's various inept successors; as a result, the war effort against the Communist insurgency became increasingly ineffectual. The North Vietnamese regime meanwhile qualitatively upgraded its involvement in the Southern insurgency by increasing the infiltration of People's Army of Vietnam (PAVN) troops and weapons into the South. Its objective was to destroy South Vietnam's government and conquer the country before the United States could react. In the United States, the new Johnson administration, which included McNamara and most of Kennedy's top civilian advisors, remained committed to containing Communism in Vietnam. At the same time, Washington sought to avoid deepening American military involvement in the war against the insurgency.

Faced with a seriously deteriorating situation, the Johnson administration nonetheless at first remained committed to working within the limits established under President Kennedy: that is, to provide aid, including American military advisors, that would enable the South Vietnamese government to resist the Communist insurgency but not to commit American forces to combat. This approach was dictated by Johnson's determination to prioritize domestic US affairs, beginning with winning the November 1964 presidential election and then by implementing his so-called Great Society program of social reform. After his election, and with the situation in South Vietnam more precarious than ever, Johnson turned to the McNamara strategy of graduated pressure against Hanoi. McNamara intended to convince Ho Chi Minh, Le Duan, and their colleagues in North Vietnam's ruling Politburo that they could not possibly achieve their goal of taking over South Vietnam and thereby bring them to the negotiating table. Along with the assumption that graduated pressure would enable the United States to deal with Vietnam without interfering with Johnson's domestic agenda, there was a second reason the president adopted McNamara's approach to war: to avoid an American military escalation in Vietnam that might draw Communist China and possibly even the Soviet Union into the conflict, an eventuality that carried with it the dreaded risk of nuclear war. As political scientist John Dumbrell has observed, Johnson wanted "to do enough to contain communism in Indochina without risking a confrontation with the big communist powers."[1]

This chapter covers the deteriorating political and military situation in South Vietnam between late 1963 and early 1965 and how the Johnson administration came to rely on graduated pressure. It reviews the implementation of graduated pressure against North Vietnam along with its complement, the gradual escalation of the US combat effort in South Vietnam, as well as the failure of the overall US policy to produce the desired results. Specifically, between 1965 and 1968 that effort involved the Rolling Thunder bombing campaign over North Vietnam; search and destroy on the ground, backed by air power, in South Vietnam; and assorted American military efforts in Laos and Cambodia. Finally, this chapter covers the 1968 Communist Tet Offensive and its impact on the war in Vietnam and on public opinion in the United States.

SOUTH VIETNAM, LATE 1963 TO EARLY 1965

The government that succeeded the Diem regime, a junta of generals, lasted only three months. Quickly undermined by its incompetence, this junta was in its turn overthrown in a nonviolent coup by yet another general. As one historian has aptly observed, the "coup season" had arrived in South Vietnam.[2] The year 1964 would see several more coups

---

[1] John Dumbrell, *Rethinking the Vietnam War* (Basingstoke: Palgrave Macmillan, 2012), 64. The Politburo was the highest body of North Vietnam's ruling Vietnam Workers' Party, the formal name for the party until it took the name Communist Party of Vietnam in 1976.

[2] Moss, *Vietnam: An American Ordeal*, 160.

and a total of seven governments in South Vietnam. These transient governments removed many of Diem's best military officers and civilian officials, people who had played a key role in successfully prosecuting the war against the Vietcong, and replaced them with less able personnel. Not until the middle of 1965 would one of South Vietnam's feuding military factions, a group led by Air Vice-Marshall Nguyen Cao Key and General Nguyen Van Thieu, succeed in establishing a semblance of a stable South Vietnamese government, the ninth the country had seen in less than two years.

Given the political turmoil in Saigon, it is not surprising that during the year and a half after Diem's overthrow, the war effort against the Communist insurgency practically collapsed. In March 1964 Secretary of Defense McNamara reported to President Johnson that the Vietcong had significantly expanded its control in many rural regions of South Vietnam. Contrary to orthodox accounts that trace these developments to Diem, the fault clearly lay with Diem's successors. Thus a deeply worried McNamara reported that because of the replacement of Diem's officials (including thirty-five of forty-one province chiefs), the "political control structure extending from Saigon down to hamlets disappeared following the November coup."[3] The key fact McNamara was referring to, that the war effort in general and the strategic hamlet program in particular deteriorated only after the coup, has been made convincingly by Mark Moyar in *Triumph Forsaken* and subsequent writings. Moyar marshals compelling evidence, not only from US sources but also from Communist sources, that the strategic hamlet program, so maligned by orthodox historians, played a crucial role in enabling the South Vietnamese government to extend its control over rural territory and its population, including during the summer and fall of 1963, just prior to the November coup against Diem. The decline of the strategic hamlets, as reported by the CIA, began after that date. Citing official Communist histories of two coastal regions in South Vietnam, Moyar adds that because of Diem's successes against the Vietcong, in some regions Diem's strategic hamlets remained strong until mid-1964.[4]

---

[3] Robert McNamara, "Memorandum for the President," March 16, 1964, *The Pentagon Papers: The Defense Department History of United States Decision Making in Vietnam*, Senator Gravel Edition, Volume III (Boston: Beacon Press, 1971), 501. This is Document 158, 499–510.

[4] See Moyar, *Triumph Forsaken*, 248, 280–87 and "Section II Response," in *Triumph Revisited*, 162–63, 215.

The trouble in Saigon, however, only partly explains the increasing success of the insurgency. The rest of the explanation is provided by actions taken in Hanoi. As early as 1963, when Diem was still in power, infiltrators from North Vietnam already constituted the base of the Vietcong armed forces and technical personnel in South Vietnam.[5] During 1964 the insurgency was dramatically strengthened by increased infiltration of PAVN units into South Vietnam via the expanded and improved Ho Chi Minh Trail, most of which ran through Laos. Modern arms for Vietcong forces also arrived via that route. These newly arrived PAVN units, notes military historian Dale Andrade, "formed the core of the burgeoning North Vietnamese main force presence in the South, in particular the PAVN 325th Division, which moved south in March 1964."[6] By January 1965 the situation had deteriorated to the point where General Taylor, now US Ambassador to South Vietnam, warned of the imminent collapse of the South Vietnamese government. Having opposed the November coup, Taylor now lamented that Washington had failed to appreciate Diem's success in keeping "centrifugal political forces under control" and added that there was "no adequate replacement for Diem in sight."[7] Meanwhile, the pressure on Washington to do something of consequence spiked in February 1965 when the Vietcong attacked the US Marine base at Pleiku in the central part of the country, killing 9 Americans, wounding more than 100, and damaging more than 20 aircraft of various types.

JOHNSON AND MCNAMARA, THE JOINT CHIEFS OF STAFF, AND GRADUATED PRESSURE

The Johnson administration's reaction to the events between November 1963 and the crisis in early 1965 that led to the policy of graduated pressure has been best chronicled by General H. R. McMaster. McMaster documents how Johnson's domestic political agenda, beginning with securing his election in November 1964, dictated US military policy in Vietnam. Prior to the election, President Johnson wanted to be seen as the moderate candidate with regard to Vietnam, in

---

[5] See Chapter 4.

[6] Dale Andrade, "Westmoreland Was Right: Learning the Wrong Lessons from the Vietnam War," *Small Wars and Insurgencies*, 19, no. 2 (June 1968): 153. "Main force" refers to traditional military ground units, which use conventional tactics, as opposed to guerrilla units, which are lightly armed and rely heavily on small-unit, hit-and-run tactics.

[7] Quoted in Moyar, *Triumph Forsaken*, 352.

contrast to his Republican opponent Senator Barry Goldwater, and therefore he was only willing to approve measures that would enhance that image. Once elected, Johnson's first and overriding commitment was to his Great Society program of social reform. This in turn meant that he was only prepared to commit forces to Vietnam sufficient to keep the Saigon regime from losing the war. These priorities were reinforced by the low opinion of America's military leaders Johnson, a man with no military experience, shared with Kennedy and McNamara. McMaster chronicles McNamara's contempt for the professional military officers and his confidence, completely unjustified as events would show, that he and his civilian advisors understood how to wage war better than military professionals. McMaster criticizes Johnson and his civilian advisors for ignoring the military advice they received from the Joint Chiefs of Staff (JCS). He documents how McNamara, aided by General Maxwell Taylor, chairman of the JCS from 1962 until 1964, prevented the views of the other Joint Chiefs from reaching the president. McMaster points out that as early as January 1964, the Joint Chiefs, writing to McNamara, made it clear that the US military strategy based on graduated pressure could not succeed. The JCS urged that "victory" be the goal in South Vietnam and wanted to develop a military campaign, including bombing North Vietnam and mining its ports through which military supplies arrived from the Soviet Union and China, to secure that goal. That recommendation was not acted upon because even by early 1964 the JCS on the one hand and Johnson and his civilian advisors on the other, in McMaster's words, "had started down different paths."[8]

McMaster, to be sure, does not give the Joint Chiefs a pass. Despite their firm conviction that the Johnson/McNamara military policy in Vietnam could not succeed, he writes, the Joint Chiefs could not overcome their interservice differences and personal bickering and become effective advocates for a military strategy they believed was necessary to defeat the Communist insurgency in Vietnam. Perhaps their most egregious failure occurred in July 1965 when the Joint Chiefs, minus their chairman, General Earle Wheeler, who was in South Vietnam at the time, met with members of the House Armed Services Committee and avoided answering questions about the level of force that would be required to win the war.[9]

---

[8] H. R. McMaster, *Dereliction of Duty: Lyndon Johnson, Robert McNamara, the Joint Chiefs of Staff, and the Lies That Led to Vietnam* (New York: Harper Collins, 1997), 63–65, 309–11.

[9] Ibid., 309–10.

McMaster points out that the Joint Chiefs hoped that graduated pressure would evolve into a different strategy "more in keeping with their belief in the necessity of greater force and its more resolute application." But by failing to confront the president with their objections and attempting to work within the McNamara strategy, they gave "tacit approval" to graduated pressure during the critical time when it was first implemented.[10]

McMaster's chronicle of events raises the question of what the Joint Chiefs could have effectively done while Johnson was in the White House, given the realities of the American political system under which civilian authorities control the military, to end the reliance on graduated pressure. That is one reason revisionist commentators vary in their evaluations of the JCS. Some offer generally negative assessments. General Bruce Palmer Jr., who served in Vietnam as overall commander of Field Force II (one of the four US military regions in South Vietnam) and later as deputy to General Westmoreland, criticizes the JCS but not as harshly as McMaster. In *The 25-Year War*, a volume published thirteen years before McMaster's, Palmer chastises the JCS for its inability to "articulate an effective military strategy that they could persuade the commander-in-chief to adopt." But he also suggests that the JCS were limited in their objections to the Johnson/McNamara strategy by the military's "can do" spirit and because they did not want to seem disloyal. Robert E. Morris criticizes the Joint Chiefs because they "acquiesced as strategy was formulated by the whiz kids and implemented in haphazard fashion."[11]

Other revisionists are more charitable to the Joint Chiefs. Christopher Gacek, in reviewing the decision making in Washington during late 1964, finds it "hard to imagine how a government could contemplate going to war and have such disregard for the opinions of its military leaders." Jacob Van Staaveren served for more than twenty years as a historian for the US Air Force history program. Among his many studies is *Gradual Failure: The Air War Over North Vietnam, 1965–1966*, a classified work written in the 1970s that was not published until 2003; it remains the most comprehensive and authoritative history of the Rolling Thunder campaign during those years. In *Gradual Failure* Staaveren chronicles how as early as 1964 the Joint Chiefs stressed the necessity of strong measures against North Vietnam and how by the fall of that year they were "exasperated and dismayed" by Johnson's and McNamara's failure to heed their

---

[10] Ibid., 328.
[11] Bruce Palmer, *The 25-Year War*, 45–46, 213, n.26; Robert E. Morris, "Why We Lost the War in Vietnam," 394.

advice. He notes how on November 1, 1964, General Wheeler told McNamara that most of the Joint Chiefs believed that failing additional military action the United States should withdraw from Vietnam. Mark Moyar stresses the difficulties the Joint Chiefs faced in dealing with McNamara and Johnson and the limited options available to them. He concludes, specifically mentioning McMaster in a footnote, that by working with Johnson while trying to influence him, the Joint Chiefs "chose the best of the inferior options available."[12]

GRADUATED PRESSURE AND GRADUAL
ESCALATION IN PRACTICE

The first airstrikes against North Vietnam, in August 1964 and again in February 1965, were intended as strictly retaliatory measures in response to North Vietnamese attacks against US forces, in the former case an American destroyer on patrol in the Gulf of Tonkin (the Gulf of Tonkin Incident) and in the latter American bases in South Vietnam. However, by early 1965 President Johnson and his top advisors, aware that without a strong demonstration of US support the government of South Vietnam could collapse, understood they had to go beyond mere reprisals. The campaign to apply graduated pressure against Hanoi via systematic and sustained bombing, known as Rolling Thunder, therefore began in March 1965. Rolling Thunder had two complementary goals: first, to raise the cost of North Vietnam's sponsorship of the insurgency in South Vietnam to the point where Hanoi would be convinced it could not succeed and therefore would agree to negotiations; and, second, to inhibit the infiltration of troops and supplies into South Vietnam to the point where the insurgency there could be defeated. Johnson's civilian advisors who formulated the Rolling Thunder bombing campaign against North Vietnam did not address what should be done at that time in South Vietnam.[13] However, because the situation on the ground in South

---

[12] Gacek, *The Logic of Force*, 190–91; Jacob Van Staaveren, *Gradual Failure: The Air War Over North Vietnam, 1965–1966* (Washington, DC: Air Force History and Museum Program, 2002), 54–55, 58–59; Moyar, *Triumph Forsaken*, 331–32, 483, n.12. For an assessment similar to Moyar's, see Lewis Sorley, *Honorable Warrior: General Harold K. Johnson and the Ethics of Command* (Lawrence: University Press of Kansas, 1998).

[13] William C. Gibbons, *The U.S. Government and the Vietnam War: Executive and Legislative Roles and Relationships, Part IV, July 1965–January 1966* (Washington, DC: US Government Printing Office, 1994), 53. The controversial Tonkin Gulf Incident involved two events. On August 2, 1964, North Vietnamese torpedo boats

Vietnam was so urgent, Johnson decided to send the first US combat troops to South Vietnam (Marines tasked with defending the important Da Nang airfield), with the first units arriving within days of the start of Rolling Thunder. The president and some of his advisors seem to have believed that sending a small number of combat troops to South Vietnam would be another way, albeit indirect, to apply graduated pressure on North Vietnam and force Hanoi into negotiations. Instead, when Hanoi did not respond as hoped, the United States was forced to begin a policy of gradual escalation in South Vietnam. As McMaster aptly puts it, Johnson's decisions of early 1965 "transformed the conflict in Vietnam into an American war."[14]

Rolling Thunder

Rolling Thunder was one of several US bombing campaigns during the Vietnam War. It lasted from March 1965 to November 1968 and was carried out by US Air Force and Navy aircraft. Among the other campaigns, Barrel Roll (December 1964–March 1973) supported the Royal Laotian government against Communist forces in northern Laos and also attacked the Ho Chi Minh Trail to stop North Vietnamese infiltration of troops and supplies into South Vietnam. Steel Tiger (April 1965–November 1968) attempted to interdict North Vietnamese infiltration via the Ho Chi Minh Trail in the northern part of the Laotian panhandle. Tiger Hound (December 1965–November 1968) did the same in the southern part of the Laotian panhandle. Commando Hunt (November 1968–April 1972) was the successor to Tiger Hound. Menu (March 1969–May 1970) attacked PAVN and Vietcong base camps inside Cambodia; it was followed by Freedom Deal (May 1970–August 1973), which supported the Cambodian government's struggle against local Communist guerrillas. Linebacker I was directed against North Vietnam during Hanoi's 1972 Easter Offensive against South Vietnam. It was closely followed by Linebacker II, the so-called Christmas Bombing launched in December 1972 to force Hanoi to make concessions in negotiations going on in Paris. American, South Vietnamese, and other allied warplanes dropped about eight million tons of bombs in Indochina during the Vietnam War, with US aircraft accounting for about 82 percent of

attacked a US destroyer. A second alleged attack, on August 4 against two US destroyers, is clouded by poor weather conditions and probably never took place.
[14] McMaster, *Dereliction of Duty*, pp. 203, 217.

that total. About half the total tonnage, approximately four million tons, was dropped in South Vietnam in support of military operations there. Much of the rest were dropped in Laos and Cambodia as part of US efforts to interdict North Vietnamese troops and supplies en route to South Vietnam. Only slightly more than a tenth, about 880,000 tons, actually were dropped on North Vietnam.[15] However, Rolling Thunder was the main means by which the United States attempted to systematically apply graduated pressure on North Vietnam and therefore merits extensive discussion.

Orthodox and revisionist commentators agree on one salient point: Rolling Thunder failed. It did not force North Vietnam to the negotiating table, and it did not sufficiently interdict the North Vietnamese infiltration effort into South Vietnam. However, the respective commentators do not agree on why Rolling Thunder failed. Orthodox historians generally argue that North Vietnam, with its largely agricultural economy, was not a suitable target for strategic bombing, which was based on US doctrine developed during World War II in campaigns against Germany and Japan, both heavily industrialized nations. North Vietnam's military supplies came from outside patrons (the Soviet Union and the People's Republic of China [PRC]), so its ability to wage war would not be damaged by bombing as was Germany's and Japan's. Orthodox commentators also argue that interdiction of North Vietnamese infiltration into South Vietnam was futile since Communist forces fighting a guerrilla war there needed so few outside supplies that their needs could be satisfied even if only a small percentage of what Hanoi sent actually reached its destination. This point, however, as some of these same commentators acknowledge, only applies to the situation as it existed up to the early 1960s, that is, before large PAVN forces equipped with heavy weapons and requiring a wide range of supplies were in the South. Finally, orthodox commentators stress that North Vietnam was too determined to attain its objective of conquering South Vietnam to be intimidated by American bombs. These factors, orthodox commentators conclude, made North Vietnam immune to US conventional strategic bombing.[16]

---

[15] These statistics are from Turley, *The Second Indochina War*, 124–25. Two million tons were dropped on Laos and 539,000 tons on Cambodia.

[16] Hess, *Vietnam: Explaining America's Lost War*, 86–89. One author frequently cited on these points is military historian Mark Clodfelter. See his study *The Limits of Airpower: The American Bombing of North Vietnam* (New York: The Free Press, 1989). See also Earl H. Tilford Jr., *Crosswinds; The Air Force's Setup in Vietnam* (College Station: Texas A&M University Press, 1991). On the requirements of PAVN forces in the South by 1965,

The revisionist response has two essential parts. First, revisionists argue that North Vietnam was vulnerable to a properly carried out bombing campaign. Rolling Thunder therefore could have been effective and achieved its goals. Second, they explain the reasons why the United States did not successfully exploit North Vietnam's vulnerability.

C. Dale Walton has effectively summarized the first part of the revisionist argument. He points out that North Vietnam's lack of industry made it dependent on military imports to carry on the war, and that dependence actually increased its vulnerability to airpower. These vital military supplies came from the Soviet Union and China, with the former supplying heavy and sophisticated weaponry such as fighter planes, tanks, antiaircraft artillery, antiaircraft missiles, radar systems, trucks, and field artillery (which together eventually comprised 80 percent of all imported North Vietnamese supplies) and the latter supplying the bulk of North Vietnam's small arms and ammunition. Closing down North Vietnam's ports, in particular mining the port of Haiphong, Walton argues, "alone would have virtually eliminated the Soviet Union's freedom to supply its client." Attacks on key railroads and highways, along with mining inland waterways, "would have severely constrained the PRC's ability to assist the DRV." Airpower simultaneously could have been used to shatter vital North Vietnamese infrastructure, including storage facilities, supply depots, factories engaged in war production, military bases, airports, and government buildings. Air power therefore could have crippled North Vietnam's ability to wage war against South Vietnam had it been properly used.[17]

The second part of the revisionist response, the reason North Vietnam's vulnerability to air power was not exploited, has several components. Revisionists place most of the blame for the failure of Rolling Thunder on the Johnson administration for imposing restrictions on the bombing of North Vietnam that made it impossible for the campaign to succeed. These restrictions included, but were not confined to, limits on the targets US warplanes could attack, rules of engagement (ROEs) that made it more difficult for American pilots to hit their targets while exposing them to

---

see Turley, *The Second Indochina War*, 68. See also note 71 for a comment by Prados on the importance of the Ho Chi Minh Trail.

[17] Walton, *The Myth of Inevitable U.S. Defeat in Vietnam*, 114–16. The information on specific weapons supplied respectively from Russia and China comes from various sources. For a useful bibliographic overview of how military historians and officers have evaluated Rolling Thunder see Ronald B. Frankum Jr., *Like Rolling Thunder: The Air War in Vietnam, 1964–1975* (Lanham: Rowman & Littlefield, 2005), 174–177.

greater risk, and the timing under which targets were attacked. At the same time, some commentators who offer these and related arguments, including serving US Air Force officers, also echo the orthodox case by criticizing senior US Air Force commanders for failing to assess the situation they faced and remaining wedded to World War II doctrine that had been designed for attacking industrialized countries and therefore was unsuited for the task at hand. However, those offering this particular critique do not always provide suggestions for how the US Air Force – and presumably the US Navy – should have modified its doctrine.[18]

Robert E. Morris has characterized America's overall military effort in Vietnam as a policy of "escalation and de-escalation, an 'on again off again' knee-jerk reaction that varied with the intuitive whims of President Johnson and his advisors."[19] That observation is particularly apt with regard to the Rolling Thunder. Rolling Thunder was the key pillar of graduated pressure because it was the main way in which the war was taken directly to North Vietnam itself, as opposed to the military effort being conducted against Hanoi's proxy forces and PAVN troops in South Vietnam. Presumably a campaign that would start slowly and deliver its message to Hanoi by increasing pressure in carefully calibrated increments, Rolling Thunder's "on again, off again" implementation included seven major bombing halts (plus smaller ones that brought the total to sixteen) instituted with the hope of serving as the carrot that along with the stick of bombing would bring North Vietnam to the negotiating table. The effect of this erratic approach was the opposite. North Vietnam made it clear from the start that it was not interested in any negotiations that would interfere with the goal of taking control of South Vietnam. Meanwhile, the pauses, the "graduated" increase in the intensity of the bombing, and Washington's restrictions on the bombing of many significant military targets bolstered Hanoi's resolve. In *A Soldier Reports*, his memoir on the war, General Westmoreland ruefully wonders how anyone could have expected the North Vietnamese to negotiate "when the only thing that might hurt them – the bombing – was pursued in a manner that communicated not determination and resolution but weakness and trepidation?" He adds, "The signals we were sending were signals of our own

---

[18] For example see Colonel John K. Ellsworth, "Operation Rolling Thunder: Strategic Implications of Airpower Doctrine" (US Army War College, Carlisle Barracks, PA, 2003); Colonel Dennis M. Drew, "Rolling Thunder 1965: Anatomy of a Failure" (Montgomery, AL: Air University Press, 1986). Available online at www.au.af.mil/au/awc/awcgate/readings/drew2.htm

[19] Robert E. Morris, "Why We Lost the War in Vietnam," 391.

distress." Graduated American bombing also enabled the North Vietnamese to disperse their most important resources, including their oil supplies, and otherwise prepare for future attacks while also exploiting the bombing for propaganda purposes by focusing attention on civilian casualties and damage. Perhaps worst of all, bombing pauses and targeting restrictions enabled the North Vietnamese to build a sophisticated air defense system.[20]

The ROEs the Johnson administration imposed on US aircraft attacking North Vietnam compounded the problems caused by Rolling Thunder's gradualist strategy. These ROEs have been widely and often bitterly criticized by revisionist commentators.[21] They were of two kinds, geographical and operational. Geographical limits placed key areas out of bounds, initially all of North Vietnam above the 20th parallel, which left Hanoi, Haiphong, and the rest of the country's heartland immune from US attacks. Even when the 20th parallel limit was lifted, important geographic restrictions remained, most importantly restricted and prohibited zones around Hanoi and Haiphong. Operating restrictions included totally or partially prohibiting attacks against targets the military wanted to hit. Usually these were considered civilian targets, although at times that designation was questionable. Also, attacks on military targets near protected civilian targets also were strictly limited. Making matters worse, the ROEs were complicated and frequently changed, to the point where at times it was difficult for pilots to know on a day-to-day basis what they actually were. The ROEs made inherently difficult missions even more dangerous. They made it impossible to wage the air war according to US Air Force doctrine, which called for inflicting maximum damage on enemy forces and the infrastructure that supported them by attacking vital targets in the enemy's heartland essential to its ability and will to fight. On a more fundamental level, the ROEs made it extremely difficult to adhere to two key principles of waging war: security, never allowing the

---

[20] Charles Tustin Kamps, "The JCS 94-Target List: A Vietnam Myth That Distorts Military Thought," *Aerospace Power Journal*, Spring 2001: 71–72; Ronald B. Frankum Jr., "'Swatting Flies With a Sledgehammer': The Air War," in *Rolling Thunder in a Gentle Land: The Vietnam War Revisited*, ed. Andrew Wiest (London and New York: Osprey Publishing, 2006), 216–18; William C. Westmoreland, *A Soldier Reports* (New York: Dell, 1980), 153; Walton, *The Myth of Inevitable U.S. Defeat in Vietnam*, 115.

[21] For example, see Staaveren, *Gradual Failure*; William M. Momyer, *Air Power in Three Wars (WWII, Korea, Vietnam)* (Washington, DC: Office of Air Force History, 1985; John T. Correll, "Rolling Thunder," *AIR FORCE Magazine*, March 2005; Wayne Thompson, *To Hanoi and Back: The U.S. Air Force and North Vietnam* (Washington, DC and London: Smithsonian Institution Press, 2000).

enemy to acquire an unexpected advantage; and surprise, striking the enemy at a time and place or in a manner for which it is unprepared.[22]

All of this was done against the advice of the administration's military advisors, most notably the Joint Chiefs of Staff, who from the start of Rolling Thunder were urging a much more intensive campaign than that approved by the president. The original JCS plan, to be directed at ninety-four targets during a four-phase operation over thirteen weeks, was rejected, notwithstanding the support it received from both General Westmoreland and Admiral Ulysses S. Sharpe, commander-in-chief of the US Pacific Command. General Taylor, by then ambassador to South Vietnam, took the middle ground, favoring stronger attacks than those authorized by President Johnson but not at the level recommended by the JCS. Air Force Chief of Staff John P. McConnell favored an even more intense twenty-eight-day campaign. As early as February 1965, just before the onset of Rolling Thunder, Admiral Sharpe wrote to the JCS that the administration's proposed "graduated reprisal" campaign was inadequate. In April 1965, a month into Rolling Thunder, JCS Chairman General Earle G. Wheeler warned Secretary of Defense McNamara that US strikes had "not curtailed DRV military capabilities in any major way."[23] CIA Director John McCone voiced the same concern. In a memo that same April to the president's top advisors, McCone warned that United States had to "change the ground rules of the strikes against North Vietnam. We must hit them hard, more frequently, and inflict greater damage."[24]

This advice was repeated frequently in 1965 and in the years that followed. The failure to heed professional military advice became, and has remained, a sore point among senior military officers who served during the war as well as with revisionist commentators who believe the air campaign against North Vietnam could have made a substantial contribution to the war effort. General McConnell, upon retiring in 1969,

---

[22] Major Ricky James Drake, "The Rules of Defeat: The Impact of Aerial Rules of Engagement on USAF Operations in North Vietnam, 1965–1968" (Maxwell Air Force Base, AL: Air University Press, 1992), 7–10; Frankum "Swatting Flies with a Sledgehammer," 218; Ellsworth, "Operation Rolling Thunder,"18.

[23] Gacek, *The Logic of Force*, 198–201. Wheeler is quoted in Joseph R. Cerami, "Presidential Decisionmaking and Vietnam." *Parameters: The U.S Army War College Quarterly* Winter 1996–97. Available online at http://strategicstudiesinstitute.army.mil/pubs/parameters/Articles/96winter/cerami.htm. For details on the so-called 94 Target List and the overall JCS plan see Kamps, "The JCS 94-Target List," 77–78; Drew, "Rolling Thunder 1965," 9.

[24] Quoted in Gacek, *The Logic of Force*, 205.

told the National Security Council that Rolling Thunder's lack of success stemmed from "restrictions placed upon the Air Force."[25] In his history of the war, General Phillip B. Davidson writes that "gradualism forced the United States into a lengthy, indecisive air war of attrition – the very kind which best suited Ho and Giap."[26] Colonel Joseph R. Cerami has noted, "the progressive, slow squeeze option succeeded only in preventing the attainment of U.S. strategic objectives."[27] US Air Force Reserve Colonel John K. Ellsworth makes a more fundamental point: the Johnson administration, following McNamara's theories, "did not understand airpower or military doctrines. Consequently, it did not utilize air power the way it was intended to be used." Specifically:

[President] Johnson showed that he did not understand the inherent nature of airpower as an offensive weapon. Aerial combat is much different from ground warfare: the vastness of airspace promotes offensive actions rather than defensive or protective measures. Defensive tactics are counter-productive. Since you can be attacked from any direction by airpower, it is therefore imperative that air leaders be allowed to force the fight and take the offensive to the enemy. Bombing halts and cease-fires hindered a continuous and concentrated strategic bombing campaign; they allowed the North Vietnamese to reconstitute their forces, reestablish their lines of supply, and generally outlast the American effort.[28]

Finally, Dale Walton makes an equally fundamental point when he notes that US policy makers made a "critical strategic error" when they used the air campaign against North Vietnam as a tool of diplomacy rather than as an instrument to weaken the DRV's ability to continue the war. This forced the Americans into the absurd position of leaving the most important targets untouched so they could be used as leverage to force Hanoi to the bargaining table. And this in turn "undermined the effectiveness of the entire air war" because it enabled the North Vietnamese to adjust to the bombing, disperse their most valuable resources, and build their formidable air defense system.[29]

The matter of what should have been done about North Vietnam's air defenses is a particularly sore point because of the enormous toll they ultimately took on American airmen. As of late 1964, North Vietnam had a relatively unsophisticated air defense system based on 1,400 antiaircraft artillery pieces. Its air force had only thirty-four fighter aircraft,

---

[25] Quoted Hess, *Vietnam: Explaining America's Lost War*, 94.
[26] Davidson, *Vietnam at War*, 339.
[27] Cerami, "Presidential Decisionmaking and Vietnam."
[28] Ellsworth, "Operation Rolling Thunder," 6, 16.
[29] Walton, *The Myth of Inevitable U.S. Defeat in Vietnam*, 108.

old MiG-15s and MiG-17s. It was after the first Rolling Thunder bombing pause, which began in May 1965, that North Vietnam began integrating Soviet-built SA-2 surface-to-air missiles (SAMs) into its air defense system. By 1966, Hanoi and other strategic centers in North Vietnam were protected by a sophisticated, world-class air defense system that included SAM missiles, antiaircraft artillery, and Soviet-built MiG fighters. By November 1968, when Rolling Thunder ended, that air defense system included 200 SAM sites, more than 8,000 antiaircraft artillery pieces, more than 400 radars of various types, and an air force of 75 fighters that included advanced MiG-21s as well as MiG-19s and MiG-17s.[30]

The antiaircraft artillery pieces alone were dangerous enough. The North Vietnamese, taking advantage of the delay in US reprisals, had almost 1,000 antiaircraft artillery pieces deployed at likely bombing targets by February 1965; by December 1965 there were more than 2,200, and, as noted earlier, by 1968 more than 8,000. These weapons took a heavy toll on US aircraft during the reprisal raids of February 1965 and the early Rolling Thunder attacks that followed. Ultimately they would account for 68 percent of all the US aircraft lost in Vietnam during the war. Meanwhile, although the United States learned early in April 1965 that SAM sites were being built, Washington did not permit attacks against them until July, and then only against sites outside the Hanoi/Haiphong region. In *A Soldier Reports*, General Westmoreland reported an incident, widely cited in the secondary literature on the war, which took place in Saigon shortly after the United States discovered SAM construction. Westmoreland and his air commander, General Joseph H. Moore, wanted to bomb the SAM sites before they were completed. They raised the matter with John McNaughton, an assistant secretary of defense. He responded: "You don't think the North Vietnamese are going to use them! Putting them in is just a political ploy by the Russians to appease Hanoi." That response echoed a memo McNaughton had written to McNamara, which opined, "We won't bomb the sites, and that will be a signal to North Vietnam not to use them," an assessment McNamara shared. Westmoreland, not surprisingly, was furious, and in *A Soldier Reports*

---

[30] Kamps, "The JCS 94-Target List," 72; Patrick K. Barker, "Air Defense: Democratic Republic of Vietnam," in *The Encyclopedia of the Vietnam War: A Political, Social, and Military History*, ed. Spencer C. Tucker (Oxford: Oxford University Press, 1998), 6.

denounced what he called this sending of signals by the "clever civilian theorists in Washington."[31]

As Leslie H. Gelb and Richard K. Betts, two orthodox commentators, noted in *The Irony of Vietnam: The System Worked*, "McNaughton turned out to be wrong. The DRV was soon using SAMs to knock down large numbers of U.S. warplanes."[32] US pilots had various techniques to avoid or defeat the SAMS, from jamming and destroying the radars that guided them to dropping down to lower altitudes, and relatively few aircraft were lost to North Vietnamese SAMs. But the SAMs still affected missions over North Vietnam. Even when these missiles missed their targets, combat aircraft that dropped to a lower altitude to avoid them were forced into what long-time *AIR FORCE Magazine* editor John T. Correll has called the "lethal shooting gallery of the [antiaircraft] guns."[33]

Even when attacks against SAMs were permitted, rules of engagement imposed by Washington severely limited their effectiveness. Airmen often could only attack SAMs actually firing on them. Therefore, in one incident when US Navy pilots found 111 SAMs being transported on railcars, they could not attack them. "We had to fight all 111 one at a time," one pilot recalled. The North Vietnamese, well aware of US rules of engagement, took advantage of them. To protect their SAM bases, they located as many

---

[31] McNaughton's memo to McNamara is cited in Correll, "Rolling Thunder," 61–62. On McNaughton also see Westmoreland, *A Soldier Reports*, 153. On the antiaircraft artillery statistics, which vary a bit from source to source, see Barker, "Air Defense: Democratic Republic of Vietnam," 6; and Van Staaveren, *Gradual Failure*, 313. On aircraft losses to antiaircraft fire see Momyer, *Air Power in Three Wars*, 123. The percentage of losses to antiaircraft fire is higher than Momyer's figure when Indochina as a whole is considered. Orthodox historian John Prados has called Westmoreland's reporting of the McNaughton incident a "much simplified version of reality," presumably because the question of whether to bomb the SAM sights had not yet been decided and was, in fact, discussed by President Johnson and his advisors in May 1965. The reality, however, especially from the perspective of the pilots who had to go into harm's way to bomb targets in North Vietnam, is that by not deciding immediately to bomb the SAM sites and deliberating instead, Johnson and his advisors decided to give the North Vietnamese (and their Soviet benefactors) time to complete several sites. In late July a SAM scored its first kill on a US warplane, at which point Johnson authorized the bombing of some, but *not* all, of the SAM sites. See John Prados, "The '65 Decision: Bombing Soviet SAM Sites in North Vietnam," *The Veteran*, January/February 2006. Available online at www.vva.org/archive/TheVeteran/2006_01/FeaturesSAM.htm

[32] Leslie H. Gelb and Richard K. Betts, *The Irony of Vietnam: The System Worked* (Washington, DC: The Brookings Institution, 1979), 138.

[33] Correll, "Rolling Thunder," 62.

as they could within ten miles of Hanoi since that city normally was safe from attack. SAMs could attack aircraft as far as twenty-seven miles from Hanoi, and that put many American aircraft attacking targets along the transportation system moving troops and supplies southward within their range. In fact, most of the targets along that transportation network in North Vietnam were within thirty miles of Hanoi. Thus, notes General William W. Momyer, who commanded the US Seventh Air Force in Vietnam from 1966 to 1968, "the SAMs could hit us whenever we came after one of their more significant targets near Hanoi, but our rules of engagement prevented us, in most cases, from hitting back."[34]

In addition, by April 1965 US aircraft on bombing raids were being engaged by North Vietnamese MiGs, but Johnson and McNamara did not permit attacks against the airfields those MiGs flew from in North Vietnam.[35] They thereby ignored US airpower doctrine, which sensibly called for striking enemy airfields at the beginning of a campaign. This enabled North Vietnamese MiGs, first MiG-17s and within a year advanced MiG-21s, to challenge US aircraft, which then had to engage them in aerial battles. The most important North Vietnamese MiG base was Phuc Yen airfield, about twenty miles northwest of Hanoi. The pleas of the military commanders in Vietnam and Joint Chiefs notwithstanding, US aircraft were forbidden to attack Phuc Yen or any other North Vietnamese airbase for two years. Until 1967 US pilots attempting to destroy enemy aircraft literally had to watch enemy airfields and wait until the MiGs stationed there took off and attacked them before taking action. Thomson notes that the lesson of this failure was learned, albeit too late for many pilots who flew in Vietnam: "In Rolling Thunder the Air Force had been forbidden to attack enemy airfields for two years. In Desert Storm [the 1991 campaign against Iraq], enemy airfields were attacked the first night."[36]

General Momyer has pointed out that in early 1965 the overall North Vietnamese system of radars, antiaircraft guns, SAMs, and MiGs was in an embryonic state and could have been destroyed with no significant American aircraft losses. That was not done because US civilian officials feared such action would be an escalation of the war that might trigger Chinese and possibly even Soviet intervention. Momyer adds that as a result the system was allowed to expand without significant

---

[34] Ibid.; Momyer, *Air Power in Three Wars*, 133.
[35] Van Staaveren, *Gradual Failure*, 314–15.
[36] Thompson, *To Hanoi and Back*, 34, 284; Drake, "The Rules of Defeat," 6.

US interference until the spring of 1966, when methodical attacks were permitted against parts it. "We were never allowed to attack the entire system," he concludes with understandable frustration.[37]

The issue of possible great power military intervention – the real concern was China, Soviet intervention was considered far less likely – was legitimate, especially given China's intervention in the Korean War less than fifteen years earlier. Revisionist commentators acknowledge this. Walton, for example, notes it would have been "irresponsible for decision makers not to consider the possibility that China would intervene on North Vietnam's behalf." However, Walton makes a strong case that the risk of this happening was low; he maintains that there was sufficient evidence that the United States "with considerable confidence" could have escalated the war against North Vietnam. Mark Moyar has seconded this conclusion with additional evidence, including comments by Mao Zedong to journalist Edgar Snow published in February 1965 in *The New Republic*. Snow summarized Mao's viewpoint as follows: "China's armies would not go beyond her borders to fight. That was clear enough. Only if the United States attacked China would China fight. Wasn't that clear?"[38] This assumption about Chinese intentions is especially true if one considers only Rolling Thunder, as opposed to the suggestion that the United States should have invaded the southern part of North Vietnam. For example, Chen Jian has noted that in June 1965 the Chinese made it clear to their comrades in Hanoi that as long as the war remained in its "current status" – meaning US military actions in South Vietnam while using only air power to bomb North Vietnam – the Vietnamese would have to fight by themselves, albeit with Chinese military and other aid. Xioming Zhang, covering the same period, citing Zhou Enlai, notes that Beijing "under the current circumstances" was not going to provoke a direct Sino-American confrontation.[39] As Walton puts it, "China did not trap US policy makers – because of their extreme risk aversion, those leaders trapped themselves."[40]

---

[37] Momyer, *Air Power in Three Wars*, 118.

[38] Walton, *The Myth of Inevitable U.S. Defeat in Vietnam*, 94–100; Moyar, *Triumph Forsaken*, 360–61 and "Section I Response," in *Triumph Revisited*, 69–71; Edgar Snow, "Interview with Mao Zedong," *The New Republic*, February 26, 1965. Available online at https://newrepublic.com/article/89494/interview-mao-tse-tung-communist-china

[39] Chen Jian, "China's Involvement in the Vietnam War, 1964–1969," *The China Quarterly* 142 (June, 1995): 369; Xiaoming Zhang, "The Vietnam War, 1964–1969: A Chinese Perspective," *The Journal of Military History* 60, no. 4 (October 1996): 751.

[40] Walton, *The Myth of Inevitable U.S. Defeat in Vietnam*, 101.

Limits imposed by Washington also severely hindered interdiction. Johnson's refusal to bomb key railways, highway bridges, and storage facilities in the northern part of North Vietnam, and, above all, mine North Vietnam's ports, especially Haiphong, its most important port, made it impossible to sufficiently interdict the flow of military supplies destined for Communist forces in South Vietnam. Thompson has summed up the situation the US Air Force and Navy faced in attempting to interdict the flow of weapons and supplies into South Vietnam. Approximately a third of North Vietnam's imports came by railroad running northeast into China while most of the rest arrived via the port of Haiphong. Since North Vietnam imported most of its military supplies, General Momyer deemed it essential to close the Haiphong port and sever the northeast railroad link with China. However, President Johnson refused to permit the US Navy to bomb and mine the port of Haiphong because, with Soviet ships there, he feared an incident that might lead to a wider war. The US Air Force was permitted to bomb the northeast railroad but not the largest bridges across the Red River at Hanoi because Johnson wanted to avoid civilian casualties. Effective bombing of the railroad yards was precluded because Johnson refused to permit the use of B-52 bombers, the aircraft that could carry the heavy bomb loads required for the job. There were other restrictions as well.[41]

The result was that US airpower was used in a manner for which it was not suited. In discussing the general problem of using air power for interdiction, Momyer later wrote that reducing an enemy's supply line to zero is "virtually impossible so long as he is willing to pay an extravagant price in lost men and supplies." The object therefore should be to reduce the supply flow as much as possible and raise the cost as high as possible. This means focusing an air campaign on the most vital supply targets such as factories, power plants, refineries, marshalling yards, and transportation lines that carry supplies in bulk. Waiting until the enemy "has disseminated his supplies among thousands of trucks, sampans, rafts, bicycles, and then to send our multimillion-dollar aircraft after these individual vehicles – this is how to maximize our cost, not his."[42] Yet, to Momyer's great frustration, this is exactly what the United States did in Vietnam during Rolling Thunder. The Johnson administration forced its airmen to interdict North Vietnamese supplies retail rather than wholesale.

[41] Thompson, *To Hanoi and Back*, 26; Momyer, *Air Power in Three Wars*, 174–75.
[42] Momyer, *Air Power in Three Wars*, 174–75, 338.

It has repeatedly been pointed out that ultimately the United States attacked almost every target on its Air Force's original target list. The overall destruction was massive: 65 percent of North Vietnam's POL (petroleum, oil, lubricants) storage capacity, 60 percent of its power-generating capacity, half of its major bridges (at one point or another), 10,000 trucks, 2,000 railroad cars, and 20 locomotives.[43] It also is constantly repeated that the United States dropped more tonnage on Vietnam, North and South, than was dropped by all combatants during the entirety of World War II. However, these statistics, in Walton's words, "prove nothing." The reason is that the "most lucrative targets in North Vietnam ... were intentionally left undisturbed by the Johnson administration." These included North Vietnam's industrial infrastructure, the port of Haiphong, key railroads and bridges, and the seat of government in Hanoi. Going beyond North Vietnam, Walton adds that the United States restricted "the wrong part of the air war." It is precisely bombing in *South Vietnam* that should have been "carefully circumscribed," while the campaign against North Vietnam should have been "nearly unrestricted."[44] Thompson makes essentially the same points. He notes that in North Vietnam "the bombs kept falling on less important targets" and that much of the bombing in Southeast Asia as a whole "did nothing but tear up jungle."[45] To which Staaveren adds, with reference to 1965 but applicable to the entire Rolling Thunder campaign, "combat pilots took many risks and often suffered high losses by striking and restriking a large number of relatively unimportant targets."[46]

Two additional perspectives, one American and one North Vietnamese, merit serious consideration in evaluating graduated response and the failure of Rolling Thunder. Douglas Pike served for many years as a US Foreign Service officer and, after his retirement, as director of the Indochinese Studies Project at the University of California, Berkeley. He was one of America's leading experts on Vietnam and probably its leading civilian expert on the Vietnamese armed forces. At a symposium in 1983, Pike compared the results of Rolling Thunder under President Johnson to those of the massive US air assault against Hanoi and Haiphong under Richard Nixon in December 1972, when most of the restrictions of the earlier campaign were removed. In his view, "while conditions had

[43] Earl H. Tilford Jr, "Rolling Thunder, Operation," in *The Encyclopedia of the Vietnam War: A Political, Social, and Military History*, 359.

[44] Walton, *The Myth of Inevitable U.S. Defeat in Vietnam*, 110, 113.

[45] Thompson, *To Hanoi and Back*, 284.   [46] Staaveren, *Gradual Failure*, 316.

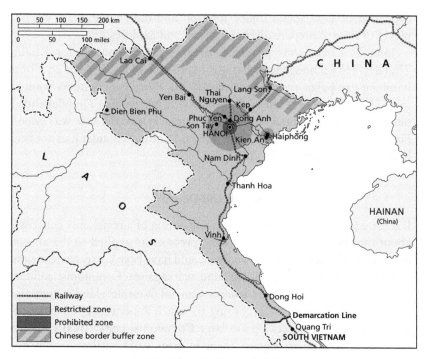

MAP 5 Rolling Thunder Restricted Zones, 1967

changed vastly in seven years, the dismaying conclusion to suggest itself
from the 1972 Christmas bombing is that had this kind of air assault been
launched in 1965, the Vietnam war as we know it might have been over
within a matter of months, even weeks."[47] Bui Tin served as a colonel on
the general staff of the North Vietnamese army and as a war correspondent; as the highest-ranking officer on the scene in Saigon on April 30,
1975, he received the South Vietnamese government's surrender. (He later
became disillusioned with the Vietnamese Communist movement and
moved to France.) Bui Tin's view from the other side lends considerable
support to Pike's assessment. In an interview with the *Wall Street Journal*
in August 1995, Bui Tin was asked about the US bombing of North
Vietnam. He answered as follows: "If all the bombing had been concentrated at one time, it would have hurt our efforts. But the bombing was

[47] Quoted in Mackubin Thomas Owens, "A Winnable War: The Argument against the
Orthodox History of Vietnam" [Book Review] *Weekly Standard*, January 5, 2007.
Available online at www.weeklystandard.com/Content/Public/Articles/000/000/013/13
3ccyfj.asp

expanded in slow stages under Johnson and didn't worry us. We had plenty of time to prepare alternate routes and facilities."[48]

John T. Correll has provided an appropriate epitaph for Rolling Thunder. He acknowledges that it is impossible to know what an all-out bombing campaign in 1965, as the US Air Force commanders wanted, would have achieved. That said, he insists, "when Rolling Thunder ended, our best chance of knocking North Vietnam out of the war was gone." Finally, he cogently and ruefully observes, "Rolling Thunder had not been built to succeed, and it didn't."[49]

Search and Destroy

If it is reasonable to say that there is something of a revisionist consensus about the shortcomings of graduated pressure as applied to the air war against North Vietnam and how they could have been corrected, the same cannot be said regarding the ground war against Communist military forces in South Vietnam. At issue is General Westmoreland's campaign of "search and destroy," according to which American combat troops focused primarily on seeking out large Communist units, usually in difficult jungle terrain, to engage them in large-scale battles. Search and destroy, it should be noted, was not graduated pressure in the same sense as Rolling Thunder. First, it was confined to South Vietnam and therefore did not directly affect North Vietnam. Second, although the US troop buildup in South Vietnam took place gradually over three years (1965–1968), it was undertaken in response to the requirements of the military situation on the ground, not as part of a strategy of systematically increasing pressure on the enemy. Third, inside South Vietnam – as opposed to the Washington's stricture that US and South Vietnamese forces not enter Laos, Cambodia, or North Vietnam – search and destroy was not subject to strict limitations and micromanagement from Washington as was Rolling Thunder. However, as with Rolling Thunder, search and destroy was pursued as part of the overall military policy of gradual escalation, an approach that rejected the option of seeking a decisive military victory as quickly as possible in favor of creating a situation that would force North Vietnam into negotiations in which it would have to accept the independence of South Vietnam.

[48] Bui Tin, "How the North Won the War." Interview with Stephen Young. *Wall Street Journal*, August 3, 1995. Available online at www.viet-myths.netbuitin.htm
[49] Correll, "Rolling Thunder," 65.

Search and destroy was the primary American approach to the ground war from the arrival of US combat troops in South Vietnam in March 1965 until after the Communist Tet Offensive of early 1968. It relied heavily on American technology, which among other advantages provided unprecedented mobility via the use of helicopters to quickly transport large American infantry units into combat areas, and on superior US firepower, both ground based and airborne, to overwhelm Communist forces. Search and destroy was essentially a strategy of attrition, the goal being to wear down the enemy and ultimately reach the so-called cross-over point, where Communist casualties would exceed the ability to replace them, and thereby force Hanoi to give up its effort to conquer South Vietnam. That goal was not achieved. The only cross-over point that was reached during the search and destroy era was that American casualties, although far lower than those suffered by North Vietnam, eventually reached the point where they were no longer acceptable to the American public.

The debate among revisionists over search and destroy is a continuation of a clash of viewpoints that began during the war; it is now more than half a century old. A key point of contention is what kind of war North Vietnam was waging to conquer South Vietnam – was it primarily a guerrilla insurgency or a conventional war? – and, therefore, how the United States should have responded militarily. The opposing poles in this disagreement among revisionists as it evolved after the war are provided by two US Army officers who served in Vietnam, Lieutenant Colonel Andrew Krepinevich, author of *The Army in Vietnam* (1986), and Colonel Harry Summers, author of *On Strategy* (1982), the former making the case for guerrilla insurgency and the latter for conventional war. There are, as there were during the war, all sorts of gradations, combinations, and variations in between, only some of which can be discussed in the limited space available here. The viewpoints of Krepinevich and Summers are covered first because they in effect frame the scope of the debate and because each makes, respectively, the best-known statement of the guerrilla insurgency and conventional war case.

The case for a counterinsurgency strategy goes back to the early days of US involvement in Vietnam. A variety of civilian and military officials argued that key to winning the war was to defeat the guerrilla insurgency in South Vietnam and that this required a counterinsurgency strategy. They included three prominent and charismatic military figures: Lieutenant Colonel Edward Lansdale, who first served in South Vietnam as a close advisor to Ngo Dinh Diem and then, between 1965 and 1968, as a civilian pacification specialist; Lieutenant Colonel John Paul Vann, who served for about eight years in Vietnam, first as an US Army officer and then as a civilian advisor, before being killed in a helicopter crash in 1972; and Colonel David Hackworth, whose public criticism of the US Army's approach to the war led to his retirement in 1971. The Marine Corps entered the fray in 1965 by implementing its own version of counterinsurgency in a number of areas in South Vietnam, albeit in the face of criticism from Westmoreland and other top Army commanders on the scene. After the war, the Marine case was made forcefully by General Victor H. Krulak, the overall commander of Marine forces in the Pacific from March 1964 to May 1968.[50]

Picking up this line of thinking, Krepinevich argues that the US Army failed in Vietnam because it overemphasized conventional warfare when in fact it faced a guerrilla war in South Vietnam that required a multi-faceted counterinsurgency strategy to ensure victory. He puts the bulk of the blame for this on what he calls the "Army Concept," which called for waging conventional war and using massive firepower to minimize US casualties. This approach grew out of the US Army's successes in its previous twentieth-century wars, the threat posed by the Soviet Union during the Cold War, and numerous contingencies the US Army faced during the Vietnam years with limited resources.[51] The trouble, says Krepinevich, is that the US Army's conventional tactics were highly destructive and unsuited to defeating the main threat to the government of South Vietnam: a guerrilla insurgency that drew its strength from the discontent of the peasants. Emphasis therefore had to be placed "first and foremost, on the *internal* [italics added] threat to the stability and legitimacy of the government of South Vietnam." Defeating this guerrilla insurgency required more than destroying main-force guerrilla units through attrition, as conventional US tactics were intended to do; it also required eliminating smaller units and the guerrilla political infrastructure, and thereby separating the guerrillas from the rural population. By focusing on attrition rather than counterinsurgency, the

---

[50] Victor H. Krulak *First to Fight: An Inside View of the US Marine Corps* (Annapolis: Naval Institute Press, 1984). Significantly, while Krulak stressed the need for counter-insurgency against Communist forces in South Vietnam, he emphasized the necessity of blocking North Vietnam from resupplying the insurgents in the South, a point also made by Colonel Harry Summers in building his case for conventional warfare.

[51] Andrew F. Krepinevich Jr., *The Army in Vietnam* (Baltimore and London: Johns Hopkins University Press, 1986), 4–6.

US Army "missed whatever opportunity it had to deal the insurgent forces a crippling blow at low enough cost to permit a continued U.S. presence in Vietnam in the event of external, overt aggression." Making matters worse, the massive use of firepower "alienated the most important element in any counterinsurgency strategy – the people." The result, Krepinevich concludes, was that the US Army not only failed to defeat the most dangerous threat to South Vietnam – the internal one – but in the process undermined public support for the war in the United States.[52]

The argument for counterinsurgency has been made in a variety of ways by a number of revisionists. Three of the most notable commentators are historian Guenter Lewy (*America in Vietnam*, 1978), Lieutenant Colonel John A. Nagl (*Learning to Eat Soup with a Knife: Counterinsurgency Lessons from Malaya and Vietnam*, 2002), and General Lewis Sorley (*Westmoreland: The General Who Lost Vietnam*, 2011). Lewy argues that search and destroy "badly underestimated" North Vietnam's ability to escalate in response to US measures and that this in turn forced Washington to continue its buildup "with no end in sight." Search and destroy tactics alienated the population in the countryside; in particular, America's "lavish use of firepower" inhibited the efforts of the South Vietnamese government to win the allegiance of the people. Lewy further criticizes the strategy of attrition for neglecting the "crucial importance" of pacification and ignoring that "the enemy whom it was essential to defeat was in the hamlets and not in the jungles." Finally, he stresses that the war had to be won in South Vietnam by the South Vietnamese themselves.[53]

Nagl stresses the failure of Westmoreland and other US Army commanders in Vietnam to get beyond the lessons they learned on the battlefields of World War II – using terms such as "institutional culture" and "organizational culture" rather than Krepinevich's "Army Concept" to sum up doctrine that embodied those lessons – despite the fact that they faced a very different war in Vietnam. Nagl notes that there were younger people, both civilian and military, who understood the need to fight a counterinsurgency in South Vietnam but that they were unable to influence the US Army's approach to the war. Unfortunately, the US Army continued to use the "hammer" of "firepower and maneuver, battalions and divisions" it had previously used with such success instead of the necessary "political-military-economic screwdriver" suggested by innovative thinkers.[54]

---

[52] Ibid., 12–13, 231–34, 259, 268.   [53] Lewy, *America in Vietnam*, 51, 437–38.
[54] John A. Nagl, *Learning to Eat Soup with a Knife: Counterinsurgency Lessons From Malaya and Vietnam* (Westport: Praeger, 2002), 200–203.

Lewis Sorley, like Krepinevich, served in Vietnam. As the title of his biography of Westmoreland makes clear, Sorely places the primary blame for search and destroy and its shortcomings on Westmoreland. He cites General Bruce Palmer, who served as Westmoreland's deputy in Vietnam, to make the point that search and destroy was Westmoreland's strategic concept, not an approach imposed on him by Washington. Sorley maintains that in focusing on search and destroy, and therefore on attrition, Westmoreland neglected "two other crucial aspects of the war, improvement of South Vietnam's armed forces and pacification." A crucial and controversial twist in Sorely's account, which is discussed Chapter 6, is that he credits Westmoreland's successor, General Creighton Abrams, with remedying Westmoreland's failures and, in effect, winning the war by 1972.[55]

Colonel Summers, the author of *On Strategy*, disagrees fundamentally with the case that counterinsurgency was the key to victory in Vietnam. He argues that what the United States faced in South Vietnam, notwithstanding the local Vietcong guerrilla insurgency, was a North Vietnamese invasion of that country that in fact was a conventional war. In other words, contra Krepinevich, Summers sees the real threat to the government of South Vietnam as *external*, not internal. Although the overall North Vietnamese campaign opened with a guerrilla attack, he argues, the nature of the war changed during 1963 and 1964 when Hanoi began sending regular army troops south. The guerrilla insurgency thus was a "tactical screen masking North Vietnam's real objectives (the conquest of South Vietnam)."[56]

The problem was that the United States responded as if it were dealing with an insurgency: "Instead of orientating on North Vietnam – the source of the war – we turned our attention to the symptom – the guerrilla war in the south." As for search and destroy, limited as it was to South Vietnam itself, to Summers it was an "intense" version of counterinsurgency. Rather than searching for Communist forces scattered about South Vietnam, the United States should have committed its forces to "isolating the battlefield": that is, cutting off the routes by

---

[55] Lewis Sorley, *Westmoreland: The General Who Lost Vietnam* (Boston and New York: Houghton Mifflin Harcourt, 2011), 73, 91–107. See also Sorley's "To Change a War: General Harold K. Johnson and the PROVN Study," *Parameters*, Spring 1998: 93–109 and his best-known work, *A Better War: The Unexamined Victories and Final Tragedy of America's Last Years in Vietnam* (San Diego: Harcourt, 1999), where Sorley makes his case for General Abrams.

[56] Summers, *On Strategy*, 125–31.

which North Vietnam sent soldiers and supplies into South Vietnam. Such an effort would have included cutting the Ho Chi Minh Trail by deploying US, South Korean, and ARVN troops along the 17th parallel from the coast across South Vietnam and extending across Laos to its border with Thailand along with using air and sea forces to cut sea-based infiltration routes. The United States also could and should have maintained a credible threat of an amphibious assault against North Vietnam, thereby tying down significant North Vietnamese troops in coastal defense. By adopting the "negative aim of counterinsurgency" instead of the "positive aim of isolation of the battle field," Summers argues, the United States left North Vietnam in control of the war while, in the words of Clausewitz, it found itself "simply waiting on events." In broader military terms, Summers notes that the United States adopted what military experts call the "strategic defensive" in opposing Communist forces in Vietnam. The problem is that adopting "strategic defensive in pursuit of a negative aim" requires that "time is on your side." In Vietnam, this was not the case. This "fatal flaw" of allowing North Vietnam to control the war crippled the American effort to defend South Vietnam.[57]

A complicating factor in the revisionist debate over search and destroy is that the relatively clear waters regarding counterinsurgency versus conventional warfare have been muddied by input from expert commentators who find both positions flawed. That assessment generally is based on the argument that the Communist effort in South Vietnam was not simply an invasion or an insurgency but *both*, that is, both a guerrilla insurgency in the South based on the Vietcong and a conventional invasion from the North by the PAVN. These interlocked campaigns were initiated and controlled by the Communist regime in Hanoi. In addition, Hanoi varied its strategy, depending on the circumstances, between emphasizing guerrilla warfare and conventional

---

[57] Ibid., 127–28, 164–73, 227–34. The Clausewitz quotation is on page 169. Another issue that divides revisionists is exactly who is to blame for the US search and destroy tactics that failed in Vietnam. This once again contrasts with the revisionist view of the air war, whose failure is overwhelmingly blamed on the civilian leadership in Washington. With regard to search and destroy, some revisionists – such as Summers – blame the civilian leadership in Washington rather than the top US Army brass in general or Westmoreland in particular. Others – such as Krepinevich – blame the top US Army brass as a whole, including Westmoreland. Yet others – most notably Lewis Sorely – lay the blame directly on Westmoreland, the officer Sorley calls "The General Who Lost Vietnam." See Krepinevich, *The Army and Vietnam*, 4–6; Summers, *On Strategy*, 34; Sorely, *Westmoreland*, 91–107.

warfare.[58] Also at issue is whether or not Westmoreland responded properly to the challenges he faced.

An excellent example of this line of thinking comes from military historian Dale Andrade. In his article "Westmoreland Was Right: Learning the Wrong Lessons from the Vietnam War" (2008), Andrade takes issue with both Summers and Krepinevich. According to Andrade, what the United States faced in South Vietnam was not simply a conventional war or a guerrilla war: it was a "simultaneous guerrilla and main force war." Andrade characterizes this "ideal melding of guerrilla and main force capabilities" as a "perfect insurgency" and argues that any strategy that ignored one or the other – Andrade sees Summers neglecting the former and Krepinevich the latter – was "doomed to failure."[59]

As Andrade sees it, when Westmoreland took command in June 1964, he faced a situation in which, contra Krepinevich, enemy main-force units, not small guerrilla groups, constituted the main threat to the government of South Vietnam. Andrade approvingly quotes Westmoreland himself on the point that the "enemy had committed big units and I ignored them to my peril." In concert with other revisionist commentators, Andrade argues that this "perfect insurgency" existed entirely because of North Vietnam: "Hanoi controlled the insurgency's leadership, Hanoi mustered the bulk of the main force units, and Hanoi sent the supplies south to keep the war going." This is also the view of counterinsurgency expert Andrew Birtle, who notes that the war in Vietnam, far from being a classic guerrilla insurgency, was a "kaleidoscopic conflict" in which the enemy consisted not only of traditional guerrillas but "of large, professional military forces directed and reinforced by an external power" determined to destroy South Vietnam.[60]

To that end, as Andrade documents using North Vietnamese sources, PAVN units began infiltrating into the South as early as 1963. The first battalion crossed the 17th parallel and entered combat in the spring of 1963; it was joined by a second battalion in 1964, and by December 1965, just nine months after the first US combat troops arrived in South Vietnam, North Vietnamese units accounted for 55 of the 160

---

[58] For an excellent overview of this subject, see James R. Ward, "Vietnam: Insurgency or War," *Military Review* 69 (January 1989): 14–23. Ward characterizes the war in the South as "two separate but interlocked conflicts – both an insurgency and an invasion."

[59] Andrade, "Westmoreland Was Right," 147–48.

[60] Ibid., 148–52; Andrew J. Birtle, "PROVN, Westmoreland, and the Historians: A Reappraisal," *The Journal of Military History* 72 (October 2008): 1247.

main-force Communist military units – the Vietcong fielded both guerrilla and main-force units – in South Vietnam and just across the border in Laos and Cambodia. Contra Krepinevich, from the very beginning US forces faced an opponent that was using both guerrilla and main-force units. Furthermore, and again contra Krepinevich, it was the PAVN and Vietcong main-force units that were the major threat to the South Vietnamese regime and, in fact, the threat that caused the Johnson administration to send American combat troops to South Vietnam in the first place. That said – and this time contra Summers, who criticizes Westmorland for scattering troops throughout South Vietnam in support of counterinsurgency – General Westmoreland understood the situation and properly used his troops and resources to meet it. Quoting an official US Army history of the war, Andrade argues that Westmoreland's approach to the situation he faced when he arrived in Vietnam was "sound within the strategic limitations under which he had to work."[61]

Andrade's reference to "strategic limitations" in effect makes the point that search and destroy, which was a strategy of attrition, could not bring the United States victory in Vietnam. He does not fault Westmoreland for this, at least not entirely, although he does criticize Westmoreland for failing to adjust to changes in Communist tactics – which increasingly emphasized attacks by small units rather than large ones – beginning in 1967. The reason Andrade mutes his criticism of Westmoreland is that the "roots of the attrition strategy lay in Washington," as it was the White House that placed Communist base areas in North Vietnam, Cambodia, and Laos off-limits to attack.[62] Or, as political scientist Christopher Gacek puts it, search and destroy was the "residual strategy" the US Army was left with once Washington denied it the option of going into Laos and Cambodia to cut the Ho Chi Minh Trail, and thereby stop infiltration from North Vietnam, and also deny Communist forces already in the South their sanctuaries.[63]

The result, Andrade maintains, echoing Summers, was that the "allies were always on the strategic defensive in South Vietnam, awaiting attacks from the North Vietnamese, who could limp across the border to recover whenever they were bloodied." To support this strategic limits argument,

---

[61] Ibid., 148–53. The quotation about Hanoi controlling the war in the South is on page 151. Andrade's sources regarding North Vietnamese troop infiltration into South Vietnam come straight from the horse's mouth: two volumes published by the People's Army Publishing House in Hanoi. For Summers's criticism of Westmoreland's alleged overemphasis on counterinsurgency see *On Strategy*, 233–34.

[62] Andrade, "Westmoreland Was Right," 162.   [63] Gacek, *The Logic of Force*, 226.

Andrade turns to Westmoreland and Admiral Sharp, who in 1968 in their joint "Report on the War in Vietnam" argued that US policy of forbidding attacks against Communist base areas in North Vietnam, Laos, and Cambodia "made it impossible to destroy the enemy's main forces in a classic or traditional sense." Driving this point home, Andrade also cites the North Vietnamese army, whose official history affirms that these base areas were of "decisive importance to our army to mature and win victory." Little wonder then that Andrade himself asserts that in making Communist base areas immune to attack, "the United States gave North Vietnam an unbeatable advantage."[64] As if that were not enough, the North Vietnamese had the vital support of "two powerful sponsors," the Soviet Union and the People's Republic of China. He concludes: these factors, when supplemented with the ability to attack South Vietnam over and over again with no threat of serious retaliation, gave North Vietnam an "unprecedented advantage."[65]

Finally, the guerrilla insurgency/conventional war waters are muddied further by differing assessments of how successful the strategy of search and destroy actually was. A case in point is the assessment that search and destroy actually was succeeding during 1966 and 1967. However frustrating search and destroy was to many American observers and the US troops who had to carry it out, many commentators have noted that by the middle of 1966 North Vietnam's leaders were discouraged and concerned about the situation on the South Vietnamese battlefield and, equally important, seriously divided about how to respond. For example, historian James Wirtz writes in his history of the Tet Offensive that by 1967 both Vietcong and North Vietnamese units in the south "were suffering from a gradual erosion of combat capability" because of falling morale and the loss of their supplies to US search and destroy operations. Former US Army major and intelligence analyst Thomas Cubbage II adds that by 1967 "the United States and the Government of Vietnam forces were winning – winning slowly to be sure, but steadily." Colonel Gregory Daddis – whose overall viewpoint in *Westmoreland's War* (2014) actually places him much closer to the orthodox than to the revisionist camp – has observed, "By mid-1966, Hanoi arguably had lost, though not irretrievably, the military initiative to American and allied forces, forcing the

---

[64] Andrade, "Westmoreland Was Right," 162. Andrade does not argue that American policy alone led to the defeat in Vietnam. He credits North Vietnam's strategy, which "arguably was like no other in history" (174).

[65] Ibid., 174.

Politburo leaders to reassess their strategy." Lt. Colonel James H. Willbanks holds views that overlap both camps but can be considered revisionist because in the end he suggests that South Vietnam could have been saved had the United States done things differently. He writes in *The Tet Offensive* (2006) that search and destroy operations during the first half of 1967 badly disrupted the Communist logistic system and forced the PAVN and Vietcong to move bases and supplies into Cambodia. James S. Robbins, a former special assistant in the Office of the Secretary of Defense and author of *This Time We Win: Revisiting the Tet* Offensive (2010), adds that by the spring 1967 US ground strength and air mobility were taking their toll on both guerrilla and PAVN units, with the result that "Hanoi knew it had serious problems."[66]

Bui Tin, the former PAVN colonel, provides a North Vietnamese perspective on search and destroy. He reports that between 1965 and 1967 US forces and ARVN forced "our troops into a defensive mode" and that by 1967 the party leaders in Hanoi believed "something spectacular was needed to regain the initiative and reverse the situation if possible."[67]

How did that situation come to exist? General Davidson explains in some detail what occurred in *Vietnam at War*, in this writer's opinion the best military history of the Vietnam War. Davidson acknowledges that search and destroy operations – the first major one took place in January 1966 – had serious shortcomings and usually did not achieve the desired results. Nonetheless, these operations disrupted Communist operations, drove their main forces away from population centers, and inflicted heavy casualties on both main and guerrilla Communist forces. As early as spring 1966, Davidson writes, search and destroy operations had "seized and held the tactical initiative in South Vietnam." Operations conducted during 1966 and early 1967 maintained and

---

[66] James Wirtz, *The Tet Offensive: Intelligence Failure in War* (Ithaca: Cornell University Press, 1991), 49; Thomas L. Cubbage II, Review of The Tet Offensive: Intelligence in War, by James Wirtz, *Conflict Quarterly*, Summer 1993: 80; Gregory A. Daddis, *Westmoreland's War: Addressing American Strategy in Vietnam* (Oxford: Oxford University Press, 2014), 81; James S. Robbins, *This Time We Win: Revisiting the Tet Offensive* (New York and London: Encounter Books, 2010), 63–64; James H. Willbanks, *The Tet Offensive: A Concise History* (New York: Columbia University Press, 2006), 4–5. The main difference between these commentators regarding the mood and outlook in Hanoi is about how desperate North Vietnamese leaders were. Were they worried about their ability to sustain the war or confident in their ultimate success? See Willbanks on this point.

[67] Bui Tin, *From Enemy to Friend; A North Vietnamese Perspective on the War*, trans. Nguyen Ngoc Bich (Annapolis: Naval Institute Press, 2002), 62.

extended that initiative. Especially important in this regard were two division-sized, and often criticized, operations: Cedar Falls (January 1967) and Junction City (February–May 1967). Together they represented a change in US strategy because their tasks included attacking and destroying Communist base areas inside South Vietnam. (The crucial base areas in Laos and Cambodia, however, were out of bounds to US and South Vietnamese forces.) Davidson acknowledges that by refusing to defend their base areas and retreating, Communist forces prevented Westmoreland from achieving his main objective, which was to engage and destroy enemy main-force units. This saved most of these units – Junction City did destroy three Vietcong regiments – but at the price of driving them away from populated areas and into sanctuaries in remote border areas. It also separated the main-force units from guerrilla units, depriving the latter of vital support. Guerrilla forces near the populated areas also lost key sources of arms and ammunition, and their morale suffered. Meanwhile, intensified Rolling Thunder bombing operations, including attacking sixteen critical targets around Hanoi, raised the price of the war in North Vietnam, which now began to suffer from economic dislocation and hardship that included shortages of food, clothing, and medicine.[68]

This situation convinced North Vietnam's leaders that the ground war in South Vietnam was turning against them and that a new strategy was required. It precipitated a major debate in Hanoi during the spring and summer of 1967 about how to respond. One side called for a major new military campaign, which would be an all-out assault, to break the stalemate and achieve a "decisive victory"; this faction was led by Le Duan, the party general secretary, who by then had supplanted the aging and ailing Ho Chi Minh as the most powerful Communist Party leader. He was supported by General Nguyen Chi Thanh, the field commander of all Communist forces in South Vietnam (who died while the debate was going on, to be replaced as Le Duan's most important military ally by General Van Tien Dung). The opposition to this risky idea was led by General Giap, North Vietnam's most respected military leader and a longtime political opponent of both Le Duan and General Thanh, and by the increasingly fragile Ho. Giap argued such an offensive was premature and would be defeated by American firepower and mobility. The issue essentially was decided in Le Duan's favor by July. Le Duan then carried out a purge in which hundreds of party officials (although

[68] Davidson, *Vietnam at War*, 417–37.

not the iconic Giap, who was charged with putting together the plan for the offensive) were arrested. The ultimate result was the Tet Offensive of early 1968.[69]

Strategic Limits and the Ground War

The matter of how much damage the strategic limits imposed by Washington did to the war effort provides a meeting place for several of the divergent revisionist streams, at least with regard to the problem of infiltration of North Vietnamese troops and supplies into South Vietnam. Prominent military officers who fought in the war, whatever their other differences, often agree on this point. As already noted, Summers stresses the need to "isolate the battlefield" by blocking the Ho Chi Minh Trail with ground troops deployed along the 17th parallel across Laos to the border of Thailand. He points out that the Joint Chiefs of Staff advocated doing precisely that in 1965 and that General Westmoreland had his staff draw up a similar plan in 1967. Westmoreland himself reports in his memoirs that he suggested such a plan as early as 1964; his first "Commander's Estimate of the Situation," issued in March 1965, also advocated operations in the Laotian panhandle. Westmoreland also had plans to block the Ho Chi Minh Trail in Laos drawn up in 1966 and again in 1968, shortly after the Tet Offensive. General Davidson, who criticizes Westmoreland for neglecting pacification, approvingly notes that Westmoreland had several "detailed plans" to cut the Ho Chi Minh Trail in Laos but was prevented from doing so "for political reasons." Davidson quotes the ancient Chinese strategist Sun Tsu to illustrate Westmoreland's "plight": "To put a rein on an able general while at the same time asking him to suppress a cunning enemy is like tying up the Black Hound of Han and then ordering him to catch elusive hares."[70]

Marine General Victor Krulak, a critic of search and destroy and staunch advocate of counterinsurgency, also stresses the need to stop the

---

[69] Ibid., 440–41; Willbanks, *The Tet Offensive*, 8–10; Lien-Hang T. Nguyen, *Hanoi's War: An International History of the War for Peace in Vietnam* (Chapel Hill: University of North Carolina Press, 2012), 69–92.

[70] Summers, *On Strategy*, 165; Westmoreland, *A Soldier Reports*, 191, 352–57; Colonel Charles F. Brower IV, "Strategic Reassessment in Vietnam: The Westmoreland 'Alternative Strategy' of 1976–1968," Naval War College, June 1990, 11. Available online at www.dtic.mil/dtic/tr/fulltext/u2/a227314.pdf; Davidson, *Vietnam at War*, 352–53. In ancient China, the black hounds of Han were famed for their speed. One traditional story has one of these hounds chasing a "wily hare" until both collapse and die from exhaustion.

flow of weapons "pouring down" the Ho Chi Minh Trail. Krulak wanted to do this before those weapons reached Laos; his recommendation, as he told the assistant secretary of state for Far Eastern affairs in 1966, was to use air power to "destroy the port areas, mine the ports, destroy the rail lines, destroy power, fuel, and heavy industry" in North Vietnam. Advocates of counterinsurgency often cite a US Army study commissioned by Army Chief of Staff Harold K. Johnson and issued in March 1966 known as PROVN (Program for the Pacification and Long-Term Development of South Vietnam) to support their arguments, and PROVN did recommend an increased counterinsurgency effort with pacification as a priority. At the same time, as Birtle points out, the PROVN study also stressed that the "bulk" of US forces "must be directed against the base areas and lines of communication in South Vietnam, Laos, and Cambodia." Among PROVN's "possible escalatory policies" was the "long term ground occupation of a strip across the Laotian Panhandle and the DMZ."[71]

This consensus extends to some revisionist commentators writing long after the fact. Walton, who calls the Ho Chi Minh Trail the "logistic enabler" for North Vietnam's war in South Vietnam, argues that cutting it (and the less-important "Sihanouk Trail," which began at the Cambodian port of Sihanoukville and ran through Cambodia into South Vietnam) should have been "the primary combat mission" of US forces in Vietnam. Robert E. Morris points out that during the "decisive phases of the war, 1965 to 1968," the United States allowed supplies from the Soviet Union and China to "sail with impunity into Haiphong harbor" and then be shipped to Hanoi over vulnerable railway bridges the US "refused to bomb" before they arrived at the Ho Chi Minh Trail. Mark Moyar argues that cutting that trail was a "promising strategic option that did not carry large risks in 1964 or in succeeding years."[72]

---

[71] Krulak, *First to Fight*, 233; Davidson, *The Vietnam War*, 352–53, 436; Birtle, "PROVN, Westmoreland and the Historians," 1223; *A Program for the Pacification and Long-Term Development of South Vietnam (Short Title: PROVN)*, 5–12. Available online at http://oai .dtic.mil/oai/oai?verb=getRecord&metadataPrefix=html&identifier=AD0377743
   For a summary of Westmoreland's various plans to block the trail, see John Prados, "The Road South: The Ho Chi Minh Trail," in *Rolling Thunder in a Gentle Land*, 94. Prados, an orthodox historian, after stating that the trial was "probably not" important for the guerrilla war of the early 1960s, says that it was "important" after 1965 and "vital" after 1971.

[72] Walton, *The Myth of Inevitable Defeat in Vietnam*, 62, 71; Robert E. Morris, "Why We Lost the War in Vietnam," 387–88; Moyar, *Triumph Forsaken*, 322–24.

Moyar turns to Bui Tin to back up his argument, and that former North Vietnamese colonel has provided some of the most convincing evidence that the Ho Chi Minh Trail was a vulnerable lifeline that could have been cut. At least, Bui Tin reports, this was how the North Vietnamese themselves saw it. In *From Enemy to Friend*, he reports that the "greatest fear" in Hanoi was that the United States would use troops to occupy part of the Ho Chi Minh Trail or a key part of the Laotian panhandle. Bui Tin quotes the general in charge of the route as saying, "The Americans could bomb us as much as they wanted. That hardly bothered us at all." What made him "scared to death" was that the United States would use troops to occupy "even a small part" of the trail. That general, Dong Sy Nguyen, who later rose to the post of prime minister of a united Vietnam, noted that the North Vietnamese soldiers stationed along the trail were skilled at logistics but not experienced combat troops. "Under attack," he said, "they would have scattered like bees from a hive." When Bui Tin traveled the trail in 1975, he heard ordinary soldiers expressing their relief that the American ground troops had not come. Bui Tin's contacts on the North Vietnamese general staff agreed. They told him that all the United States had to do was send two or three divisions – American and South Vietnamese – to occupy a part of the trail, at which point the North Vietnamese would be "in trouble." That the North Vietnamese were worried is not surprising since, as Bui Tin estimates, by mid-1967 about 98 percent of all equipment reaching the South did so via the Ho Chi Minh Trail.[73]

Several versions of a more drastic and riskier strategic option have been suggested by a number of revisionists including Bruce Palmer, Summers, Walton, and Moyar, among others: threatening to invade (Palmer) or to invade and occupy (Walton and Moyar) the southernmost part of North Vietnam. While rejecting an invasion as too risky, Palmer suggests that "a clear amphibious threat of the coast of North Vietnam ... could have kept the North Vietnamese off balance and forced them to keep strong troop reserves at home." Summers hedges his bets on the issue. While discussing isolating the battlefield, he approvingly mentions both landing troops in the southernmost part of North Vietnam according to a plan suggested in 1965 by General Cao Van Vien, South Vietnam's highest-ranking military officer, as well as threatening to do so according to Palmer's proposal, noting that the latter proposal did not involve invading North Vietnam

[73] Moyar, *Triumph Forsaken*, 322; Bui Tin, From Enemy to Friend, 41, 74–75; Bui Tin, "Fight for the Long Haul," 69–70.

and therefore the risk of PRC intervention. Walton and Moyar maintain that occupying the region known as the Dong Hoi panhandle just north of the 17th parallel would have tied down a significant part of the North Vietnamese army, making it impossible for Hanoi to continue its aggression against South Vietnam. As for how China would have reacted to a US invasion of southern North Vietnam, Walton and Moyar argue that in the 1960s China feared the United States and that Washington should have realized that Beijing was in no position to send combat troops to North Vietnam in response to such a US action.[74]

Bui Tin firmly supports this assessment, citing as evidence his conversations with top North Vietnamese military officials. For example, General Le Trong Tan, deputy commander of the decisive campaign that ended the war in 1975 and later Vietnam's chief of staff and vice-minister of defense, told Bui Tin that a US strategy of invading North Vietnam slightly above the 17th parallel would have been "lethal" to Hanoi's plans. "The Americans needed to deploy no more than a division to occupy the Dong Hoi panhandle temporarily," the general commented. The Chinese "would have sat idly by while our troops were pinned down defending our rear ... The configuration of the war would have flipped completely." Perhaps viewing what the United States might have done through the prism of what North Vietnam itself did in the South when it moved its troops back and forth across South Vietnam's borders with Cambodia and Laos, General Tan added, "The United States with impunity could have invaded and withdrawn, invaded and withdrawn, with its mobility guaranteed by the covering fire of its Seventh Fleet." General Tan was not alone in having these concerns. General Giap expressed the same fears when speaking with the military editors of the North Vietnamese army newspaper where Bui Tin worked. This concern extended to other generals on North Vietnam's general staff.[75]

THE TET OFFENSIVE

At the end of January 1968, after almost three years of Rolling Thunder and search and destroy, the decisions North Vietnam's leaders made in

---

[74] Bruce Palmer, *The Twenty-Five Year War*, 177; Summers, *On Strategy*, 165–72, 227; Walton, *The Myth of Inevitable Defeat in Vietnam*, 85–102; Moyar, *Triumph Forsaken*, 320–23, "Section I Response," 69–70.

[75] Bui Tin, *From Enemy to Friend*, 81–82; Bui Tin, "Fight for the Long Haul," 68–69. The Tan and Giap quotations are from "Fight for the Long Haul."

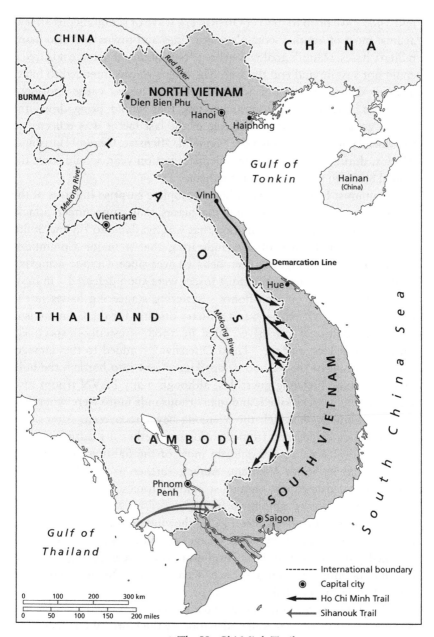

MAP 6 The Ho Chi Minh Trail

mid-1967 gave birth to the Tet Offensive, a wave of simultaneous attacks against most of South Vietnam's major cities and towns and also many military bases. Hanoi's goal was to break the military stalemate it feared it could not sustain and end the war. The offensive was intended to inflict a major defeat on US and South Vietnamese forces, cause enormous casualties, and spark a general uprising that would bring down the Saigon government. The crucial role of the last factor was reflected in the official name of the campaign: "General Offensive, General Uprising." All this, during an American presidential election year, would force the United States to withdraw from Vietnam.

Communist forces achieved almost complete surprise in terms of the exact timing of the attacks and the places that came under attack. Exactly why, given the information that was available to US and South Vietnamese intelligence officers indicating that a major Communist effort was in the offing, has been debated ever since. Despite achieving surprise, the attacking Communist forces were soon defeated – in most places within days or even hours – suffering staggering losses in the process. The Tet Offensive was a military disaster for the Communists, and two additional offensives later in 1968 – usually respectively called "Little Tet" and the "Third Offensive" – added to the damage. More than half of the 84,000 troops Hanoi sent into battle – the bulk of whom were Vietcong guerrillas, although many PAVN troops also were involved – were killed, and many thousands more were wounded. It was a blow from which the Vietcong never recovered. After 1968 PAVN troops dispatched from the North, whether organized in guerrilla or main-force units, would do most of the fighting on behalf of Communism in South Vietnam. Adding further to the damage, the defeat extended beyond Communist military forces. The Vietcong suffered grievous losses among its political cadres who staffed its so-called Vietcong Infrastructure (VCI), the underground network that had operated so effectively in the villages since the 1950s. These cadres emerged into the open in both rural and urban areas during the fighting and became easy targets once Vietcong and North Vietnamese forces had been defeated.

Official statements both during and after the war notwithstanding, the disaster that was Tet was well understood by the North Vietnamese. For example, in April 1969 the Central Office for South Vietnam (COSVN), Hanoi's headquarters inside South Vietnam for managing the war effort, issued the following directive: "Never again, and under no circumstances, are we going to risk our entire military force for just an offensive." This directive was secret, but after the war prominent Communist officials spoke openly about Tet. One of them was General Tran Van Trah, who commanded the attack on Saigon during Tet and would do so again, with very different results, in 1975. After the war he wrote in his memoirs that the entire venture was a "flawed application of the idea of revolutionary offense" that followed from "an illusion based on our subjective desires." For that frank assessment, as well as for other information they revealed, Tran Van Trah's memoirs were banned in Vietnam and the general himself was forced into retirement and kept under house arrest for three years. In another postwar assessment, a former top Vietcong official called Tet "catastrophic to our plans." General Giap, a general not known for his concern about casualties, called Tet "yet another costly lesson in blood and bone." In 1995 Bui Tin, by then living in Paris, told a journalist that "our losses were staggering and a complete surprise ... Our forces in the South were nearly wiped out by the fighting in 1968." He added that when the Communists finally were able to reestablish their presence in the South in 1971, "we had to use North Vietnamese troops as local guerrillas."[76]

Revisionists and orthodox commentators alike agree that Tet was a military defeat for the Communists. They also agree that what for Hanoi was a major tactical defeat on the battlefield in South Vietnam became an even more important strategic victory in the political arena in the United States: Tet seriously undermined support for the war in the United States, demoralized President Johnson, causing him to end his policy of sending more troops to Vietnam and to withdraw from the 1968 presidential race, and thereby led to the process of US disengagement from the war. But whereas the orthodox argument maintains that this reaction was reasonable since Tet demonstrated the war was in fact unwinnable, many revisionists counter that, given the scale of the Communist defeat, by turning from escalation to disengagement the United States forfeited a chance for victory in Vietnam. They see the military victory as a potentially decisive one that not only virtually destroyed both the Vietcong's military forces but also severely damaged its underground political apparatus. The victory also strengthened the South Vietnamese government, whose army had performed very well, and often heroically, during Tet and which was now buoyed by increased popular support. The United States was in a position to defeat North Vietnam,

---

[76] Curry, *Victory at Any Cost*, 272; Robbins, *This Time We Win*, 296–97; Bui Tin, "How North Vietnam Won the War."

assuming it finally abandoned the premises of graduated pressure that had been self-defeating thus far.

However, most revisionists argue, because the American public now turned against the war – in large part because the media portrayed Tet as a US/South Vietnamese fiasco that demonstrated the war was not being won and, more important, because Lyndon Johnson again failed as a military leader – this opportunity was wasted. As W. Scott Thompson and Donaldson D. Frizzell put it, "After Tet there was a golden opportunity to exploit the weakness of the enemy ... Instead, our resolve obviously wavered, we [the United States] began to fold our hands and started looking for a way out of the war."[77] Other revisionists making that argument in one form or another include Dave Richard Palmer in *Summons of the Trumpet* (1978), Bruce Palmer in *The 25-Year War* (1984), Philip B. Davidson in *Vietnam at War* (1988), and, more recently, James S. Robbins in *This Time We Win: Revisiting the Tet Offensive* (2010).

The element of surprise merits further discussion, as both the United State and South Vietnamese on the one hand and the North Vietnamese and the Vietcong on the other received major surprises during Tet. Ironically, perhaps, a key reason for the former's surprise was faulty North Vietnamese planning. As a number of military historians have pointed out, the Tet Offensive was badly planned. General Giap, who planned and directed the campaign despite his serious doubts about its prospects, underestimated the mobility of US forces, which enabled them to move quickly from Vietnam's borders back to its cities and towns when needed. Giap's plan was too complicated to permit adequate coordination, a fault made worse when he attacked in too many places at once, thus weakening his troops everywhere. Most important, the attacks on the cities and towns exposed Communist forces to US and South Vietnamese firepower, thereby achieving what Westmoreland had been trying to do for several years. In other words, Giap played into his enemy's strengths, and this military error is what so surprised the American military leaders since they expected him to do what made military sense and attack South Vietnam's two northernmost provinces. US intelligence officers were expecting a Communist offensive, but *not* where it occurred because the cities and towns were the wrong places for Giap to attack. As General Davidson comments, "One never attributes folly to his enemy – but then,

[77] W. Scott Thomson and Donaldson D. Frizzell, eds., *The Lessons of Vietnam* (New York: Crane, Russak & Co., 1977), 108.

of such stuff surprises are made." That the offensive took place during Tet, rather than just before or after the holiday, also was a surprise given Tet's importance to the Vietnamese people, although a much lesser surprise.[78]

The place where the Tet Offensive caused the greatest surprise was not in Vietnam but in the United States, where the American people had been led to believe that progress in the US war effort had made such an offensive impossible. The guilty parties here, for failing to prepare the American people for what they knew was coming in one form or another, included President Johnson, General Westmoreland, and other top government officials. Another guilty party, at least in revisionist eyes, was the American press, which failed to report warnings that did crop up, such as a statement by General Wheeler in December 1967 about a possible "Communist thrust" similar to the World War II German effort in the Battle of the Bulge. However, a far great failing on the part of the American press, most revisionists agree, was its distorted and inaccurate reporting that in effect turned a US/South Vietnamese military victory into a major defeat, at least in the eyes of the American people. By 1968 most US journalists were critics of the war effort, and this was reflected in their reporting.[79]

Peter Breastrup is the author of *The Big Story*, a two-volume study of reporting during the Tet Offensive that is the definitive work on the subject. He writes that reporting by American journalists as a whole amounted to "a distortion of reality – through sins of commission and omission – on a scale that helped shape Tet's political repercussions in Washington and the Administration's response." Breastrup adds that bad as the print media was, "TV was much worse. TV was always worse. The emotive demands of the medium and the commercial demands of holding an audience worked against calm and dispassionate reporting." Many revisionists extend this critique of press coverage from Tet to most or all of the war, a case made in great detail by Robert Elegant, a correspondent who spent several years in Vietnam, in a 1981 article called "How to Lose a War: The Press and Vietnam." In any event, most revisionists agree that what was crucial during the Tet maelstrom was

---

[78] Willbanks, *The Tet Offensive*, 80–81; Davidson, *Vietnam at War*, 478–79. Davidson adds that an offensive against South Vietnam's two northern provinces would not have contributed to the desired and vital popular uprising, which is "probably" why the North Vietnamese did not adopt it (481).

[79] Davidson, *Vietnam at War*, 483.

presidential leadership, and that once again Lyndon Johnson failed the test. Davidson, his critique of the press notwithstanding, makes this point in *Vietnam at War*, as does Robbins in *This Time We Win* in a chapter bluntly titled "Johnson Surrenders."[80]

Meanwhile, the leaders of North Vietnam experienced major surprises of their own. In complete contrast to what Hanoi expected and counted on, no "General Uprising" occurred. Nor did the ARVN crumble. Instead, the South Vietnamese people supported the Saigon government, and the ARVN fought well. Interestingly, the ARVN's performance during Tet also surprised the Americans. As Andrew Wiest points out, since 1965 when American combat troops had arrived in South Vietnam, the ARVN, whose overall performance often was found wanting, in many ways had been pushed aside as US troops increasingly took on the burden of fighting Vietcong and PAVN forces. Nonetheless, during 1965–1968 the ARVN engaged in constant combat, suffering heavier casualties than US forces. Even as the US combat role grew, the ARVN conducted its own campaigns and participated in some way in every major American operation; while Wiest concedes that its performance "varied widely," he maintains that "in general the ARVN acquitted itself well in battle."[81]

A key factor, often overlooked or ignored by the ARVN's detractors, is that prior to Tet the ARVN often lacked modern weapons comparable to those fielded by the PAVN or Vietcong. By Tet some ARVN units finally were equipped with modern weapons that matched those in the hands of the Vietcong and PAVN troops, in particular the M-16 rifle. As military historian Martin Loicano has observed, during Tet well-equipped ARVN units were able to stand up to larger Communist forces and "push their enemy out of towns and cities in a manner of hours or, at most, days." In the city of Hue, where fighting lasted a month, the ARVN fought particularly well. As to why the South Vietnamese people as a whole

---

[80] Robbins, *This Time We Win*, 109, 248, 261, 263–79. The Breastrup quote is on page 248; Davidson, *Vietnam at War*, 483–88; Robert Elegant, *"How to Lose a War: The Press and Viet Nam,"* *Encounter* (London) LVII, no. 2, August 1981, 73–90. See also Peter Breastrup, Lyndon Baines Johnson Library Oral History Collection, March 1, 1982. Available online at www.lbjlib.utexas.edu/johnson/archives.hom/oralhistory.hom/Braestrup/Braestrup.PDF. Some commentators, regardless of their views on the war, have pointed to the negative impact of television on a democracy's ability to wage war. They note that the increasingly difficulty of fighting a war when the carnage appears on a daily basis on TV screens. See Davidson, *Vietnam at War*, 489–90.

[81] Wiest, "The 'Other' Vietnam War" in *America and the Vietnam Was: Re-examining the Culture and History of a Generation* eds. Andrew Wiest, Mary Kathryn Barbier, and Glenn Robins (New York and London: Routledge, 2010), 60–61.

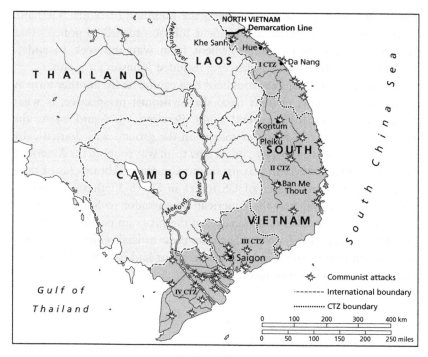

MAP 7 The Tet Offensive, 1968

reacted as they did, Lewis Sorley observes that the "firsthand encounter with the enemy's destructiveness" that occurred during Tet – including the massacre of several thousand civilians in Hue, a city the PAVN controlled for a month – demonstrated the Communists' cruelty toward those they presumably were going to "liberate." This in turn "radically changed the outlook of South Vietnam's populous" and after Tet enabled the South Vietnamese government to mobilize the population for the war effort, which included almost doubling the size of its military forces.[82]

It has already been noted that revisionists, who justifiably argue that the Tet Offensive resulted in a major US/South Vietnamese military victory, were and remain frustrated that the Johnson administration did not take advantage of the situation. The US military had plans to go on the offensive that included finally attacking North Vietnam's supply lines in

---

[82] Martin Loicano, "The Role of Weapons in the Second Indochina War: Republic of Vietnam Perspectives and Perceptions," *Journal of Vietnamese Studies* 8, no. 2 (Spring 2013): 43–44; Sorley, *A Better War*, 14–15.

Laos and Cambodia and intensifying the bombing of North Vietnam. These plans were rejected, as President Johnson turned to policies that would begin America's disengagement from war and seek to end it through negotiations. Those measures included Johnson's announcement on March 31, 1968, that he would not be a candidate for another term as president. The irony, at least from the revisionist perspective, is what happened over the next several years. Between 1968 and 1972, the US role in the war in terms of troops on the ground was dramatically reduced. At the same time, by 1969 a new team was running the American war effort. Richard Nixon was president; Creighton Abrams (as of mid-1968) was the commander of US forces in South Vietnam; Ellsworth Bunker (as of 1967) was the American ambassador to South Vietnam; and William Colby had taken charge of the program pacification in the country's villages and hamlets. Together these officials enjoyed successes to the point that in 1972, many argue, the war had been won. How that happened is the subject of next chapter.

6

The Vietnamization of the War

A fundamental revisionist complaint about how President Johnson conducted the Vietnam War is that he subordinated America's military effort to two agendas, one domestic and one international. The former was the Great Society program of social reform. The latter was the imperative of avoiding actions that might lead to Chinese or possibly even Soviet involvement in the war. As a result, revisionists argue, Johnson put restrictions on the US forces in Vietnam that made it impossible to win the war.

This subordination of Vietnam War policy to both a domestic and an international agenda continued under President Nixon. Nixon was a longtime supporter of US intervention in South Vietnam, but now as president he had to operate within constraints at home imposed by the declining popular support for the Vietnam War in general and the influence of the antiwar movement in particular. His domestic agenda therefore was to reduce or mute antiwar sentiment as much as possible while boosting support for his management of the war. This required, as Nixon put it, ending the war "as quickly and honorably as possible."[1] Nixon's concerns about antiwar sentiment on a number of occasions influenced him to reject or place limits on military options in Vietnam. One example is his rejection of the so-called Duck Hook plan of 1969, which would have involved a new bombing campaign against North Vietnam with an expanded target list and the mining of the port of Haiphong. Another is the 20-mile "tether" placed on allied forces during the 1970 incursion into Cambodia,

[1] Quoted in Walton, *The Myth of Inevitable U.S. Defeat in Vietnam*, 135.

a limit that helped the North Vietnamese in the path of those forces organize their defenses.[2]

Nixon's international agenda reinforced the imperative to withdraw US armed forces from Vietnam. But while Nixon's domestic and international concerns both required a US withdrawal, it was his approach to US foreign policy as whole – his overall international agenda – that determined *how* that withdrawal had to be done. That agenda was détente, the policy of relaxing tensions with the Soviet Union, which Nixon crafted along with Henry Kissinger, his national security advisor and, later, secretary of state. Détente was the Nixon/Kissinger strategy for adjusting US foreign policy to the new international conditions of the late 1960s. On the one hand, in historian Robert Beisner's apt phase, the United States was a "wounded power" that needed "new leverage" for its policy of containment; on the other hand, that leverage existed because of the growing spilt between the Soviet Union and the People's Republic of China (PRC).[3]

Détente was designed to reduce the cost of the Cold War, facilitate an agreement that would limit nuclear arms, and encourage the Soviet Union to follow policies that would reduce its expansionist tendencies in return for economic benefits. Its implementation was linked to a diplomatic initiative to the PRC, which Washington still did not officially recognize although that regime had been in power since 1949. That measure, taking advantage of the emerging Sino-Soviet split, was designed to promote a normalization of relations between the United States and the PRC while providing a lever to induce Moscow to reach the accommodations Nixon and Kissinger believed were essential to American national interests. Nixon and Kissinger believed that the United States could only deal with the Soviets from a position of strength. That in turn required the United States to extradite itself from the Vietnam War, but only while ensuring the continued existence of a non-Communist regime in South Vietnam. American credibility, which would be severely undermined if the United States simply abandoned South Vietnam to its fate, was essential to implementing détente, and this meant that the US exit from Vietnam could not be tainted with the stain of defeat. In Nixon's words, implementing détente required that Washington exit from Vietnam having first secured "peace with honor."

---

[2] The term "tether" is Dave Richard Palmer's. See Dave Richard Palmer, *Summons of the Trumpet: A History of the Vietnam War from a Military Man's Viewpoint* (New York: Ballantine Books, 1978), 299.

[3] Robert Beisner, "History and Henry Kissinger," *Diplomatic History* 14, no. 4 (Fall 1990): 522.

Making matters more complicated, Nixon and Kissinger took office with very few options or room to maneuver regarding Vietnam. This is a point on which orthodox and revisionist commentators agree, and it helps explain why upon entering office Nixon directed Kissinger to form a special study group to examine the situation in Vietnam and why it took several months during 1969 for the Nixon/Kissinger overall Vietnam policy to emerge. George Donelson Moss, author of *Vietnam: An American Ordeal,* provides a typical orthodox analysis when he notes the main reasons why US options were so limited: the battlefield stalemate, North Vietnam's strategy of protracted war and determination to conquer South Vietnam, the Soviet Union's refusal to push Hanoi to end the war, domestic US constraints, and the South Vietnamese regime's determination to avoid a settlement that would endanger its survival. From a revisionist perspective, while these factors certainly were important, Nixon's lack of options was primarily the result of Johnson's mismanagement of the war. As Dave Richard Palmer points out, while fighting the war ineptly Johnson nonetheless escalated the fighting "quite beyond the point of public tolerance," and Nixon therefore could not increase US strength on the battlefield. In addition, during 1968 Johnson had stopped bombing Hanoi and begun negotiations with North Vietnam, "so both of these powerful levers were denied to Nixon." In *Ending the Vietnam War,* his defense of how he and Nixon handled the war, Kissinger points out, "the liberal Establishment, which had launched America into the quagmire, had become demoralized and left the field to the radical protesters." Many conservatives also "had abandoned the cause of Indochina in frustration." The Nixon administration, Kissinger continues, had inherited a dilemma: "The possibility of victory had been given up by our predecessors," yet "simple abandonment was precluded by our concept of honor." The United States had to somehow stabilize the situation in South Vietnam while gradually withdrawing American forces so that international stability was not threatened and America's role in defending its allies was undamaged. Overall, as Dave Richard Palmer succinctly puts it, "No American president before had ever faced so complex a war situation with so few options remaining."[4]

---

[4] Moss, *Vietnam: An American Ordeal,* 328; Dave Richard Palmer, *Summons of the Trumpet,* 272–73; Henry Kissinger, *Ending the Vietnam War: A History of America's Involvement in and Extradition from the Vietnam War* (New York: Simon and Schuster, 2003), 10, 550. Or, as Kissinger more caustically told *Der Spiegel* in 2005, "Leading members of the government which had started the war later joined the peace movement." See www.spiegel.de/international/spiegel/spiegel-interview-henry-kissinger-on-europe-s-falling-out-with-washington-a-379165-druck.html

Nixon dealt with this dilemma by turning to measures Johnson had refused to take. Even as Nixon withdrew US forces from Vietnam, while negotiating with North Vietnam to reach an agreement that would ensure the survival of a non-Communist South Vietnam, and even as he at times placed limits on his American forces in Vietnam, he also rejected some key restraints that Johnson had imposed on the American war effort as he sent those forces there. Specifically, Nixon refused to confine US ground operations to South Vietnam given the importance of North Vietnam's use of Cambodia as a supply route and sanctuary for its troops. He refused to permit southern Laos, the site of the main part of the Ho Chi Minh Trail, to remain immune from an effort by South Vietnamese ground forces to cut that route. Finally, when in 1972 negotiations stalled and Nixon resumed the bombing of North Vietnam, he removed most of the limits Johnson had imposed during the Rolling Thunder campaign of 1965–1968.

VIETNAMIZATION AND THE LOST VICTORY

Nixon's strategy of withdrawing from Vietnam while attempting to guarantee the survival of South Vietnam produced the policy known as Vietnamization. Aside from serving American needs outside Vietnam, the withdrawal of US troops was viewed, in the words of a Military Assistance Command, Vietnam (MACV) report, as "a necessary method of compelling the South Vietnamese to take over the war."[5] Vietnamization meant turning over the responsibility for waging the war to the South Vietnamese. It had several components: strengthening and expanding the South Vietnamese army; pacification, or spreading and solidifying government control of rural areas, an approach that included land reform and permitting local self-government; and improving the South Vietnamese government and its ability to deliver services to its people. While assessments of Vietnamization among revisionists vary widely, some argue that the team of Abrams, Bunker, and Colby responsible for Vietnamization achieved a major success. Between 1969 and 1972, the Saigon regime became stronger and more stable, the Army of the Republic of Vietnam (ARVN) improved considerably as a fighting force, the pacification program spread and solidified the government's control of the countryside, and Communist forces inside South Vietnam became considerably weaker, a fact Hanoi acknowledged in commentaries published after its victory. Many

[5] Quoted in Sorley, *A Better War*, 113.

revisionists thus agree with Colby, who was in charge of pacification from 1968 to 1971, that as of 1972, "On the ground in South Vietnam, the war had been won."[6] The victory was forfeited, Colby argues, when the United States abandoned South Vietnam between 1973 and 1975; hence the title of his book on the subject, *Lost Victory* (1989).

The most comprehensive and widely cited endorsement of the lost victory thesis is Lewis Sorley's monograph *A Better War: The Unexamined Victories and Final Tragedy of America's Last Years in Vietnam* (1999). Sorley, a Vietnam veteran, argues that between 1968 and 1973 the United States, by adopting new tactics, both on the battle-field and in the villages and hamlets in the countryside, essentially defeated the Communist effort in South Vietnam. *A Better War* supplements, updates, and expands on *Lost Victory* – the reviewer in *Parameters*, the scholarly quarterly published by the US Army War College, called it "in many ways a companion volume" to Colby's work[7] – as well as on earlier revisionist accounts such as Dave Richard Palmer's *Summons of the Trumpet*. *A Better War* has been strongly endorsed by some revisionist commentators, including military officers who like Sorley served in Vietnam. They include Colonel Stuart A. Herrington, the reviewer in *Parameters*, and Mackubin Thomas Owens, a US Marine infantry officer in Vietnam during 1968–1969 and later a professor of national security affairs at the Naval War College.[8] Various aspects of Sorley's case have been supplemented by other scholars, among them John W. Shaw, whose monograph *The Cambodian Campaign: The 1970 Offensive and America's Vietnam War* (2005) argues that this offensive into Cambodia was a major success, and Martin Loicano, whose article "The Role of Weapons in the Second Indochina War," defends ARVN's performance once it was properly armed with weapons that matched those of the Vietcong and the People's Army of Vietnam (PAVN).[9]

---

[6] Colby, *Lost Victory*, 321.

[7] Colonel Stuart A. Herrington (USA, ret.), review of *A Better War: The Unexamined Victories and Final Tragedy of America's Last Years in Vietnam*, by Lewis Sorley, *Parameters*, Autumn 2000. Available online at http://strategicstudiesinstitute.army.mil/pubs/parameters/Articles/ooautumn/aut-rev.htm

[8] Mackubin T. Owens, "The Vietnam War: Winnable After All," Ashbrook Center at Ashland University, 1999. Available online at http://ashbrook.org/publications/oped-owens-99-vietnamwar/

[9] John M. Shaw, *The Cambodian Campaign: The 1970 Offensive and America's Vietnam War* (Lawrence: University Press of Kansas, 2005); Martine Loicano, "The Role of Weapons in the Second Indochina War," 37–80.

Some revisionists have a less positive view of what Vietnamization achieved between 1969 and 1972. For example, General Davidson argues that in 1972 South Vietnam suffered from too many of the "same old faults" that had undermined its war effort for years and overall remained too dependent on the United States for survival.[10] Other disagreements include conflicting evaluations regarding the differences between Westmoreland's and Abrams's respective approaches to the war, as well as about how successful each general was. Thus, in peering through the overall revisionist looking glass, one at best sees unclearly and sometimes darkly. Nonetheless, a strong case can be made that in the wake of the Tet Offensive, the anti-Communist position improved dramatically in South Vietnam.

US FORCES: FROM SEARCH AND DESTROY
TO CLEAR AND HOLD

The gradual withdrawal of US troops from Vietnam began in mid-1969. From a peak of 540,00 in 1968, US troop strength in Vietnam declined to 480,000 by the end of 1969, 335,000 by the end of 1970, 157,000 by the end of 1971, and 27,400, almost none of whom were combat troops, by the end of 1972. Meanwhile, the US troops remaining in South Vietnam began to be used in a different way.

Exactly why that occurred, and how significant the change really was is a matter of debate among revisionists. Sorley argues that the change began in mid-1968, when General Abrams took over as head of MACV from Westmoreland, who returned to the United States to become Army Chief of Staff. Sorley quotes General Fred Weyand, Abrams's successor (in 1972) as MACV commander, who said, "tactics changed within fifteen minutes of Abrams taking command." What Abrams did, Sorley writes, was to abandon Westmoreland's search and destroy war of attrition in favor of what was called "clear and hold." Under clear and hold, large-unit sweeps designed to engage the enemy in major battles as part of an attrition strategy were deemphasized in favor of thousands of small-unit patrols and ambushes. These small-unit operations were done repeatedly in the same populated area to provide permanent security to the rural population. In contrast, search and destroy had involved moving from one area to another in search of hidden enemy main forces. Since prior to launching attacks the Communists pre-positioned supplies, from weapons

[10] Davidson, *Vietnam at War*, 711–12.

and ammunition to rice and other essentials, Abrams's small-unit patrols sought out and destroyed these supply caches, thereby making it more difficult, or even impossible, to carry out attacks. Abrams called this cutting off the enemy's "logistical nose." In Sorley's words, the point was "to screen the rural population from the enemy." Sorley approvingly quotes a journalist's distinction made in 1971 between the Westmoreland and Abrams approaches: "Where Westmoreland was a search-and-destroy and count-the-bodies man, Abrams proved to be an interdict-and-weigh-the-rice man." And this interdiction was done successfully. During 1969, for example, US and South Vietnamese forces seized almost 3,000 enemy caches, 50 percent more than in 1968. The supplies seized included 1,855 tons of ammunition, twice that of 1968, and 12,000 weapons.[11]

Davidson views the change, at least why it occurred, somewhat differently. He maintains that Abrams would have preferred large-unit battles but was unable to get them because in mid-1968 the North Vietnamese, in the wake of the Tet defeat, abandoned their large-unit strategy and returned to small-unit guerrilla warfare. Thus it was "not Abrams who changed American strategy for the ground war, but Giap and Troung Chin [a leading member of the Politburo]." The new American approach debuted in the spring of 1969 when Abrams, "thwarted by the enemy's refusal to fight in large units ... had to change his tactics to meet Giap's."[12] Two other factors that discouraged or made it difficult for Abrams to undertake large operations were decreasing manpower as US troops gradually were withdrawn and a specific order he received in July 1969 from Washington "to conduct the war with a minimum of American casualties."[13]

Abrams did undertake several large-unit operations during 1968 and 1969. The best known, and most controversial because of the high casualties US forces suffered, was the sweep in May 1969 by several thousand troops of the 101st Airborne Division into the A Shau Valley along the Laotian border. Dale Andrade views this and other operations as essentially a continuation of search and destroy. Davidson sees it differently. In his view, although Abrams had a new strategy, it did not

---

[11] Sorley, *A Better War*, 2, 199; Sorely, "Could the War Have Been Won?" in *The Real Lessons of the Vietnam War*, 406–7.

[12] Davidson, *Vietnam at War*, 572, 613.

[13] Andrew J. Birtle, "PROVN, Westmoreland, and the Historians: A Reappraisal," *The Journal of Military History* 72 (October 2008): 1226; Andrade, "Westmoreland Was Right," 169.

prevent major clashes between large US and North Vietnamese units. Sorley has yet another perspective. He argues that the A Shau Valley campaign, which culminated in a bloody battle for some high ground that American troops, with considerable bitterness, dubbed "Hamburger Hill," was an extension of clear and hold. As Abrams saw it, Sorely reports, along with small-unit patrols in populated areas, it was necessary for large US units to attack North Vietnamese base areas in remote, lightly populated areas because these were the places where major caches of supplies were stored in preparation for large-scale attacks on populated areas. In this particular case, the target was called Enemy Base Area 611. Abrams believed it was essential to disrupt enemy logistical preparations and bases near the Laotian border. As he put it, "we destroy his [the North Vietnamese] tediously-prepared logistical arrangements and thus in the end deny large-scale attacks on the populated areas." Sorley argues that Abrams's overall strategy of "getting into the enemy's system" gave the major battles such as the one in the A Shau Valley "a coherence they lacked in the earlier days of the war." With regard to the A Shau Valley operation in particular, that fight and the continued presence of US troops in the area for the next three years served Abrams's purposes by preventing the North Vietnamese from preparing any operations against the major population centers to the east.[14]

THE CAMBODIAN CAMPAIGN

The time and place where Abrams's efforts to cut the North Vietnamese "logistics nose" melded neatly with Nixon's willingness to exceed the limits established by President Johnson was the 1970 offensive into Cambodia. The target area was Cambodian territory just across the South Vietnamese border. Orthodox commentators often assert that Nixon "widened," "extended," or "escalated" the war to describe what took place during that action.[15] Revisionists view that characterization as inaccurate or at best misleading. Kissinger notes that Cambodia's official "neutral" status was a sham. In fact, the offensive's target territory "was no longer Cambodian in any practical sense ... Cambodian officials had been excluded from the soil of their own country; most, if not all, of the

---

[14] Andrade, "Westmoreland Was Right," 164–65; Davidson, *Vietnam at* War, 614–15; Sorley, *A Better War*, 138–41.

[15] For example, see Moss, *Vietnam: An American Ordeal*, 348.

population had been expelled." These were "illegally occupied territories" under control of the North Vietnamese. Dave Richard Palmer calls the situation as of 1968 a North Vietnamese "military occupation on parts of Cambodia." There were fourteen North Vietnamese military bases inside Cambodia, some no more than thirty-five miles from Saigon. About two-thirds of South Vietnam's population was exposed to attack from these bases. As long as the North Vietnamese bases in Cambodia remained immune from attack, "it was as if a loaded and cocked pistol was being held to the head of South Vietnam." Most fundamentally, as noted previously, Andrade points out that Cambodian bases, immune from attack along with those in Laos and North Vietnam, were part of the "unbeatable advantage" the United States had long given North Vietnam.[16] This situation gave Nixon his first, and primary, reason to move against Hanoi's forces in Cambodia.

The sequence of events that led to the Cambodian invasion dates from 1965. That was when Norodom Sihanouk, Cambodia's longtime ruler, first allowed the North Vietnamese the use of his country's port of Sihanoukville as an entry point for shipments destined for Communist forces in the southern part of South Vietnam. At the same time, hoping to keep his country from becoming entirely engulfed by the Vietnam War, beginning in 1969 Sihanouk also allowed the United States to secretly bomb North Vietnamese bases and lines of communication in Cambodia. This campaign (Operation Menu), however, could not stop the flow of supplies or eliminate the North Vietnamese military threat to the southern part of South Vietnam. Finally, in 1970 Sihanouk was overthrown in a coup led by his country's prime minister, Lon Nol. The main reason for the coup was widespread resentment of the North Vietnamese occupation of Cambodian territory, which Sihanouk was blamed for tolerating and abetting. Lon Nol immediately closed the port of Sihanoukville to the North Vietnamese, a serious blow to their efforts to supply their troops in the southern part of South Vietnam. When the North Vietnamese responded to the coup by seizing more territory and threatening the existence of Lon Nol's pro-Western government, Nixon had a second reason to attack their forces in Cambodia.

The Cambodian "incursion," as Nixon called it,[17] involved both US and ARVN forces. At home it provoked a serious of major antiwar

---

[16] Kissinger, *Ending the Vietnam War*, 198–99; Dave Richard Palmer, *Summons of the Trumpet*, 292–93; Andrade, "Westmoreland Was Right," 162.

[17] For Nixon's speech informing the American people of the operation, see www.presidency.ucsb.edu/ws/?pid=2490

demonstrations, especially on college campuses, that apparently rattled Nixon and led him to maintain tight limits on how far allied troops were allowed to go. This and other factors, including a delay in the start of the operation, compromised its effectiveness. This is reflected in the evaluations it has received. Dave Richard Palmer's assessment that overall the operation was a "distinct military success – though falling short of delivering the enemy a decisive blow" is shared by many revisionists. The campaign, Palmer writes, delivered a "jolting setback" to the North Vietnamese. Even more important, a large part of that jolt was delivered by the ARVN, which took the offensive against Hanoi's PAVN units and defeated them "at every turn." Not surprisingly, South Vietnamese morale soared.[18] Davidson is less upbeat. He points to the persistence of the "fundamental defects of the ARVN system" even during "almost ideal conditions" and laments that the main North Vietnamese troops managed to flee, meaning that "there was no great battle," as Nixon and Abrams had hoped. Still, Davidson's assessment is highly positive. Allied forces, he reports, killed or captured thousands of enemy troops, seized huge quantities of weapons and ammunition of all sorts, and confiscated fourteen million pounds of rice. The amount of small arms ammunition alone was equal to what Communist forces used in an entire year. Davidson cites estimates that North Vietnamese offensive plans were set back at least a year, possibly two. The operation thus was "quite successful militarily." It "struck the Communists a stunning blow by destroying their stores and bases in Cambodia"[19] and bought time both for Vietnamization and the US withdrawal from South Vietnam. Army veteran and military historian John M. Shaw, author of a comprehensive and well-received volume on the subject, offers a similar assessment. Shaw considers the campaign "fully justified and reasonably well executed." While hardly perfect, it seriously weakened the North Vietnamese, bolstered South Vietnamese morale, strengthened Vietnamization, and bought the United States time to complete an orderly military withdrawal.[20]

Even as they cite these successes, revisionists point to shortcomings in the Cambodian operation in terms of when it took place and its long-term impact. Dave Richard Palmer comments that the cross-border operations into Cambodia and Laos (the latter, against the Ho Chi Minh Trail, took place in 1971) were "moves of the strategic chessboard which should have been made in 1966 and 1967." Even Sorley, perhaps the most positive

[18] Dave Richard Palmer, *Summons of the Trumpet*, 299–301.
[19] Davidson, *Vietnam at War*, 625–30.   [20] Shaw, *The Cambodian Campaign*, 3, 170.

analyst of Abrams's "better war," mentions that the operation's impact was "ephemeral" and that in the "long run" it caused only a "temporary disruption" to North Vietnam's campaign to control South Vietnam, Laos, and Cambodia.[21] However, as Sorley and other revisionists stress, the events that were decisive in South Vietnam's defeat in the long run were far from inevitable. The Cambodian campaign achieved a great deal and could have contributed to a different outcome of the war had US policy after 1973 been different: that is, had Washington fulfilled the commitments it made to the government of South Vietnam.

ARMING THE ARVN

There is a widespread consensus that ARVN suffered from multiple shortcomings and often performed poorly during the course of the Vietnam War. That consensus extends from many of the military men who fought the war, to journalists who covered the war, to scholars of all stripes who wrote about the war after it was over. American criticism of the ARVN dates from the arrival of US advisors during the Diem era: in discussing that period, Andrew Birtle refers to "the South Vietnamese Army's well-known dysfunctional behavior." Orthodox historian George C. Herring points out that the ARVN became an "object of ridicule" among US officers as American troops increasingly assumed the burden of the fighting after 1965. Orthodox commentators attribute ARVN's persistent problems of corruption, poor leadership, and lack of fighting spirit to the shortcomings and alleged ultimate illegitimacy of the South Vietnamese regime it was trying to defend. At least in part, this outlook extends to the revisionist camp. Even Lewis Sorley, in an article in which he defends the ARVN ("Reassessing ARVN"), acknowledges that deficiencies such as poor leadership and corruption were problems the ARVN "never really solved."[22]

There are, however, matters of degree, and some revisionists make a strong case that ARVN's improvement from the late 1960s through the early 1970s was significant to the point of being potentially decisive. The key point is that the previously mentioned faults, which after all are found in many armies, were not the only causes of ARVN's combat

---

[21] Dave Richard Palmer, *Summons of the Trumpet*, 308; Sorley, *A Better War*, 213.

[22] Andrew J. Birtle, "Triumph Forsaken as Military History," in *Triumph Forsaken*, 124; Herring, *America's Longest War*, 199–200; Lewis Sorley, "Reassessing the ARVN" (a lecture), 7. Available online at http://nguyrntin.tripod.com/arvn-sorley-2.htm

failures in the period up to 1968. Sorley points to another major problem: the inferior firepower of the rifles and carbines dating from World War II that the United States initially provided to the South Vietnamese when compared to the AK-47 assault rifles and other modern weapons the Soviets and Chinese had delivered to North Vietnam.[23] This deficiency existed for the ARVN not only when it faced regular PAVN units but also when it was in combat with supposedly lightly armed Vietcong guerrillas. The lack of proper armament was an important factor in the ARVN's inadequate performance during much of the war, at least until the late 1960s.

Military historian Martin Loicano focuses on this matter in "The Role of Weapons in the Second Indochina War." His basic point is that "orthodox paradigms," which assume sociopolitical factors doomed the South Vietnamese regime and therefore the ARVN from the start, are inadequate because they do not take into account newly available sources and what new generations of scholars have concluded from them. Sociopolitical factors certainly "played a prominent role in the outcome of the war," but outcomes on the battlefield also depended heavily on "material factors," by which Loicano means the weapons each side had at its disposal.[24]

Loicano points out that from 1965 until the end of 1969, Communist soldiers, both Vietcong and PAVN, enjoyed a "substantial tactical advantage in firepower" over their ARVN opponents. By 1965 Communist forces were equipped not only with the AK-47 automatic rifles but also with modern machine guns and "devastating" rockets. When facing an enemy equipped with the AK-47, ARVN troops had to make do with outdated rifles that often placed them "on the receiving end of around ten times the firepower they could put out in response." This advantage, almost impossible to overcome in large engagements, was even more pronounced in the small skirmishes that made up most of the fighting in South Vietnam. Making matters worse, and adding insult to injury, some

---

[23] Lewis Sorley, "The Conduct of the War," in *Rolling Thunder in a Gentle Land,* 179; Sorley, "Could the War Have Been Won?" 411–12. The AK-47 is a modern Soviet-developed assault rifle that is widely regarded as the world's best such weapon. The American equivalent of the AK-47 is the M-16. Its debut when it was issued to some US troops in Vietnam in 1965 was marred by a variety of serious problems, including jamming, and to this day a debate continues about whether it is superior to the M-14, the rifle it replaced as the standard weapon for US troops. That debate, however, is beyond the scope of this book.

[24] Loicano, "The Role of Weapons in the Second Indochina War," 39–41.

of the older rifles supplied to the South Vietnamese were too large for the typical ARVN soldier. American tanks supplied to the ARVN were out-dated and outmatched by those fielded by the PAVN, and there were similar problems with other weapons. In short, in combat with PAVN troops and even with many Vietcong units, ARVN troops were armed with inadequate weapons well into 1968.[25]

The finances of military aid to North and South Vietnam add to this picture. Between the late 1950s and the winter of 1967, Communist forces received about $1.895 billion in military aid from the Soviet Union, PRC, and other Communist benefactors. That compares to $1.476 billion in direct military aid received by South Vietnam between 1950 and 1968, a period about twice as long. In 1967, North Vietnam's allies provide it with $950 million versus $625 million received by South Vietnam. Loicano adds that recent studies suggest that aid to North Vietnam may have been "far greater" than the figures just cited.[26]

Sorley credits General Abrams, who became deputy commander of US forces in Vietnam in 1967, with changing this untenable situation. As a result, a small number of ARVN elite units received modern M-16 assault rifles during 1967, and they subsequently outperformed other units in combat. These elite units fought well in 1968 during the Tet Offensive, although it is also true, to the surprise of both US and Communist observers, that so did many under-equipped units. Meanwhile, Tet finally convinced Washington of the need to properly supply the ARVN, and within days of a report to President Johnson in February 1968, a total of 100,000 M-16 rifles were on their way to ARVN troops. By mid-1969, more than 700,000 M-16s were in ARVN hands, as were other modern weapons such as the M-79 grenade launcher, M-60 machine guns, and new radios for operating in the field.[27]

Despite these improvements, between 1969 and 1972 ARVN's fire-power disadvantages were not eliminated, even as Washington withdrew most US ground forces from the war zone and turned over the bulk of the fighting to the South Vietnamese. During 1968 new and more powerful Russian tanks, self-propelled guns, mortars, recoilless rifles, and artillery arrived on the South Vietnam battlefield. The PAVN, Loicano notes, had become a "formidable conventional fighting force." Prior to 1972, when

[25] Ibid., 41–47. See also Sorley, "Reassessing ARVN," 2.
[26] Loicano, "The Role of Weapons in the Second Indochina War," 46.
[27] Sorley, "Reassessing the ARVN," 2; Loicano, "The Role of Weapons in the Second Indochina War," 46–47.

the United States belatedly began a new round of weapons upgrading, ARVN forces had to fight PAVN units armed with T-54 tanks, long-range rockets, and heavy artillery without comparable weapons. ARVN's light-weight tanks and personnel carriers "were simply no match for PAVN armor and artillery." PAVN weapons turned ARVN's armored personnel carriers into "deathtraps." And even though Hanoi's air force played little role in the fighting until 1975, it had been modernized to include MiG-21s that were superior to the ARVN's propeller aircraft and "low-end" jets.[28] Overall, as Andrade points out, by 1971, with PAVN units armed with Soviet T-34 and T-54 tanks and powerful new artillery pieces, the ARVN and remaining US troops in Vietnam were up against "a much more sophisticated and well-trained fighting organization than that faced by General Westmoreland."[29]

The modernization of the ARVN that began in 1967 and intensified after Abrams replaced Westmoreland was not without its problems. Loicano and Davidson both point out that the modernization program operated against severe time constraints – the last US troops left Vietnam in early 1973 – that made complete success, in Loicano's words, "all but impossible." Davidson notes the "monstrous problems" that stalked Vietnamization in general, pointing out that it was "caught between the United States troop withdrawal ... and the North Vietnamese timetable for aggression."[30]

Nonetheless, between 1968 and 1972 there was real progress. The total strength of the South Vietnamese armed forces, which included not only regular (army, navy, air force, and marines) forces but also irregular territorial forces at the local level, rose from about 700,000 to about 1.1 million. This expansion, along with much else, was in part made possible by Tet, which had sparked an upsurge of patriotism in South Vietnam that allowed President Thieu to mobilize additional troops. The expansion was accompanied not only by new arms but also by intense training programs that, despite continued firepower shortcomings, allowed not only ARVN troops but also the territorial troops to face the enemy on something that finally resembled an even playing field. As early as June 1968, a MACV analysis of the impact of providing ARVN troops with M-16 rifles reported significant improvements in ARVN operational

[28] Loicano, "The Role of Weapons in the Second Indochina War," 43–45.
[29] Andrade, "Westmoreland Was Right," 171.
[30] Loicano, "The Role of Weapons in the Second Indochina War," 53; Davidson, *Vietnam at War*, 605, 607.

capability and morale. This improvement continued over the next three years. Probably the most striking progress was in the territorial forces. Because local territorial forces were essential to providing day-to-day security to villages and hamlets, arming them with modern weapons was a high priority; during 1969 they often received the prized M-16s before ARVN units. By 1972 these forces, numbering about 550,000, had played a crucial role in bringing most of rural South Vietnam under government control. As Sorley stresses, playing that role had implications beyond the battlefield; as the rural population of South Vietnam defended their homes and farms against the North Vietnamese and Vietcong, they demonstrated their support of and loyalty to the government in Saigon.[31]

LAM SON 719

By most assessments, ARVN, and by extension Vietnamization as whole, suffered its most serious setback in early 1971 in a campaign knows as Lam Son 719, ARVN's attempt to temporarily cut the Ho Chi Minh Trail. The plan was to move westward just south of the demilitarized zone into Laos for about twenty-five miles to the important trans-shipment town of Tchepone. South Vietnamese forces would destroy supplies stored in the region and remain in Laos for ninety days, thereby severing the Ho Chi Minh Trail until the upcoming rainy reason slowed traffic along the route. Because by then Congress had forbidden the use of US ground troops in Laos (and Cambodia), the operation had to be conducted with South Vietnamese troops only, albeit with considerable US air support and artillery support from inside South Vietnam. About 16,000 South Vietnamese troops were committed to the operation. In part because the North Vietnamese had anticipated such an assault after the Cambodian operation and therefore had made preparations where they thought it was most likely to occur, the ARVN eventually would face about 22,000 PAVN troops, a number that grew considerably by the time its troops exited Laos.

The operation initially went well but then was hampered by bad weather. At that point, only a month into the operation, President Thieu, acting against advice from General Abrams, ordered a withdrawal. That

[31] Loicano, "The Role of Weapons in the Second Indochina War," 48; Dave Richard Palmer, *Summons of the Trumpet*, 280; Davidson, *Vietnam at War*, 603; Sorley, "Reassessing the ARVN"; Sorley, "Could the War Have Been Won?" 414–16; Sorley, *A Better War*, 306.

two-week operation turned into a disorderly and, in General Davidson's words, "agonizing affair," complete with demoralizing press pictures of desperate South Vietnamese troops hanging on to the skids of US helicopters assisting the retreat. General Bruce Palmer says that the retreat became a "nightmare" but also adds that US air support and helicopter operations enabled the South Vietnamese troops to get out of Laos "generally intact and in fairly good order." Kissinger makes basically the same point while also noting that the photographs of South Vietnamese troops were "untypical." By then the North Vietnamese had about 40,000 troops engaged in battle, sometimes attacking in human waves. Losses on both sides were extremely heavy. About 40 percent of the South Vietnamese force became casualties (killed or wounded) or were listed as missing; North Vietnamese losses, often the result of attacks by huge B-52 bombers, may have reached 20,000. Although no US ground forces participated in the operation, more than 250 Americans were killed and more than 1,100 wounded, mainly helicopter crew members.[32]

Orthodox commentators cite Lam Son 719 as irrefutable evidence of the failure of Vietnamization, and that assessment, albeit in moderated form, extends to the revisionist camp. James H. Willbanks saw combat in Vietnam during the 1972 Easter Offensive and currently is director of the Department of Military History at the US Army Command and Staff College. While critical of some central revisionist positions, he shares, with caveats, the fundamental revisionist position that the war could have been won with a different US approach. Willbanks argues that Vietnamization failed because it began too late and did not address several major problems that plagued the South Vietnamese government and its armed forces. This, along with the flawed Paris Peace Accords of 1973, America's determination to exit Vietnam, and the resultant withdrawal of US support for South Vietnam, "set the stage" for the collapse of Saigon's military forces. With regard to Lam Son 719, Willbanks maintains that although it temporarily disrupted the PAVN buildup in Laos and inflicted severe losses on the North Vietnamese, in the end the operation was "a defeat for ARVN and a setback to Vietnamization."[33]

---

[32] Most of these statistics are from Davidson, *Vietnam at War*, 649–50. See also James H. Willbanks, *A Raid Too Far: Operation Lam Son 719 and Vietnamization in Laos* (College Station: Texas A&M University Press, 2014), 59–63.

[33] James H. Willbanks, *Abandoning Vietnam: How America Left and South Vietnam Lost its War* (Lawrence: University Press of Kansas, 2004), 114–15, 286–87.

Davidson essentially agrees; he finds that the operation demonstrated that "while Vietnamization had made progress," both the South Vietnamese government and the ARVN still had "deep flaws" that would require "years, probably decades" to resolve. He adds that US and ARVN planners should have known beforehand that the extremely difficult terrain, North Vietnamese capabilities, and South Vietnamese deficiencies meant the operation could not succeed. Dave Richard Palmer is somewhat more positive, calling the results of Lam Son 719 "a mixed bag" since despite shortcomings, it delayed a North Vietnamese invasion by a year. He adds that, as with the Cambodian campaign, an operation such as Lam Son 719, presumably with the participation of US ground troops, should have taken place in 1966 or 1967. Bruce Palmer uses the word "mixed" and notes that the ARVN's shortcomings "did not bode well for the future." At the same time, he points out that together the Cambodian and Laos operations disrupted North Vietnamese activities to the point where they saved South Vietnam from defeat at Hanoi's hands during the 1972 Easter Invasion, a point also made by Kissinger.[34]

Sorley offers the most positive assessment. Aside from pointing out the PAVN losses in men and equipment, he cites a Polish (i.e., Communist) source regarding how Lam Son 719 hurt the North Vietnamese and how the French military mission in Hanoi reported a "devastating" effect on both civilian and military morale in North Vietnam. He also cites a message from General Abrams to Westmoreland in August 1971 that reported lower enemy military activity and infiltration since the operation. Sorley also acknowledges the generally negative evaluations of the operation and the "residual deficiencies" in ARVN that it revealed.[35]

MILITARY OPERATIONS AND VIETNAMIZATION

Sorley credits Abrams for conceiving and implementing the new overall strategy that won the war after 1968; however, other revisionist commentators point out that the circumstances created by the Tet Offensive made that strategy possible. According to Andrade, Tet created an environment that allowed Abrams to do what had been denied to Westmoreland.

[34] Davidson, *Vietnam at War*, 654–56; Dave Richard Palmer, *Summons of the Trumpet*, 308; Bruce Palmer, *The 25-Year War*, 113–14; Kissinger, *Ending the Vietnam War*, 204–5.
[35] Sorley, *A Better War*, 261–65, 270–71.

As a result of Tet, Communist main-force units had been driven away from the population centers. Hanoi moved those forces, as Birtle puts it, to "the relative safety of the hinterland and cross-border sanctuaries where they nursed their wounds and waited for America's withdrawal to create more favorable circumstances." Although these units were still a potential threat, the fact that they had been driven away from where most people lived turned the ongoing battle in the rural areas of South Vietnam into a traditional guerrilla insurgency. Meanwhile, Vietcong cadres in the villages, whose network constituted what Andrade calls "the glue that held the insurgency together," had been "decimated" during the Tet fighting. US/South Vietnamese operations therefore faced far less resistance than they had several months earlier. Andrade quotes Abrams's October 1968 comment on this development: "There's more freedom of movement throughout Vietnam than there has been since the start of the US buildup."[36]

This improved post-Tet situation benefited Vietnamization, as did the Cambodian campaign and, albeit indirectly, Lam Son 719. Willbanks points out that even if Lam Son 719 was a setback to Vietnamization, it also took a severe toll on the PAVN in terms of casualties, disrupted its buildup in Laos, and therefore bought Vietnamization desperately needed time. He quotes military historian Keith Nolan, author of a monograph on the operation called *Into Laos*, to the effect that Vietnamization "had been tested, had strained but not cracked, and now had continued room to grow."[37]

PACIFICATION

This positive impact of these military campaigns was especially evident when it came to pacification, the effort to broaden and deepen the South Vietnamese government's control over the countryside. Pacification was nothing new; it had a history going back to the Diem regime. What was new after Tet was the emphasis it received, how it was carried out, and, crucially, its success. The post-Tet pacification effort was based on an organization set up in 1967 called Civil Operations and Revolutionary Development Support (CORDS). Its first boss was Robert Komer,

---

[36] Andrade, "Westmoreland Was Right," 164–65; Birtle, "PROVN, Westmoreland, and the Historians," 1226.

[37] Willbanks, *Abandoning Vietnam*, 115. See also Keith W. Nolan, *Into Laos: The Story of Dewey Canyon II/Lam Son 719, Vietnam 1971* (Novato: Presidio Press, 1986).

a civilian whose nickname, "Blowtorch," reflected his ability to cut through bureaucratic red tape and get things done. William Colby became his deputy in February 1968. After being disrupted by Tet, the CORDS pacification effort really got off the ground in November 1968 under what was called the Accelerated Pacification Campaign (APC). This campaign was conceived by Colby, who took over CORDS that same November and led it until 1971. The APC was an intense ninety-day effort to bring 1,300 hamlets from what was called a "contested" to a "secure" state; by January 1969 more that 85 percent of these formerly contested hamlets were considered secure. This achievement provided the basis for what was accomplished during the next three years. That longer-term success in turn is at the heart of the case made by several revisionists, most notably and emphatically by William Colby and Lewis Sorley, that as of 1972 the "war was won."[38]

Post-Tet pacification started with protecting villagers from the Vietcong. Significantly, instead of first turning to the ARVN, CORDS began locally by arming villagers so they could protect themselves. In *Lost Victory*, Colby points out that the Vietcong had long used terror and murder to intimidate villagers and force them to pay taxes and otherwise support the insurgency. Terror was a tool for undermining the government's authority. Colby reports that unarmed rural communities could be entered and controlled by five-man Vietcong squads, who could then collect taxes, gather supplies, and recruit local people. Therefore, as soon as Colby began working for CORDS, he made the formation of armed local self-defense units his first priority. This required the approval of the South Vietnamese government, a potential stumbling block because some top Saigon government officials were worried about the villagers' loyalty. President Thieu thought otherwise and in April 1968 ordered the creation of the People's Self Defense Force (PSDF). This took place in the wake of the Tet Offensive, after which thousands of South Vietnamese had asked the government for arms so they could protect themselves. During the APC that began in November 1968, what Colby calls "a three-month blitz," about 170,000 weapons were distributed. By 1971 approximately 500,000 weapons had been distributed to villages, where they were held by village chiefs and used by more than four million volunteers on a rotating basis. Above the PSDF were territorial forces at the local and regional levels (Popular Forces and Regional Forces), whose more than 400,000 members were part-time soldiers attached to ARVN and who, as

[38] Sorley, "The Conduct of the War," 191; Andrade, "Westmoreland Was Right," 167.

mentioned earlier, increasingly were equipped with modern weapons, including M-16 rifles.[39]

Another crucial part of pacification was the Phoenix program, which was designed to uproot the Vietcong infrastructure (VCI) in the villages. Despite the damage the VCI suffered during Tet, as of 1968 it still retained what Sorley calls an "iron grip" in many rural areas, a fact confirmed by its continuing campaigns of terrorism and assassination. The Phoenix program was established by Colby in mid-1968 in cooperation with the South Vietnamese government. Phoenix, unfairly, has been tarnished by accusations that it was an assassination program. The reality is that Phoenix was an intelligence-gathering program, and while abuses may have occurred, Colby specifically and in writing prohibited assassination. Indeed, as Sorley points out, the goal was to capture Vietcong operatives alive to make use of the intelligence they could provide. Colby and others have stressed that in seeking to identify an assassination campaign in rural South Vietnam, one should look first and foremost to the Vietcong and the PAVN. While numbers regarding Vietcong/PAVN terrorism are necessarily imprecise, Summers estimates that Communist forces assassinated 61,000 South Vietnamese civil servants and village officials between 1958 and 1966; Colby gives figures of 6,000 officials and citizens killed and 15,000 wounded in 1969, "figures ... rather lower than those of 1968." Whatever the exact numbers, Andrade reports that in 1969, to "compensate for the losing situation" they faced, the Communists responded with a "greater emphasis on terrorism."[40]

Once Phoenix gathered intelligence, operations against the VCI were undertaken by military or police units: in Colby's words, by "all the forces engaged in the war" in South Vietnam. This meant that most VCI personnel who were killed lost their lives in combat situations. Combat occurred because, as Mark Moyar explains in *Phoenix and the Birds of*

---

[39] Colby, *Lost Victory*, 242–43, 254–60; Sorley, *A Better War*, 77–78; Brian M. Jenkins, "A People's Army for South Vietnam: A Vietnamese Solution" (Santa Monica: Rand, 1971), 14. One problem in discussing pacification in South Vietnam is that the word "pacification" can be misleading in terms of what the program actually was and attempted to do. The dictionary definition (usually given after something like "to pacify or appease") is the forcible suppression of a hostile population. As Colby describes in *Lost Victory*, pacification in South Vietnam meant something very different: protecting the rural population from the Vietcong. Pacification certainly involved violence, but mostly against enemy guerrillas and armed cadres.

[40] Sorley, *A Better War*, 144–45; Colby, *Lost Victory*, 246–47, 330–31; Harry G. Summers Jr., *The Vietnam Almanac* (Novato: Presidio Press, 1985), 284; Andrade, "Westmoreland Was Right," 168.

Prey, by the late 1960s the ability of US and South Vietnamese forces to reach villages and hamlets often made it impossible for VCI cadres to live among the peasants. VCI cadres had to enter the villages accompanied by armed guerrillas, and they usually were armed themselves. Thus operations against VCI cadres often merged with those against Communist armed forces. As Moyar puts it, the favored "rifle shot" approach of targeting a single important VCI cadre often had to give way to the "shotgun" approach of apprehending or killing a large group of insurgents to net a few important ones. But the shotgun approach was not assassination. In a jointly written article on "counterinsurgency lessons," Andrade and Willbanks point out that more than two-thirds of the 81,000 Communist cadres "neutralized" between 1968 and 1972 were captured; of those killed, 87 percent died in combat operations.[41]

The Phoenix program was a major success, although it was less effective after 1969, the year the CIA withdrew from participation in it. According to Andrade and Willbanks, by eliminating so many Communist cadres between 1968 and 1972, Phoenix destroyed the VCI infrastructure in many places. This contributed mightily to the pacification effort as a whole. Estimates are that the number of VCI personnel shrank from about 85,000 in August 1967 to about 56,000 in February 1972. The number of guerrillas dropped to 25,000, one-third their number in January 1968; their ranks had to be replenished by PAVN soldiers from the North. Meanwhile, according to one authoritative estimate, the percentage of peasants living in government-controlled hamlets went from 42 percent in 1967 to 80 percent in 1972.[42] Other estimates for the latter figure are higher, approaching or exceeding 90 percent, depending on how one reads various sets of statistics.[43] Communist sources confirm Phoenix's successes. For example, the general who was second in command in South Vietnam called

---

[41] Colby, *Lost Victory*, 250; Mark Moyar, *Phoenix and the Birds of Prey: Counterinsurgency and Counterterrorism in Vietnam* (Lincoln and London: University of Nebraska Press, 1997), 370–71; Dale Andrade and Lieutenant Colonel James H. Willbanks, "CORDS/Phoenix: Counterinsurgency Lessons from Vietnam for the Future," *Military Review*, March–April 2006, 20; Richard A. Hunt, "Pacification," in The *Encyclopedia of the Vietnam War*, 315. Hunt is the author of *Pacification: The American Struggle for Vietnam's Hearts and Minds* (Boulder, CO: Westview Press, 1995).

[42] Andrade and Willbanks, "CORDS/Phoenix," 20–21; Hunt, "Pacification," 315. See also Colby, *Lost Victory*, 331.

[43] Andrade, "Westmoreland Was Right," 168, 178; Brig. Gen. Tran Dinh Tho, *Pacification*, (Washington, DC: US Army Center of Military History, 1980), 164–65.

Phoenix "extremely destructive," while a former Vietcong minister wrote in his memoirs that it was "dangerously effective." Moyar adds that the inability of the VCI to collect taxes, gather intelligence, and perform other services was a factor in the failure of the North Vietnamese 1972 Easter Offensive.[44]

The final and crucial piece of the pacification puzzle was put in place in 1970 when President Thieu announced his "Land to the Tiller" program. Within three years, with US financial help, the South Vietnamese government distributed almost three million acres of land to 950,000 families. The peasants received their land free of charge, while the government paid the former landowners. This act reduced tenancy in South Vietnam from about 60 percent to only 10 percent. It also played a role in reducing support for the Communists while helping the government win increased support among the peasantry. Rice production soared to record levels.[45] When combined with other government programs that provided for local elections and otherwise improved local government, it is reasonable to agree with Moyar that between 1969 and 1972 the South Vietnamese government succeeded in winning the support of the majority of the peasantry. Ironically, one measure of what the Land to the Tiller program meant only became evident after 1975 and the Communist victory: the peasants of the former South Vietnam, now under Communist rule, bitterly resisted collectivization to the point that by 1980 less than a quarter of families south of the 17th parallel belonged to collectives, many of which existed only on paper. Of course, beginning in 1986 the entire inefficient and corrupt collectivization system, an utter failure in Vietnam and everywhere Communist dictatorships imposed it on unwilling peasants, was abandoned.[46]

---

[44] Andrade and Willbanks, "CORDS/Phoenix," 21; Moyar, *Phoenix and the Birds of Prey*, 392.

[45] Moyar, *Phoenix and the Birds of Prey*, 310–12, 394–96; Thomas C. Thayer, *War Without Fronts: The American Experience in Vietnam* (Annapolis: Naval Institute Press, 1985), 242–43; Sorley, *A Better War*, 149; see also Willard C. Mullar, "The Land-to-the-Tiller Program: The Operational Phase" (USAID/Vietnam, 1973). Muller at the time was the Associate Director for Land Reform for the US Agency for International Development.

[46] Michael Kirk and Nguyen Do Anh Tuan, "Exiting from Collective Agriculture: Land-tenure Reform in Vietnam," in *Millions Fed: Proven Successes in Agricultural Development*, eds. David J. Spielman and Rajul Pandya-Lynch (Washington, DC: International Food Policy Research Institute, 2009), 139–40.

"THE WAR IS WON"

It is important to understand exactly what Sorley, Colby, and other revisionists mean when they argue that by 1972 "the war is won."[47] They do *not* mean that the fighting was over or that the Communists had conceded defeat. Rather, as Sorley puts it, it was that the South Vietnamese had achieved the ability to "maintain their freedom and independence of action." Sorley stresses that this in turn was dependent on the promise of continued American support, "similar to the support still being rendered to American allies in West Germany and South Korea,"[48] the two other countries divided as a result of the Cold War.

In terms of specifics, Sorley says that the South Vietnamese government controlled about 90 percent of the country's population as of 1969, adding that this control stayed at about that level in 1970 and 1971. He mentions the "myriad of economic improvements," including the record rice production levels achieved by 1971, and cites General Abrams on the increase in the stretches of road and number of bridges open since the low point in 1968. By 1972, Sorley argues, the ARVN had almost completed the plans for its expansion and improvement and now possessed a "formidable capability." He also cites other expert assessments, beginning with Colby's (discussed later) and John Paul Vann's. Vann was a legendary figure who served in South Vietnam for many years, first as a US Army officer advising ARVN and, after his retirement from the US Army, as a civilian advisor. He had seen the bad years first hand since the early 1960s. In January 1972, Vann commented that Vietnamization "has gone literally beyond my wildest dreams of success." He added, "We are now at the lowest level of fighting the war has ever seen." Sir Robert Thompson, the renowned British counterinsurgency expert, issued a similar upbeat assessment after touring South Vietnam in late 1970. Sorley drives home his argument by citing an authoritative North Vietnamese source, a volume on the Le Duc Tho–Kissinger negotiations published by Hanoi in 1995. Its authors admit that Communist forces "fell into a critical situation in 1969, 1970, 1971." That "situation" included the loss of many key rural areas, that "armed forces were worn out and compelled to withdraw gradually to mountain regions," and that "the war situation continued deteriorating." Le Duc Tho himself is quoted as admitting that by the end of 1968 the Communist side "had suffered

---

[47] Sorley, "Could the War Have Been Won?" 413.
[48] Sorley, "Reassessing ARVN," 11.

great losses" and that pacification caused "great difficulties" in 1969–1970. The overall situation was grim: "Our bases in the countryside were weakened, our positions shrank. Our main [force] troops were decimated and no long had footholds in South Vietnam and had to camp in friendly Cambodia."[49] All this provides is a reasonable basis for Sorley's heading of one of his works that "The War Is Won."

Rufus Phillips, who served in South Vietnam in a variety of capacities over many years, seconds Sorley's assessment. Pacification, he affirms, had largely succeeded. By 1972, most of South Vietnam, including the vital Mekong Delta area, "was not only pacified but peaceful," as was most of central South Vietnam. Phillips notes how in 1973 a South Vietnamese senator together with a retired general traveled in a civilian car, unarmed and without escort, from Saigon to Hue, almost the length of the entire country. He reports that many US officials attested to the improved security, including a National Security Council staffer who in 1973, during three visits to South Vietnam, traveled "securely" throughout the country accompanied only by an interpreter and one or two Vietnamese soldiers, "who mainly drove." Phillips's conclusion is that "a stalemate à la Korea" – meaning the South Vietnamese shouldering most of the struggle while the United States provided logistical and air support – "was not an impossible outcome."[50]

General Davidson's view of Vietnamization is more qualified. While discussing Lam Son 719 and providing a generally negative assessment of that operation, he notes that pacification "continued the great gains it had made in 1969 and 1970." Davidson acknowledges that pacification's degree of success is a matter of debate, but in the end he concludes that compared to other US efforts going on at the time, "pacification was the big winner in 1971."[51]

Moyar's perspective notes the positive impact of the Land to the Tiller program and the restoration of village and hamlet elections (which Diem had abolished) in 1969. Moyar frequently cites Communist sources to back up his argument for the success of Vietnamization. One good example is a 1971 Central Office for South Vietnam (COSVN) directive that complains about how the United States and the "puppet" (South

---

[49] Sorley, *A Better War*, 149, 219, 223, 306; Sorley, "Could the War Have Been Won?" in *The Real Lessons of the Vietnam War*, 415–17. The heading "The War Is Won" is in "Could the War Have Been Won?"

[50] Rufus Phillips, *Why Vietnam Matters: An Eyewitness Account of Lessons Not Learned* (Annapolis: Naval Institute Press, 2008), 301, 361, n.19.

[51] Davidson, *Vietnam at War*, 661.

Vietnamese) regime have "strengthened puppet forces, consolidated the puppet government," and established territorial defense forces "in many hamlets and villages." These activities, COSVN glumly reported, "caused many difficulties on friendly forces," including many defections to the South Vietnamese side. Moyar stresses that the key success in the countryside was leadership and power, and the ability of the South Vietnamese regime to provide these was vital to the success of Vietnamization. These were the main factors behind the decline the Vietcong's popularity (which began during the Tet offensive) after 1969 and the corresponding rise in the government's popularity. Thus by 1972 "in all but a few places, the large majority of hamlet dwellers had decided they preferred GVN [Government of South Vietnam] rule to Communist rule."[52]

Finally, William Colby provides an overview of Vietnamization's successes that combines the advantages of professional expertise with an eyewitness account. He explains how CORDS finally established a unified management structure for dealing with pacification and why that structure worked. As noted, he details the positive results of arming territorial forces with modern weapons and the successes of the Phoenix program. He notes the positive impact of the restoration of local village elections in 1969 and the effectiveness of a new national training center for elected village chiefs and other local officials. Colby praises the Land to the Tiller program, noting that it avoided the pitfall of Diem's program – which had required peasants to pay for their land – by giving the land to the peasants free of charge. In describing the situation as of Tet 1971, three years after the Tet Offensive, Colby reports that large areas of the countryside were sufficiently secure so that villagers could focus on economic activity and bettering their lives. Peasants could move their goods to market "free of fear that a mine planted the night before" would kill them or destroy their goods. Random attacks on cities had ceased. Colby covers various parts of the country, and he acknowledges that in several northern provinces that abutted Cambodia and Laos, while significantly improved, the situation was not as favorable as elsewhere. He is especially positive about the southern part of the country

---

[52] Moyar, *Phoenix and the Birds of Prey*, 250, 298–322. The quotations are on pages 250 and 317. The term used to describe the process of defection of Communists to the South Vietnamese side was "rallying," and those who did so were "ralliers," although how many of them and how important they were are matters of debate.

around Saigon and the Mekong Delta, commenting extensively on the increased security and economic activity in those areas.[53]

In his chapter "Tet 1971: A Ride in the Countryside," Colby describes a motorcycle ride, "to celebrate the Tet holiday," he and John Paul Vann took across the entire Mekong Delta, from the sea to a town within sight of the Cambodian border. They rode alone, albeit with helicopters overhead just in case. There was a striking contrast, Colby writes, between his and Vann's "peaceful traverse" and the "ambushes, roadblocks, and enemy battalions" they would have encountered three years earlier. "Tet 1971 in Vietnam was a different world from that of Tet 1968," he concludes.[54]

WHY AN EASTER OFFENSIVE?

The effort to destroy that "different world" demanded what Willbanks calls a "radical departure" from North Vietnam's "strategy and methods of warfare."[55] Known as the Easter Offensive, the new strategy was a conventional invasion of South Vietnam. The question is why this departure occurred, as well as how to explain its timing. After all, the US withdrawal was continuing, and soon the PAVN would not have to worry about any US ground combat troops in South Vietnam. Orthodox commentators tend to focus on international considerations, in particular the progress of détente, which Hanoi feared might cause the Soviet Union and China to decrease their military aid to the point where it could no longer sustain a war effort sufficient to conquer South Vietnam. The result was that in early 1971 Hanoi decided it had to score a "decisive victory" during 1972. A related point was the imperative of forcing a settlement before Nixon could win reelection since he was likely to stiffen his terms after that eventuality. Lien-Hang T. Nguyen had access to previously classified North Vietnamese documents in writing *Hanoi's War* (2012), which at various points supports both orthodox and revisionist arguments. She writes that Nixon's détente policy toward the Soviet Union and opening to China convinced North Vietnam's leaders of the

---

[53] Colby, *Lost Victory*, 259, 313, especially pages 260, 264, 279, 293, 300, 306, 310.
[54] Ibid., 303–7.
[55] Willbanks, "Easter Offensive (Nguyên Huê Campaign) (1972)," *The Encyclopedia of the Vietnam War: A Political, Social, and Military History*, 112. This section also draws on Willbanks's monograph *Abandoning Vietnam*, 124–29.

"urgency to change the balance of power on the ground militarily" in South Vietnam.[56]

These considerations certainly influenced Hanoi. However, orthodox commentators slight or even ignore the progress achieved by Vietnamization as a factor in North Vietnamese decision making. This is true even when Vietnamization is mentioned as something Hanoi wanted to reverse. One orthodox historian who does consider Vietnamization as a factor in Hanoi's decision making is William S. Turley. He cites a memo Le Duc Tho wrote to Communist commanders in South Vietnam in late March 1972, just days before the start of the Easter Offensive. Tho's overriding concern was to force a settlement of the war before Nixon's reelection, and he told his commanders this meant it was necessary "to basically defeat Vietnamization." Turley adds, "Tho did not say Vietnamization was succeeding, but reversing its progress clearly was a major objective."[57]

Vietnamization's successes made reversing it an urgent objective, and this in turn led Hanoi not only to change its strategy and launch a conventional invasion of South Vietnam but to do it sooner rather than later. Willbanks notes that in 1971 the North Vietnamese Politburo debated when to launch the invasion. Some members favored a delay until 1973, when most US troops would be gone. However, Le Duan and others argued for 1972, citing the progress of Vietnamization with regard to both the growing strength of the ARVN and pacification. They warned that delay would make it much more difficult to conquer South Vietnam militarily. Le Duan's argument carried the day.[58] While Le Duan's assessment of the situation in South Vietnam was hardly the same as Sorley's – he and his supporters obviously did not believe the United States and South Vietnam had won the war – what he told the Politburo at a minimum lends considerable credence to Sorley's case for the success Vietnamization. So does an assessment provided by Sir Robert

---

[56] See, for example, Herring, *America's Longest War*, 304; Moss, *Vietnam: An American Ordeal*, 369; John Prados, *Vietnam: History of an Unwinnable War*, 448–49; Duiker, *The Communist Road to Power in Vietnam*, 291–92. Also see Lien-Hang T. Nguyen, *Hanoi's War: An International History of the War for Peace in Vietnam* (Chapel Hill: University of North Carolina Press, 2012), 223–24.

[57] Turley, *The Second Indochina War*, 183–85.

[58] Willbanks, *Abandoning Vietnam*, 125–26. Willbanks bases his summary of this Politburo debate on two sources: David W. P. Elliott, *NLF-DRV Strategy and the 1972 Spring Offensive* (Ithaca: Cornell University, International Relations Project of East Asia, IREA Project, January 1974); and Ilya V. Gaiduk, *The Soviet Union and the Vietnam War* (Chicago: Iran R. Dee, 1996). See also Andrade and Willbanks, "CORDS/Pheonix," 22.

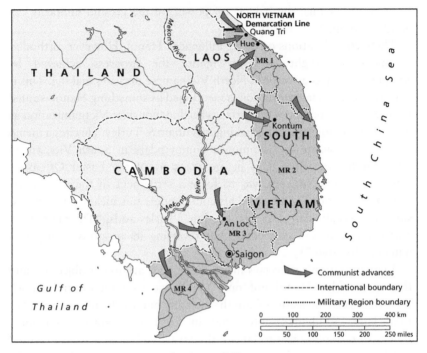

MAP 8 The Easter Offensive, 1972

Thompson. Shortly after the Easter Offensive, Thompson told a conference audience in the United States: "The result of successful Vietnamization and pacification was that by 1971 the North decided that the only thing left was to invade."[59]

"THE TEST PASSED"

"The Test Passed" is William Colby's lapidary assessment of how South Vietnam dealt with the crisis it faced during the spring and summer of 1972.[60] On March 30, 1972, North Vietnam invaded South Vietnam. Hanoi's goal was to strike a devastating blow against the South Vietnamese regime that would wreck Nixon's policies and force him to negotiate a settlement on Hanoi's terms. A successful invasion might

---

[59] Quoted in Sorley, *A Better War*, 306. On Thompson see W. Scott Thompson and Donaldson D. Frizzell, *The Lessons of Vietnam*, 103.

[60] Colby, *Lost Victory*, 314.

even cause the Thieu government to collapse. This was not infiltration, as in the past, but rather an outright full-scale invasion by a conventional army, almost the entire North Vietnamese army in fact. More than 130,000 troops, the elite of PAVN's combat forces, were thrown into battle, their numbers swelled by thousands of guerrillas. They were equipped with 1,200 tanks and armored vehicles, heavy artillery, modern surface-to-air missiles, heat-seeking antiaircraft missiles, and other state-of-the-art weaponry. This equipment had been supplied by the Soviet Union and China, mostly the former; this invasion could not have taken place without Soviet help. The invasion was three pronged: four divisions attacking across the demilitarized zone in the north, two more pushing east from Laos into the Central Highlands, and three more divisions attacking eastward from Cambodia in the south. Altogether, fourteen PAVN divisions and more than twenty-six additional regiments units participated in the operation.[61]

The ground fighting was fierce and lasted into the summer, with the ultimate outcome very much in doubt at various points. It is widely agreed that Nixon's decision to provide massive US air support to the beleaguered South Vietnamese, including bombing by B-52s, was decisive in turning the tide. For example, US fighter-bombers and B-52s were critical in enabling ARVN forces to resist and eventually repel two key sieges, one at An Loc, about sixty-five miles from Saigon, in the south and the other at the city of Kontum, in the center of the country. American advisors to ARVN also played a critical role in the ground war, at times taking de facto command of units they supposedly were only advising. Beginning in early May the use of airpower included resumed attacks against North Vietnam, but, crucially, without many of the restrictions imposed by Johnson on Rolling Thunder. This time the bombing campaign, called Linebacker, was designed to cripple North Vietnam's ability to wage war. Haiphong and ports were mined so that no ships could enter or leave, and roads and rail lines linking North Vietnam to China were hit. North Vietnam was almost entirely cut off from its Soviet and Chinese suppliers. Factories and power stations were destroyed. The accuracy of the bombing was dramatically increased by newly developed precision weapons such as laser-guided bombs. Management of the campaign, unlike under Rolling Thunder, was turned over to military commanders. For some of the men who fought in the war and later wrote about it, this important change finally

---

[61] Willbanks, *Abandoning Vietnam*, 127–28; Turley, *The Second Indochina War*, 186.

provided some satisfaction. Thus General Davidson noted, "No more would the president and secretary of defense – military neophytes – pore over target maps and bomb tonnages."[62] Or, as General Dave Richard Palmer laconically summed things up, "Linebacker was not Rolling Thunder – it was war."[63]

The Easter Offensive met its final defeat in September 1972 when ARVN forces completed their recapture of Quang Tri City, capital of South Vietnam's northernmost province, which PAVN forces had overrun in the first days of the invasion. By then the North Vietnamese had suffered about 100,000 killed and lost at least half of their tanks and large artillery. Many units were almost entirely wiped out. South Vietnamese losses, while considerably less, were still staggering: at least 25,000 killed and three times that number wounded. Not incidentally, as the fighting was slowing drawing to a close in late August, the last US combat troops in South Vietnam boarded a plane for home.

Orthodox commentators generally agree that the Easter Offensive demonstrated the futility of Vietnamization. The ARVN may have repelled the attack, they argue, but only because of American support both on the ground and in the air. South Vietnamese failings, both governmental and military, were still very much in evidence. To make matters worse, even in defeat the North Vietnamese had seized and retained a strategic strip of territory along the Laotian and Cambodian borders extending approximately from the DMZ to the northern part of the Mekong Delta; in 1975 it would provide key jumping-off points for a new invasion. Hanoi also still had tens of thousands of troops inside South Vietnam.

Revisionists vary in assessing the Easter Offensive, including what it revealed about Vietnamization. Summers calls the offensive "disastrous" for Hanoi; at the same time, comparing the Easter Offensive to Tet, he says that as with Tet, the Easter Offensive, while a "tactical failure," nonetheless was a "strategic success" because it eroded American will.[64] Davidson argues that the ARVN's victory over the North Vietnamese, while important and even heroic in many ways, also demonstrates South Vietnam's excessive dependence on US military support and that, in the

---

[62] Davidson, *Vietnam at War*, 704. After a second bombing campaign in December 1972, the bombing of North Vietnam during the Easter Offensive was called Linebacker I. The December 1972 campaign became Linebacker II.

[63] Dave Richard Palmer, *Summons of the Trumpet*, 321.

[64] Summers, *On Strategy*, 156–57, 184–85.

end, too many of "the same old faults were there, too." To Davidson, the Easter Offensive was "a stern test for Vietnamization," not the "complete test." That test, the "real trial of Vietnamization," came after America's complete withdrawal from Vietnam.[65] Andrade agrees with Davidson about the problem of South Vietnamese dependence on the United States, noting that the US/ARVN "partnership" could work, "but only as long as American firepower remained abundantly available."[66] Cecil Curry likewise notes the offensive showed that Vietnamization "seemed as if it would not work unless backed by American air support," although he adds that for North Vietnam, even combined with the new territory the PAVN now held, this revelation "was little enough reward in the face of such a serious reversal."[67]

Colby and Sorley make the most positive revisionist case for Vietnamization in the wake of the Easter Offensive. Colby notes that during the offensive, virtually no guerrilla assaults took place in most of South Vietnam, including the heavily populated Mekong Delta and coastal regions, a tribute to the success of pacification. He points out that despite the initial North Vietnamese successes after attacking across the demilitarized zone, the ARVN managed to reform its defenses, stop the PAVN advance, and save the city of Hue. Colby assigns much of the credit for this to Ngo Quang Truong, the general Davidson calls South Vietnam's "finest combat soldier," who in early May 1972 was put in charge of defending Hue by President Thieu.[68] Colby points out that it was possible for Thieu to move an elite division from its position in the Mekong Delta region south of Saigon to an area north of the capital to face the invading PAVN because Communist guerrillas in the area were capable of nothing more than "marginal harassment," which could be handled by local territorial forces. Pacification had accomplished its mission. Colby

---

[65] Davidson, *Vietnam at* War, 711–12.

[66] Dale Andrade, *America's Last Vietnam Battle: Halting Hanoi's 1972 Easter Offensive* (Lawrence: University Press of Kansas, 2001), 487–88.

[67] Curry, *Victory at Any Cost*, 288. Curry notes that Giap had opposed the offensive yet was blamed for its failure and removed as commander of PAVN, the army he had built. As Curry puts it, in effect explaining a key aspect of how North Vietnam's political system worked: "He [Giap] had been right. That was enough to condemn him."

[68] Colby, *Lost Victory*, 319; Davidson, *Vietnam at War*, 685. For General Truong's assessment of the Easter Offensive see Lt. Gen. Ngo Quang Truong, *The Easter Offensive of 1972* (Washington, DC: US Army Center of Military History, 1980), especially pages 175–81. Davidson adds that Truong "could have commanded a division or corps in any army in the world."

assigns due credit to American airpower, advisors, logistical support, intelligence, and more. But in the end, he insists, the South Vietnamese had borne the brunt of the ground fighting. They had defended Hue, repulsed the North Vietnamese in the central highlands, and defeated the attack on Saigon. "A free Vietnam had proven that it had the will and the capability of defend itself with the assistance, but not the participation of its American ally" against an enemy backed by the Soviet Union and China. For these reasons, Colby insists, "On the ground in South Vietnam, the war had been won."[69]

Sorley makes essentially the same case as Colby. To Sorley, what is "most important of all" about the Easter Offensive is the way the ARVN fought. He admits that the ARVN still had problems but insists that negative accounts of its performance by critics have obscured the fact that by 1972 it had become "a professional, agile, and determined military shield for its country." Sorley quotes Douglas Pike's assessment that "ARVN troops and even local forces stood and fought as never before." He quotes General Abrams's statement to his commanders that while US airpower was critical, "the thing that had to happen before that is the Vietnamese, some numbers of them, had to stand and fight. If they didn't do that, ten times the air [power] we've got wouldn't have stopped them [the North Vietnamese]." Sorley writes that "evidence abounds" for the ARVN's effectiveness in its battlefield performance during 1972: he adds, "South Vietnam did, with courage and blood, defeat the enemy's 1972 Easter Offensive." The point had been reached where "the war was won."[70]

To keep the war won, Sorley argues, the United States had to continue providing substantial help to South Vietnam. Unlike orthodox and even some revisionist critics of ARVN, Sorley maintains that this was not unreasonable, as it was exactly what the United States had done (and in 1972 was still doing) for West Germany and South Korea. Sorley reminds his readers, and ARVN's critics, that with the start of the Cold War, West Germany was incapable of defending itself against Soviet aggression without American help; in northeast Asia, after the armistice ended the fighting in 1953, South Korea needed US help against the continued threat from North Korea. Therefore, about 300,000 US troops remained in West Germany and 50,000 in South Korea. In 1973, having signed the Paris Peace Accords and withdrawn all US troops from Vietnam, the Nixon

[69] Colby, *Lost Victory*, 320–21.
[70] Sorley, "Reassessing ARVN," 13–14; Sorley, "The Conduct of the War," 191.

administration made a series of commitments to the South Vietnamese government for continued support in the event of renewed North Vietnamese aggression. When that aggression materialized, the United States "defaulted" on those commitments. And that, says Sorley, is the reason the war was "no longer won."[71] How this happened is the topic of the following chapter.

[71] Ibid.; Sorley, "Could the War Have Been Won?" 417. See also Sorley, "Courage and Blood: South Vietnam's Repulse of the 1972 Easter Offensive," *Parameters: The US Army War College Quarterly*, Summer 1999: 38–56. Actually, about 250,000 US troops were stationed in West Germany from the mid-1950s until the end of the Cold War. See Tim Kane, "Global US Troop Deployment, 1950–2003," Heritage Foundation, Center for Data Analysis Report #06-02 on National Security and Defense. Available online at www.heritage.org/research/reports/2006/05/global-us-troop-deployment-1950-2005

7

The Paris Peace Accords to Black April

The Easter Offensive left exhaustion and frustration in its wake from Saigon to Hanoi to Washington. One result was the resumption, in July 1972, of secret negotiations in Paris between American National Security Advisor Henry Kissinger and North Vietnamese Politburo member Le Duc Tho, which had been going on intermittently since 1970. By now both sides were prepared to make some compromises in long-held positions, the most important for Hanoi being the removal of the Thieu regime and for Washington the removal of all North Vietnamese troops from South Vietnam when all US troops withdrew. Of the two, Washington's concession was far more significant in determining the ultimate result of the Vietnam War since failure to achieve a mutual withdrawal would leave at least 150,000 thousand PAVN troops in South Vietnam once all US troops had departed. This reluctant acceptance of compromise by both sides enabled Kissinger and Tho to reach an agreement in October 1972. However, the agreement was rejected by President Thieu, who with considerable justification argued that the concession regarding North Vietnamese troops constituted a mortal threat to his government and the ability of South Vietnam to maintain its independence. Thieu's demands for modifications of this and other parts of the agreement he considered dangerous brought Kissinger back to Paris for renewed negotiations with Tho; these quickly deadlocked. Meanwhile, while pressuring Thieu to accept the agreement, Nixon offered him both increased American military aid and the assurance of US military support in the form of air power should Hanoi violate the Paris agreement.

In the end Nixon, who actually shared some of Thieu's concerns about the agreement, decided to use another bombing campaign against North

Vietnam to force Hanoi to accept at least some of the changes the US wanted in the October agreement. This campaign, Linebacker II, which began on December 18, 1972, and lasted for eleven days, was the most intensive of the war. Because it lasted through Christmas, it is also known as the Christmas Bombing. It provoked outrage in the press, among American antiwar groups and political figures, and in several European countries for allegedly being indiscriminant terror bombing directed at civilians. Among the accusations hurled at Linebacker II were that it was "a crime against humanity," "Stone Age barbarism," "war by tantrum," a "wave of terror," and worse.[1]

In fact, as even most orthodox historians now acknowledge, it was none of these things. Turley points out "the bombing was as discriminating as bombing could then be." He also notes that "the vast majority of Hanoi's buildings were never touched was plain for visitors to see, too." Moss states that Linebacker II "was not a campaign of terror that targeted cities and civilian populations." The only targets deliberately attacked were military or those in areas not heavily populated. Herring notes that "American pilots went to extraordinary lengths to avoid civilian casualties," a point also made by journalist Stanley Karnow.[2] The total civilian death toll in Hanoi and Haiphong was about 1,600, extremely light considering the scale of the bombing and when compared to past bombing campaigns. In contrast, the destruction of railroad yards, port facilities, factories, broadcasting stations, and similar actual targets was devastating. While the extent to which Linebacker II affected the North Vietnamese remains a matter of debate; on January 8, 1973, Kissinger and Tho returned to the bargaining table prepared to make some additional, if relatively minor, concessions.

The Paris Peace Accords were signed on January 27, 1973, and a cease-fire in Vietnam began that same day. The main changes from the October 1972 agreement, most commentators agree, were minor; they certainly did not have any impact on what was to follow. The point that matters most, and the main flaw from the perspective of the United States and South Vietnam, concerned troop withdrawals: the United States would withdraw all its military forces from South Vietnam (and in return American prisoners of war would be released) while North Vietnamese troops (actually not mentioned in the Accords) would remain.

---

[1] Quoted in Willbanks, *Abandoning Vietnam*, 182.
[2] Turley, *The Second Indochina War*, 192; Moss, *Vietnam: An American Ordeal*, 385; Herring, *America's Longest War*, 316.

That left more than 150,000 PAVN troops in South Vietnam, as well as another 100,000 in Laos and Cambodia. The territory those troops controlled, much of it seized and held during the Easter Offensive, stretched along South Vietnam's western border with Laos and Cambodia from the DMZ to the northern edge of the Mekong Delta. This "Third Vietnam," as Hanoi called it, provided the ideal launching point for attacking South Vietnam when the time was right. Another major flaw was that the Accords did not contain an effective mechanism for policing the cease-fire. Both North Vietnam and the United States were forbidden from sending more troops into South Vietnam, a provision that the US observed and North Vietnam violated from the start. In fact, as Willbanks points out, North Vietnam violated the Accords even before they could take effect. That sequence of events went as follows: Kissinger and Le Duc Tho initialed the Accords on January 23, but in the 48 hours before the cease-fire they mandated officially took effect (midnight January 27 Greenwich Mean Time, 8 a.m. January 28 Saigon time), PAVN forces attacked more than 400 villages and hamlets.[3] Orthodox and revisionist commentators agree that the Accords were little more than an interlude before the fighting would begin again. The revisionist perspective is aptly summed up by General Davidson: "In reality, the settlement only suspended major combat operations for the period necessary for North Vietnam to prepare her forces for the final offensive."[4]

President Thieu, who considered the Accords a "surrender agreement," was pressured by Nixon into signing the agreement by a combination of intensified threats and promises of upgraded aid and support. The threats included signing the Accords even if Thieu refused and cutting off all aid. The promises guaranteed continued diplomatic support, continued military and economic aid, and, crucially, the assurance the United States would respond "with full force should the settlement be violated by North Vietnam," a guarantee that meant the use of air power as had been done during the Easter Offensive of 1972.[5]

Both Nixon and Kissinger maintained the Paris Accords would have provided "peace with honor"; that is, they would have protected the independence of South Vietnam had Congress not undermined them by radically reducing aid to the Saigon government. Revisionists are divided

---

[3] Willbanks, *Abandoning Vietnam*, 186–88.   [4] Davidson, *Vietnam at War*, 731.
[5] Quoted in Turley, *The Second Indochina War*, 194; Willbanks, *Abandoning Vietnam*, 184–85.

on this important point. Some agree with orthodox commentators that the Paris Accords were too flawed to protect South Vietnam. Dave Richard Palmer, for example, calls them "nothing more than a device to remove the US military presence from Vietnam." These revisionists also argue that in light of the evolving Watergate scandal and the widespread desire among the American people to exit from Vietnam, Nixon's promises to Thieu were empty. Beyond that, they tend to blame South Vietnam's ultimate defeat two years later on its own internal problems, from corruption to poor leadership to ARVN's unfixable shortcomings. This essentially is General Davidson's position, although he includes the caveat that some criticism of Nixon and Kissinger is "too harsh" given the situation they faced at home and suggests that they "had to take the agreement they got."[6] Other revisionists, such as Sorley and Colby, have a different focus. Whatever problems they find with the Accords and the Nixon/Kissinger performance or with the South Vietnamese government, they argue that the primary reason for South Vietnam's collapse in 1973 was America's failure – and by this they mean that of Congress – to honor the promises made in 1973. It was, they insist, what Washington did *after* the Accords – its "abandonment" of South Vietnam – that led to what the South Vietnamese call "Black April," Hanoi's military victory that united Vietnam under a Communist dictatorship.

THE ABANDONMENT OF VIETNAM

The idea that the United States, at least to some degree, abandoned South Vietnam is present in orthodox commentaries. Scholars such as Herring, Moss, and Turley do not deny that US aid cuts undermined ARVN's fighting ability. They also cover how the American withdrawal from South Vietnam hurt the country's economy by depriving it of funds that provided thousands of civilian jobs. The impact of worldwide inflation, caused by the 1973 Arab oil boycott of Western nations and the resultant spike of oil prices, also receives mention. However, as Moss puts it in a representative comment, while the congressional aid cuts "no doubt sapped the strength and morale of the RVNAF [Republic of Vietnam (South Vietnam) Armed Forces] forces ... they were not the most important causes of the GNV's growing military weaknesses." Those causes, the ones that mattered, were to be found in the shortcomings of the Saigon

---

[6] Dave Richard Palmer, *Summons of the Trumpet*, 335; Davidson, *Vietnam at War*, 732.

regime.[7] It is this point that revisionists, at least some of them, firmly reject. In rebuttal, they argue that with continued US support at the level promised, the non-Communist regime in South Vietnam could have survived. Instead, between 1973 and 1975, piece by piece, Washington withdrew its support to the point where it can be said the United States abandoned South Vietnam. And this, not South Vietnam's failings, was the fundamental cause of Saigon's military collapse and defeat in 1975.

The revisionist case about the abandonment of South Vietnam dates from when it was happening. As one might expect, it was made by a variety of US government officials, including Nixon and Kissinger. Some of the most compelling early statements of that case came from a soldier on the scene in South Vietnam, Major General John E. Murray, the author of a series of urgent and prescient dispatches from Saigon between 1973 and 1975. In January 1973 Murray became head of the newly created Defense Attaché Office (DAO), which was charged with managing US military aid to South Vietnam after the Paris Accords. He was warning of critical shortages and a dangerous situation in South Vietnam by December of that year. Interestingly, Murray is virtually ignored in many standard orthodox accounts of the war.[8] Once the war was over, Dave Richard Palmer provided a succinct early statement of the abandonment case when he observed that "the Soviet Union and China refurbished and strengthened Hanoi's army while the United States gradually constricted its own flow of supplies to Saigon."[9]

By far the most thorough early presentation of evidence for the abandonment case is a study published by the US Army Center of Military History, *Vietnam from Cease-Fire to Capitulation*, by Col. William E. Le Gro. Le Gro served in South Vietnam as a senior officer with the MACV and then in the DAO from December 1972 until April 1975. He does not overlook the leadership shortcomings of the Thieu regime with regard to civilian and military leadership; in fact, he cites strong leadership "at the highest levels" in Saigon as one of the two key missing factors that might

---

[7] Moss, *Vietnam: An American Ordeal*, 407; Herring, *America's Longest War*, 330–31; Turley, *The Second Indochina War*, 212–13.

[8] Colonel William E. Le Gro, *Vietnam from Ceasefire to Capitulation* (Washington, DC: U.S. Army Center of Military History, 1981), 80–81. Herring, *American's Longest War*; Moss, *Vietnam: An American Ordeal*; Karnow, *Vietnam: A History*; and Anderson, *The Vietnam War* fail to mention Murray. The MACV was disbanded when the last US troops left Vietnam in March 1973. The DAO staff consisted of 50 military officers and about 1,200 civilians.

[9] Palmer, *Summons of the Trumpet*, 335.

have avoided South Vietnam's defeat. Le Gro's other key vital missing factor was "unflagging American moral and material support,"[10] and this point has become a foundational part of the revisionist case as it has evolved over the years. Sorley stresses it in making the abandonment case in several works, including *A Better War*. Citing South Vietnamese General Cao Van Vien, chief of the ARVN Joint General Staff, Sorley mentions three "vital areas" where US help was essential: air support, including troop transport; sea support; and the replacement of weapons and supplies. He adds that these areas "had always been factored into calculations of the appropriate South Vietnamese forces." The importance of American aid to Saigon's survival is also central to the most comprehensive overview of the post–Paris Accords period, George J. Veith's *Black April: The Fall of South Vietnam, 1973–1975*. Veith is a former US Army captain and the author of two other books on the Vietnam War. In writing *Black April*, he consulted extensively with Le Gro and also with Merle Pribbenow, the acclaimed translator of Vietnamese whose efforts gave Veith access to numerous sources previously unavailable to other scholars. In his treatment of the US abandonment issue, Veith seconds Sorley by noting that after the Paris Accords no major US military or civilian official believed South Vietnam could withstand another major attack without the backing of US firepower. He states that by 1973 the ARVN, its problems notwithstanding, had become a military force capable of defeating the North Vietnamese. He concludes that had the ARVN been adequately supplied and given steady American support after the ceasefire, "the outcome of the war might have been vastly different."[11]

THE "MOST MURDEROUS TRUCE"

The sequence of policies and events that doomed South Vietnam began as soon as the Paris Accords were signed. South Vietnam soon became the scene of fierce fighting, not the lasting peace called for by the Accords or even a real truce.[12] Meanwhile, Congress cut aid to South Vietnam. Antiwar political figures in Congress were able to impose these cuts when President Nixon was weakened by the Watergate scandal, which

---

[10] Le Gro, *Vietnam from Ceasefire to Capitulation*, 179.
[11] Sorley, *A Better War*, 373–75; George J. Veith, *Black April: The Fall of South Vietnam, 1973–1975* (New York and London: Encounter Books, 2012), 7, 499.
[12] For the term "most murderous truce" see Sorley, *A Better War*, 364.

emerged as a major factor in American politics in early 1973. Congress made these cuts despite the continued requests for higher levels of support by Nixon and, after he had to resign in August 1974 because of Watergate, his successor Gerald Ford. As a result of congressional cuts, US military aid to South Vietnam decreased drastically between 1973 and 1975: from $2.3 billion in fiscal year 1973 to just over $1.1 billion in 1974 to only $700 million authorized for 1975, a year in which the Ford administration requested $1.5 billion. Meanwhile, price increases and other factors such as shipping costs ate away at what that money could buy, to the point where the $700 million authorized for 1975 could purchase only one-fifth of the material provided to the South Vietnamese armed forces in previous years.[13]

In addition, as of August 1973, having already ended all funding for military operations in Laos and Cambodia, Congress ended all funding for any American military activities in Indochina, which meant that US air and naval power could not be used to support South Vietnam in the event of North Vietnamese violations of the cease-fire mandated by the Paris Accords. That cease-fire, as already noted, was a fiction, as North Vietnam violated it from the start. During 1973 North Vietnamese efforts to seize more territory – its so-called Landgrab 73 or land and population grab campaign – plus other attacks turned that year into one of the bloodiest of the war, leading French journalist Olivier Todd to call the 1973 cease-fire "the most murderous truce this century." However, despite 15,000 Communist acts of terror, the ARVN fought well, and at year's end Saigon controlled slightly more territory and people than when the Paris Accords were signed. In Davidson's words, a year after the Paris Accords South Vietnam "still held the upper hand."[14]

The declining American support for South Vietnam had a serious implication beyond its direct impact on the ARVN: it was a key factor in the decision of North Vietnam's ruling Politburo to resume full-scale warfare in the South, a decision it made in May 1973. Davidson observes that congressional cuts "freed the Politburo's hand to strike the RVN whenever it so desired." Declining US support was not the only reason for Hanoi's timing, however. As Veith points out, the Politburo, pressured as

---

[13] Davidson, *Vietnam at War*, 746; Herring, *America's Longest War*, 331. At the time, the fiscal year began on July 1 of the previous calendar year and ended on June 30 of the year with which it was numbered.

[14] Sorley, *A Better War*, 364–65; Davidson, *Vietnam at War*, 743–47; Le Gro, *Vietnam from Ceasefire to Capitulation*, 21.

always by Le Duan, believed it had a small window of opportunity to win the war. South Vietnam was plagued by economic and political weakness, as was the United States. However, neither condition was likely to last for long. The Politburo also was concerned about its relations with China, including Beijing's claims on islands near the Vietnamese coastline. As the Politburo itself observed in its study of the war two decades later, if it had waited "the situation might have become very complicated and dangerous." Therefore, in early 1973 North Vietnam began its "strategic preparations" to finish its conquest of South Vietnam.[15]

The intense combat of 1973 was possible because during that year the North Vietnamese, in violation of the Paris Accords, poured new troops and heavy weapons into South Vietnam. While the actual numbers vary from source to source, Sorley's figures, some of which are drawn from Communist sources, can be considered reliable. Sorley quotes the official North Vietnamese history of the PAVN to the effect that between January and September 1973, the quantity of supplies sent into South Vietnam reached 140,000 tons, four times that of 1972. This included 80,000 tons of military supplies, which in turn included 27,000 tons of weapons. During 1973, in terms of personnel, 100,000 soldiers and civilian cadres "marched from North Vietnam to the battlefields of South Vietnam," as the PAVN history puts it. This included two infantry divisions, an antiaircraft division, two artillery regiments, an armored regiment, an engineering regiment, and other assorted units. Despite high combat losses during 1973, the massive reinforcements that streamed down the Ho Chi Minh Trail meant that by year's end North Vietnamese forces in the South had increased by 40,000. They also were equipped with six times as many tanks and three times as many artillery pieces as before.[16] Turley, who includes figures for Vietcong main-force units and guerrillas, places the total for Communist forces in the South at 230,000.[17]

All these troops and supplies could reach Vietnam and also arrive far more quickly than before because of improvements to the Ho Chi Minh Trail. At the time of the Paris Accords, it already was an elaborate network of thousands of miles of jungle trails and roads much improved from what it had been a decade earlier. With the end of American air

[15] Veith, *Black April*, 8, 85–86. The Politburo document, published in 1995 by Hanoi's National Political Publishing House, is called *Review of the Resistance War against the Americans to Save the Nation: Victory and Lessons*; Davidson, *Vietnam at War*, 741.

[16] Sorley, *A Better War*, 363–65.   [17] Turley, *The Second Indochina War*, 210.

interdiction, Hanoi was able to expand and transform it into something akin to a modern military highway network.

It was a massive effort. A two-lane, all-weather hard-surfaced road was built in Laos stretching from just south of the 17th parallel to within less than 100 miles of Saigon, that is, almost the entire length of South Vietnam. It was one of a growing number of such modernized roads that were now part of the Ho Chi Minh Trail network. A fuel pipeline, essential to supply all the tanks, trucks, and other vehicles being shipped to South Vietnam, ran along the same route. Veith considers the eight-inch pipeline the key logistical upgrade for PAVN forces in the South because they no longer faced fuel shortages despite being equipped with more armor and other modern vehicles than ever before. There were many other major improvements as well, as Hanoi dispatched more than 30,000 people and more than 1,000 vehicles and specialized machines for north-south road construction in Laos and in territory it controlled inside South Vietnam. Building the "road to victory," according to the official PAVN history, became "the entire nation's number one priority." As a result, by 1974 the north/south route of the Ho Chi Minh Trail in Laos was supplemented by a similar route – the Truong Son Corridor, or Corridor 613 – stretching 600 miles southward from the DMZ, entirely within the mountainous western section of South Vietnam. By September 1974, that route was an all-weather thoroughfare twenty-six feet wide complete with eastward spurs to the battlefronts. North Vietnamese soldiers – 100,000 in 1973 and 80,000 in 1974 according to North Vietnamese General Hoang Van Thai, a key staff officer for General Giap – rather than walking now often rode to South Vietnam in truck convoys, some of which numbered 300 vehicles. Armor, heavy artillery, antiaircraft weapons, and other materials all rolled down the Ho Chi Minh Trail. They could be serviced at new supply depots and repair facilities along the route, which had been built because Hanoi no longer had to worry they would be attacked by US aircraft. The expanded "strategic transportation routes," as General Thai called the trail, even allowed Hanoi for the first time to evacuate badly wounded troops back to North Vietnam for proper treatment.[18]

---

[18] Davidson, *Vietnam at War*, 738; Le Gro, *Vietnam from Ceasefire to Capitulation*, 39, Veith, *Black April*, 68–69; Willbanks, *Abandoning Vietnam*, 209, 213; Cao Van Vien, *The Final Collapse* (Washington, DC: U.S. Army Center of Military History, 1985), 36–39; Military History Institute of Vietnam, *Victory in Vietnam: The Official History*

WEAPONS AND US VERSUS SOVIET AND CHINESE AID

Another important point to understand about what revisionists call the abandonment of South Vietnam is the nature and quality of the weapons North Vietnam was able to send to South Vietnam as compared to those in ARVN hands. During 1973 the number of tanks available to North Vietnamese forces in South Vietnam (or just across the border in Laos and Cambodia), including modern T-54 models, increased from 100 to 500; that number soon swelled to 650, at least twice the number available to ARVN. Orthodox commentators often stress that when it came to heavy artillery, ARVN had an advantage, but as Major George R. Dunham and Colonel David A. Quinlan point out in their survey of the US Marines in Vietnam, between 1973 and 1975 "raw statistics relating to artillery reveal how misleading the numbers game" actually is. It is true that as of 1975 the ARVN had about 1,200 artillery pieces (down from 1,600 in 1973) versus about 400 in PAVN hands. The trouble for the ARVN, as both Dunham/Quinlan and Le Gro note, was that the PAVN's main artillery pieces were Soviet 122-mm howitzers and 122mm and 130mm guns. These could be fired faster and had a longer range than the ARVN's primary artillery weapons, American 105mm and 155mm howitzers. The Soviet weapons also were highly mobile, another factor that enabled PAVN forces to counter the ARVN's numerical superiority. The ARVN did have a few long-range US 175mm guns, but at long range the Soviet 122mm howitzers and 130mm guns were more accurate than even these weapons. This essentially allowed PAVN gunners to fire on ARVN positions without fear of effective retaliation. In addition, by the end of 1973 the PAVN's twenty antiaircraft regiments in the South were equipped with advanced handheld Soviet SA-7 heat-seeking antiaircraft missiles; some units also had deadly SA-2 antiaircraft missiles mounted on mobile launchers. One antiaircraft regiment even was equipped with the Soviet ZSU-23, an ultramodern armored vehicle featuring radar-guided antiaircraft cannon, which had never before been deployed in Vietnam. These were extremely effective weapons against South Vietnamese aircraft attempting to support Saigon's ground troops.[19]

---

of the People's Army of Vietnam, trans. Merle L. Pribbenow (Lawrence: University Press of Kansas, 2002), 348.

[19] Major George R. Dunham and Colonel David A. Quinlan, *U.S. Marines in Vietnam: The Bitter End, 1973–1975* (Washington, DC: History and Museums Division, U.S. Marine Corps, 1990), 12–13; Le Gro, *Vietnam from Ceasefire to Capitulation*, 39–40, 45; Davidson, *Vietnam at War*, 738; Willbanks, *Abandoning Vietnam*, 209; Military

The ARVN's disadvantage in heavy and advanced weapons is part of the larger question of the impact US aid reduction to Saigon had on the outcome of the war. The reduction of US aid to South Vietnam is only half of a key equation regarding the years 1973 to 1975. The other half is the Soviet and Chinese aid to North Vietnam, and that aid is one of the main bones of contention between orthodox and revisionist commentators, especially in light of the disastrous impact the US aid reduction had on South Vietnam's armed forces. Some orthodox historians have argued that after the Paris Accords Soviet and Chinese aid to North Vietnam also decreased and that the aid that was forthcoming was increasingly economic rather than military. The raw aid figures they cite presumably show that Washington was no less forthcoming than were Moscow and Beijing. To cite two examples of this line of thinking, Prados contends that "Saigon may have been famished but so was Hanoi," while Turley, even while admitting that the figures on US versus Communist arms shipments "are not fully comparable," argues that the aid figures "remove any doubt about Washington's generosity in comparison with that of Moscow and Beijing."[20] This fits neatly with assertions that, contra certain revisionists, the main reasons for Saigon's collapse in 1975 cannot be blamed on US aid cuts but rather on the Saigon regime's and ARVN's multiple failings.

One does not have to be a revisionist to find serious problems with this argument. It is true that during 1974 PAVN troops in South Vietnam faced shortages in ammunition for their burgeoning number of tanks and artillery pieces.[21] But those shortages were being redressed; more to the point, at no time did they cause problems nearly as severe as those faced by the ARVN. Furthermore, during late 1974 and early 1975, the Soviets dramatically increased their aid to Hanoi, something that could not have been included in American intelligence estimates available at the time. That huge spike came after General Viktor Kulikov, the head of the Soviet general staff, visited Hanoi in late 1974; immediately after his departure, Soviet shipments by sea of war material to North Vietnam increased fourfold. As Frank Snepp, the chief CIA strategy analyst in Saigon at the time observed, Moscow was giving Hanoi "full aid and

History Institute of Vietnam, *Victory in Vietnam*, 348–49; Turley, *The Second Indochina War*, 211; Veith, *Black April*, 471.

[20] John Prados, "Response by John Prados," *H-Diplo Roundtable Review*, XI, no. 7 (2009): 31; Turley, *The Second Indochina War*, 210–11.

[21] Merle L. Pribbenow, "North Vietnam's Final Offensive: Strategic Endgame Nonpareil," *Parameters: US Army War College Quarterly*, Winter 1999–2000: 58–71; Veith, *Black April*, 103.

comfort" in its effort to finish off South Vietnam. Willbanks notes that the actual amount of Soviet aid to North Vietnam remains "subject to debate." At the same time, he points out that "the sheer volume of new equipment and weapons during the final offensive in 1975 was most impressive, demonstrating few if any shortages."[22] For example, as Veith reports, PAVN units in the southernmost part of the country (which the North Vietnamese called the B-2 Front) had 58,000 tons of supplies in mid-April as they prepared for the assault on Saigon. This was supplemented by 240 trucks en route carrying 13,000 rounds of 130mm shells; also en route were 40 trucks carrying spare parts for tanks and 150 trucks with mortar ammunition. Focusing on the 130mm rounds, which were fired from artillery guns the ARVN could not match in terms of power or range, Veith rhetorically ask how North Vietnam suddenly came up with this particular ammunition. His answer: "Only the Soviets could have supplied such ammunition."[23]

Veith finds the assertion that after the Paris Accords Hanoi received considerably less aid than Saigon "disingenuous," in part because US intelligence lacked specific information about the size and actual costs of Soviet and Chinese aid, which in turn made all estimates "guesswork."[24] US intelligence agencies acknowledged this at the time in their classified reports. For example, an interagency intelligence memorandum on North Vietnamese military imports during 1974 issued jointly by the CIA, Defense Intelligence Agency (DIA), and State Department in January 1975 states that its estimate "will undoubtedly increase as additional evidence becomes available." It further qualifies its estimates by noting that they include only the cost of the actual equipment received, not the costs of spare parts, training, and transportation, "for which there is virtually no information." The next sentence in the report points out that these items, as well as others such as rations, medical supplies, and the costs of contractor support for various services, are

---

[22] Willbanks, *Abandoning Vietnam*, 208; E. H. Hartsook, *The Air Force in Southeast Asia: The End of US Involvement, 1973–1975* (Washington, DC: Office of Air Force History, 1980), 81; Nicholas Khoo, *Collateral Damage: Sino-Soviet Rivalry and the Termination of the Sino-Vietnamese Alliance* (New York: Columbia University Press, 2011), 89. The original report of the Kulikov visit came from Frank Snepp, *Decent Interval: An Insider's Account of Saigon's Indecent End Told by the CIA's Chief Strategy Analyst in Vietnam* (New York: Vintage Books, 1977), 137–38. Prados acknowledges that CIA/DIA estimates indicate that Soviet aid to North Vietnam increased from $1 billion in 1973 to $1.7 billion in 1974 but qualifies that by noting that the majority was economic aid. See Prados, *Vietnam: The History of an Unwinnable War*, 526.

[23] Veith, *Black April*, 472.   [24] Ibid., 497.

included in US military aid totals. Another classified report issued at about the same time, this one a CIA/DIA memorandum, says that estimates of military aid to North Vietnam "are subject to a wide margin of error."[25] The problem of comparing US and Soviet/Chinese military aid, Veith stresses, is compounded by the important fact that the two military systems and sets of weapons were so different, a point also made by CIA/DIA/State Department intelligence analysts. Soviet and Chinese weapons were cheaper than US weapons and easier to maintain, which meant that Communist aid went much further than did US aid. In addition, ARVN had been trained to fight according to US doctrine, which stressed machines and firepower, a more expensive approach to warfare than the Soviet/Chinese approach, which put more emphasis on personnel.[26]

Another vital consideration, and perhaps the most important one of all, is what *each side actually needed.* While it is true that from 1973 through the end of 1974 – that is, until Kulikov's visit to Hanoi and the subsequent spike in Soviet shipments to North Vietnam – Soviet military aid to North Vietnam decreased, the essential fact is that after the Paris Accords Hanoi's military needs decreased considerably. The reason is straightforward: North Vietnam no longer had to deal with US military power. This is one of the first points made in the joint CIA/DIA/State Department report of January 1975, which states that "with no air war in North Vietnam," there was less need for "sophisticated and expensive" Soviet air defense equipment. The report adds that this equipment constituted at least a third of North Vietnam's military imports prior to the Paris Accords, and "even more" if antiaircraft munitions are included. Because Hanoi no longer had to defend against US bombing, as of January 1975 there were at most twenty-five operational SAM missile sites in North Vietnam, as compared to forty-eight two years earlier. This new situation, the CIA and DIA noted, in which Hanoi no longer had to face US airpower north of the 17th parallel, allowed Hanoi to send at least 100 Soviet-supplied SA-7 shoulder-fired antiaircraft weapons to South Vietnam, where they saw "heavy use" in

[25] CIA/DIA/US State Department, "Imports of Military Equipment and Materiel by North Vietnam in 1974," January 10, 1975 (declassified January 2005), i, 2. Available online at www.cia.gov/library/readingroom/docs/DOC_0001166498.pdf; CIA/DIA, "Communist Military and Economic Aid to North Vietnam, 1970–1974," nd (declassified January 2005), 4. Available online at www.cia.gov/library/readin groom/docs/DOC_0001166499.pdf.

[26] Veith, *Black April,* 498.

1974.[27] In other words, North Vietnamese needs actually *decreased* at the very time when South Vietnamese needs were *increasing*.

Ammunition requirements are part of this equation. Le Gro points out that the PAVN, which was on the offensive, had the great advantage of being able to accomplish its objectives with far less ammunition requirements than the ARVN, which was on the defensive. He explains:

Through careful reconnaissance, registration, and the siting of batteries in concealed locations, the attacker concentrated heavy fires on small targets, while the defender had to search great areas, cover many avenues of approach and suspected enemy positions, and use much larger amounts of ammunition in the defense. The requirements for defense of populated areas, thousands of bridges, and hundreds of miles of highway, left the RVNAF with few forces available to use in deep or prolonged offensives.[28]

Veith adds another crucial point regarding Soviet aid: the matter of training. One of the key reasons the Easter Offensive failed is that General Giap did not understand how to coordinate what is known as combined arms operations: that is, the simultaneous use of different military arms – such as infantry, armor, and artillery – in an operation. This is essential in modern warfare given the great variety of available weapons, and after 1972, as Veith notes, the PAVN "needed to become a modern army, and only the Soviets could train it in this type of warfare." Therefore, in the fall of 1973, by which time the Paris Accords precluded the United States from providing any additional advising to the South Vietnamese, several leading North Vietnamese commanders went to the Soviet Union to train in this kind of warfare. Not coincidentally, this was only a few months after the North Vietnamese Politburo had voted to resume full-scale warfare to conquer the South. There is no way to measure the value of this aid in dollars; it does not appear on any ledger. What one can say given the conventional invasion Hanoi launched against South Vietnam in late 1974 – an invasion spearheaded by armor, the "key to victory" according to Veith – is that this particular form of Soviet aid was invaluable.[29]

Veith provides a broader perspective on the question of Saigon's and Hanoi's respective aid requirement that reduces the orthodox focus on numbers to absolute meaninglessness. He explains that the geography

---

[27] CIA/DIA/US State Department, "Imports of Military Equipment and Materiel by North Vietnam in 1974," 1–3.

[28] Le Gro, *Vietnam from Ceasefire to Capitulation*, 145–46.

[29] Veith, *Black April*, 7–8, 46–47.

made it extremely difficult to defend South Vietnam from invasion. It is a long, narrow country with an exposed western flank 800 miles long. Rugged mountainous terrain and thick jungle vegetation add to the problem of defense, as does the lack of space between the mountains and the coast where the bulk of the population lives, which leaves no room to absorb an attack. Faced with this geographic challenge, the South Vietnamese armed forces, to defend their territory and, above all, their people, "had to guard everywhere, all the time." The Communists, enjoying the interior lines provided by the Ho Chi Minh Trail, could maintain smaller forces because they could mass them at will and attack at the point of their choosing. Furthermore, the South Vietnamese not only needed more troops, they also required more equipment to move troops and weapons to respond to North Vietnamese attacks. This equipment was expensive and, in the case of helicopters and fix-wing aircraft, technologically complex and costly to maintain. In short, given their respective tasks, the costs of the two military establishments were not comparable: South Vietnam needed much more aid to defend than North Vietnam needed to attack. Little wonder Veith calls the dollar-for-dollar comparisons of American and Soviet/Chinese military aid to their respective Vietnamese clients "disingenuous."[30]

Two other factors must be taken into account to understand South Vietnam's needs and the corrosive impact of American aid cuts on the South Vietnamese armed forces and government. First, as Veith notes, even before the US aid cuts, the withdrawal from Vietnam of all American troops and airpower left the South Vietnamese defending their country "with less than half the previous forces and a fraction of the firepower." Second, while Washington had expected that the cease-fire would reduce the expenses and needs of South Vietnam's armed forces, "the ceasefire never materialized."[31] South Vietnam therefore had been deprived of vital resources and support, but the situation that was supposed to enable it to survive under those circumstances did not exist.

What this meant, as Davidson puts it, is that as of 1974 South Vietnam had to fight a "rich man's war on a pauper's budget." The result was "devastating." Training in every branch of the armed forces "ceased altogether." The ability to move troops and supplies by

[30] Ibid., 7, 497–98; See also CIA/DIA/US State Department, "Imports of Military Equipment and Materiel by North Vietnam in 1974," 2. This memorandum calls the North Vietnam versus South Vietnam aid comparisons "singularly inappropriate."
[31] Ibid., 48–49, 497.

helicopters and cargo aircraft fell by 50 percent to 70 percent. The shortage of spare parts sidelined vehicles, and the cannibalization of some vehicles to supply others reduced inventories even further. The shortages of munitions became a serious problem, forcing the ARVN to reduce its artillery and mortar fire. Hand grenades were rationed, and rifle ammunition issued to troops was cut by 50 percent. Davidson cites North Vietnamese General Van Tien Dung, the commander of the 1975 offensive that ended the war, who wrote shortly after his victory that the US cuts forced President Thieu to "fight a poor man's war." The North Vietnamese general also reported that ARVN's firepower fell by nearly 60 percent and its mobility by half.[32]

Veith provides extensive additional evidence along the same lines, including how the aid cuts affected specific battles. For example, in August 1974, after the fall of the small but strategic town of Thoung Dec, which controlled an important route to the port city of Danang, aid cuts were an important factor in the ARVN's inability to retake that town. The ARVN artillery could only fire six rounds of 105mm shells and four rounds of 175mm shells per gun per day. This added up to less than 500 total rounds both in support of the attack and to protect outposts spread over a province and a half. Nor could the ARVN commander use his armor to support attacking troops because he lacked sufficient fuel. Veith notes that "in the eyes of the increasingly demoralized ARVN troops, PAVN supplies appeared plentiful."[33] Meanwhile, by the middle of 1974, South Vietnamese civilian morale – battered by inflation, general economic decline, and the mounting evidence that the United States would not reenter the war with air and naval power under any circumstances – was low and sinking further.[34]

Finally, Veith stresses that the impact of aid cuts on South Vietnam's military forces was not only predictable, but predicted. In mid-December 1973, several months after Congress first voted to cut aid funding for South Vietnam, the US Army cut off all funds for operations and maintenance for the rest of the 1973 fiscal year (which ran through June 1974). General Murray immediately warned that within six months there would be critical shortages of replacement parts, ammunition, and other supplies vital to ARVN's ability to fight. In April and May of 1974, ARVN conducted a highly successful offensive operation, a two-week campaign

[32] Davidson, *Vietnam at War*, pp. 747–49.
[33] Veith, *Black April*, 96; for additional statistics, see Sorley, *A Better War*, 370.
[34] Davidson, *Vietnam at War*, 749.

against PAVN forces on both sides of the Cambodian border northwest of Saigon. It turned out to be ARVN's last offensive operation because it was followed by ARVN's rapid decline. Le Gro, who covered the campaign in detail, explains, "severe constraints on ammunition expenditures, fuel usage, and flying hours permitted no new initiatives." To which Veith adds, "It was the exact period Murray had warned about: the point where the effects of the supply cut-off would hit."[35]

BLACK APRIL

The military struggle that took place in South Vietnam in the spring of 1975 was the largest Southeast Asian war in history fought strictly by Southeast Asians. It was fought by more than one million Vietnamese conventional, guerrilla, and militia forces and other combatants, and it claimed at least 200,000 lives, about equally divided between soldiers and combatants.[36] Almost the entire North Vietnamese army was committed to the battle, including most of the country's air defenses. The attacking PAVN force consisted of more than 300,000 combat and support troops equipped with about 700 tanks (twice the number in ARVN hands), 400 artillery pieces, and more than 200 antiaircraft weapons. To this must be added 40,000 PAVN troops in Cambodia, 50,000 support personnel in Laos, 70,000 PAVN troops in reserve in the North ready for immediate deployment in the South, and Vietcong guerrillas in South Vietnam. Compared to the weakened ARVN, this was an overwhelming force that, unlike in 1972, was backed by a modern and effective logistics system to keep it well supplied.[37] Hanoi also proved to be flexible and ready to exploit unexpected opportunities. For example, during December 1974 and January 1975 PAVN troops overran an entire province in the central part of South Vietnam. That encouraged the Politburo, but even more encouraging was the failure of the United States to respond, as both Hanoi and Saigon had expected, with airpower. As a result, new plans were drawn up for further successful major

---

[35] Veith, *Black April*, 56–57, 74–75; Le Gro, *Vietnam from Ceasefire to Capitulation*, 91–95. The campaign is known as the Svay Reing Operations.

[36] Brian P. Farrell, Review of Black April: The Fall of South Vietnam, 1973–1975, by George J. Veith, *Journal of Southeast Asian Studies* 45, no. 3: 483.

[37] Davidson, *Vietnam at War*, 791–92; Le Gro, *Vietnam from Ceasefire to Capitulation*, 145; Willbanks, *Abandoning Vietnam*, 232. These numbers, drawn from Le Gro and Willbanks, vary slightly from source to source.

attacks.[38] In March 1975 these attacks swelled into the offensive that first forced a chaotic and disastrous ARVN retreat from the territory it held in the Central Highlands, the strategic plateau along South Vietnam's border with Laos and Cambodia, and then ended with the Ho Chi Minh Campaign, which produced the conquest of Saigon, the South Vietnamese government's surrender on April 30, and the end of the war.

The details of this offensive are available in many places, most comprehensively in Veith's *Black April*, the South Vietnamese term for when Saigon fell, and will not be covered here. Instead, the focus will be on how the ARVN comported itself during the fighting. The conventional wisdom, which transcends the orthodox/revisionist divide, is that the ARVN fought poorly, with its leaders in particular coming in for criticism for making mistakes and also in many cases for deserting their troops. Willbanks writes that the ARVN at times fought well but finds these instances "the exception rather than the rule, due to abysmal combat leadership."[39] Davidson is especially scathing when he calls the ARVN's final effort "a craven, every-man-for-himself scuttle for the exits." He says this despite having noted earlier the corrosive effects of declining US aid on the ARVN's ability to maintain its fighting strength, all this while Hanoi was able to refit, reinforce, and reequip its divisions in South Vietnam and also expand and modernize the Ho Chi Minh Trail. Davidson is not entirely negative: he also cites the "epic stand" by the ARVN's 18th Division in defense of the town of Xuan Loc, about sixty miles from Saigon, to illustrate how during the Ho Chi Minh Campaign the ARVN demonstrated "for the last time that, when properly led, it had the 'right stuff.'"[40]

The consensus regarding the ARVN's leadership failures and its consequent failure to fight is widespread. Even Sorley concedes this point, albeit with important caveats. He quotes Douglas Pike's statement that the ARVN "didn't fight at all" in 1975. However, he then quotes Thomas Polgar, the highly capable CIA station chief in Saigon at the time, who assessed what happened in 1975 by contrasting it to what happened in 1972. In 1972, Polgar observed, the South Vietnamese "fought like hell" because they understood the "Americans were in it." In 1975, believing they did not have American support, "their morale gave out and they did not fight." Sorley generally follows Polgar. He writes that by 1975 the South Vietnamese "had run out of conviction." This, however, was caused by "the realization that their sometime ally the United States had

---

[38] Willbanks, *Abandoning Vietnam*, 227–28. [39] Ibid., 283.
[40] Davidson, *Vietnam at War*, 752, 786–90.

abandoned them and by the impending depletion of their means to carry on the fight." All that said, Sorley adds, "it must be admitted, they [the South Vietnamese] ran out of leadership."[41]

In referring to the heroic ARVN stand at Xuan Loc, Willbanks suggests that had such an effort been more common, the war's outcome might have been "drastically different."[42] This is a point that Le Gro, Sorley, and Veith also address, but it takes them to a more positive assessment of ARVN's performance during its last years. Le Gro notes that between the cease-fire of 1973 and the final defeat in 1975, "unit for unit" and "man for man," the South Vietnamese "repeatedly proved themselves superior to their enemies."[43] Sorley's defense of the ARVN is that it proved itself in 1972 when it had the American backing it deserved. In "Reassessing ARVN," he argues that South Vietnamese forces "performed admirably" in defeating the Tet Offensive and the smaller Communist offensives that followed during 1968. Tet was ARVN's "first real test," and it passed. Despite some setbacks, it continued to do well between 1969 and 1972, gradually taking more and more territory from the enemy. In 1972, "with courage and blood," South Vietnam defeated Hanoi's Easter Offensive. Sorley praises ARVN's performance between the Paris Accords and Hanoi's final offensive. By 1975, however, deserted by the United States, the situation was hopeless to the point where nothing better than what actually happened could have been expected. Yet he also points out that during that massive fifty-five-day onslaught "much hard fighting took place." This Sorley adds, is a tribute to the South Vietnamese, who by then had to know "what the final outcome would inevitably be."[44]

In reviewing how the ARVN has been evaluated, Sorley reminds its critics that during the Cold War the United States had to station several hundred thousand troops in West Germany "precisely because the Germans could not stave off Soviet or Warsaw Pact aggression without American help." After the Korean War, 50,000 American troops remained in South Korea for the same reason. Yet, Sorley notes with some bitterness, it was not suggested that the West German or South Korean armed forces should be "ridiculed or reviled" because they needed

---

[41] Sorley, *A Better War*, 376–80.   [42] Willbanks, *Abandoning Vietnam*, 267.
[43] Le Gro, *Vietnam from Ceasefire to Capitulation*, 179.
[44] Sorley, "Reassessing ARVN" (a lecture), 2–3, 11–14. Available online at http://nguyentin
.tripod.com/arvn-sorley-2.htm

US help. "Only South Vietnam ... was singled out for such unfair and mean-spirited treatment."[45]

The claim that the ARVN performed respectably during the 1975 fighting that culminated in Black April plays little or no role in most versions of the revisionist viewpoint on the Vietnam War. Keith Taylor devotes one sentence to the 1975 fighting in his history of the Vietnamese people. Walton and Dave Richard Palmer have slightly more to say on the fighting that year but barely mention the AVRN's performance. Bruce Palmer, Sorley, Davidson, and especially Willbanks have somewhat more to say, with the first two providing a more positive assessment of ARVN than the last two, but their main concerns in discussing the events in question lie elsewhere. The same applies to Le Gro, whose coverage of the December 1974–April 1975 fighting is comprehensive and detailed.

Veith takes a different approach. He reinforces the revisionist case by documenting, considerably more extensively than other authors, how US aid cuts after 1973 were the fundamental factor that undermined ARVN's ability to defend South Vietnam, an issue that has been discussed earlier in this chapter. He also adds another element to the revisionist case, albeit one that is a matter of debate within the revisionist camp: the argument that the ARVN, even in defeat, acquitted itself well in the four months of fighting that culminated in Black April until it was overwhelmed by superior force.

Veith argues that the evidence, including what happened from 1973 to 1975, refutes the conventional thesis that South Vietnam's armed forces were ineffectual "because of the regime's illegitimacy" and that "hence the war was unwinnable." His objective is to provide a "counterweight" to that assessment of the South Vietnamese while making sure not to "whitewash their mistakes or disregard their faults." There were "both good and poor units, excellent and lackluster leaders"; the problem is that Western commentators rarely covered or depicted the good units and leaders. Veith turns to a South Vietnamese battalion commander for context regarding two of the worst South Vietnamese disasters during the 1975 fighting, the retreat from the Central Highlands and the chaos at Danang: "We are ashamed of these things, but they do not define us." Veith's point, which he documents over hundreds of pages, is that South Vietnam's military,

[45] Ibid., 13; Tim Kane, "Global U.S. Troop Deployment, 1950–2003," Heritage Foundation, 2004. Available online at www.heritage.org/research/reports/2006/05/glo bal-us-troop-deployment-1950–2005

"particularly in the 1973–1975 period, had performed much better than anyone has realized."[46]

Space permits only a few of Veith's examples to be mentioned here. He cites a series of battles during 1975, including the 18th Division's stand at Xuan Loc, in which ARVN troops and their commanders acquitted themselves well. Some of these battles are known only to specialists, such as a South Vietnamese counterattack in early April that resulted in the recapture of several villages on the major coastal road Route 1. At Danang, where the panic that occurred at the evacuation points was "a disgrace," Veith points out that "for the most part" the South Vietnamese soldiers fought well. A variety of factors then contributed to the sudden breakdown of morale that ultimately occurred. Most involved other battlefield reverses, most notably the disastrous retreat from the Central Highlands town of Pleiku. But "also critical" was the decision by the US Congress to deny additional aid as the fighting raged. Veith also debunks the reports by many American journalists that in March and April of 1975 ARVN officers deserted their troops "in droves"; the reality is that very few officers commanding troops during the last days of fighting did so. Most of the military men guilty of leaving the country early were staff officers, not unit commanders.[47]

Veith calls on Communist leaders to help refute the notion that the final four-day battle that ended with the fall of Saigon was an easy victory. In an article written eleven years later, Le Duc Tho called the battle "fierce," adding that thousands of "sons and daughters" lost their lives just before Saigon fell. A general on the scene later commented that if he heard someone say the battle for Saigon was easy, "I will give him a shovel and have him dig the graves of our dead." In terms of specifics, a postwar Hanoi study reported that in the last stages of the war, North Vietnamese forces lost 6,000 killed and wounded.[48]

A number of expert reviewers have found Veith's case for the ARVN convincing. Tom Glenn served as an intelligence officer for many years in South Vietnam and was still in Saigon on April 29, 1975, a day before the city fell. In his view, "Veith dispels the misconception that the South Vietnamese fought poorly and disintegrated in the face of a resolute

---

[46] Veith, *Black April*, 4–5. The South Vietnamese officer is Tran Tien San, the former commander of his country's 86th Ranger Battalion.

[47] Ibid., 4–5, 329, 396, 494–96.   [48] Ibid., 496.

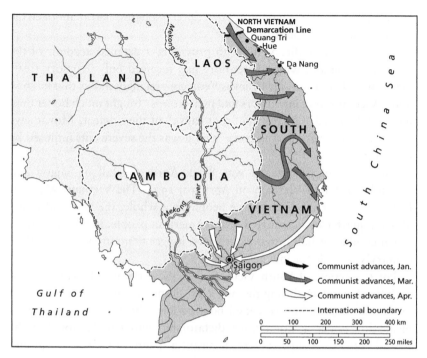

MAP 9 The North Vietnamese Spring Offensive, 1975

North Vietnamese onslaught." To the contrary, "Unit after unit fought with valor against overwhelming odds," including, of course, the 18th Division at Xuan Loc.[49] Dr. William J. Gregor, professor of Social Sciences at the School of Advanced Military Studies at the US Army Command and General Staff College, concurs with this assessment. *Black April*, he writes in his review of that book, "makes it clear that the military forces of South Vietnam were neither inept nor cowardly." Even more to the point, "during the Great Spring Offensive [of 1975] they often got the better of their North Vietnamese opponents tactically." The problem ARVN could not overcome was a combination of two years of North Vietnamese preparations and the simultaneous decline of military aid to South Vietnam. Again

---

[49] Tom Glen, Review of *Black April: The Fall of South Vietnam, 1973–75*, by George J. Veith, *Washington Independent Review of Books*, May 10, 2012. Available online at www.washingtonindependentreviewofbooks.com/bookreview/black-april-the-fall-of-so uth-vietnam-1973-75

agreeing with Veith, Gregor writes that the US Congress had abandoned the US commitment to South Vietnam.[50]

Mark Moyar credits Veith with providing a detailed account of the 1973–1975 period, which heretofore had received only "cursory treatment" from historians. He believes Veith convincingly shows that in 1975 South Vietnamese commanders and their troops "fought much better than has been believed." As for the "root cause" of their defeat, Moyar says Veith "demonstrates persuasively" that it was the severe cuts imposed by Congress in 1974.[51]

The result of that defeat was Black April: the fall of Saigon and surrender of South Vietnam on April 30, 1975. The Vietnam War was finally over. For the Vietnamese people as a whole, the war had lasted about a quarter of a century. For the American people, in terms of traditional combat, it had lasted eight years, longer than any war since their country's struggle for independence.

For the people of South Vietnam, less those thousands who escaped with the Americans during the war's last desperate and chaotic days and more than one million so-called boat people who fled subsequently, it meant life under a Communist dictatorship based in Hanoi. For the United States as a super power, it meant a major Cold War defeat and the first war this country ever lost. For everyone interested in what happened, it meant and has continues to mean a debate that, unlike the war that spawned it, shows no sign of ending.

[50] Dr.William J. Gregor, Review of Black April: The Fall of South Vietnam, 1973–75, by George J. Veith, *Parameters: The US Army War College Quarterly*, 42, no. 4; 43, no. 1, Winter/Spring 2013: 87–89.

[51] Mark Moyar, review of *Black April: The Fall of South Vietnam, 1973–75, Wall Street Journal (Online)*, May 4, 2012. Available online at www.wsj.com/articles/SB100014240 5270230445000457727736199739531 8

Summary and Epilogue

This volume is designed to present the varied viewpoints that constitute the revisionist narrative on the Vietnam War and explain why the revisionist perspective poses a serious challenge to the orthodox consensus on that war. Because multiple and sometimes conflicting viewpoints comprise the revisionist narrative, it seems appropriate to conclude by summarizing some key points that have been covered in this reexamination of the war. The epilogue will explore why developments since 1975 provide an additional compelling reason to reexamine the Vietnam War.

SUMMARY

The revisionist case begins with a survey of Vietnamese history. It reveals that as the Vietnamese expanded southward, significant differences emerged between the people of northern and southern Vietnam, to the point where for more than 200 years beginning in the mid-sixteenth century Vietnam was divided de facto into two rival dynastic states. The dividing line between these states was approximately the 17th parallel, the same dividing line established by the 1954 Geneva Accords. These differences between north and south in effect contradict the contention that there could be only one legitimate vision of Vietnamese nationalism. Aside from the version based on Marxism-Leninism, an alien ideology imported from Europe, others were based on a variety of ideas. The preeminence by the 1940s of Marxist nationalism in Vietnam – that is, the totalitarian Stalinist version adopted by Ho Chi Minh and his comrades – was due largely to outside help from an international movement based in the Soviet Union and the use of force against rival nationalist groups. Further, for Ho and his comrades, the commitment to Marxism's goal of a world socialist revolution took precedence over Vietnamese nationalism. The Communists' most effective nationalist opponent turned out to be Ngo Dinh Diem, a leader of stature who after 1954 headed a regime in South Vietnam that constituted a legitimate and potentially viable alternative to Ho's Stalinist dictatorship in North Vietnam.

With regard to America's involvement in Vietnam, the decision in 1954 to defend the existence of an independent, non-Communist South Vietnam was based on a reasonable assessment of national interests given the geopolitical realities of the Cold War. From the start, the Communist insurgency in South Vietnam, far from being an independent movement, was initiated and controlled by the government of North Vietnam. The Kennedy administration's decision to support Diem's overthrow in 1963 was a huge blunder, possibly the worst mistake the United States made during its involvement in Vietnam. Graduated pressure, the tenet upon which the Johnson/McNamara approach to the war was based, violated the basic principles of warfare worked out by practitioners and theorists of war over many centuries. Once the United States became directly involved in combat, graduated pressure produced the policy of gradual escalation from 1965 to 1968. Gradual escalation was a costly failure that wasted three crucial years at great expense and pain to the American people. It crippled Rolling Thunder, the bombing campaign against North Vietnam, and hampered the ground war effort inside South Vietnam.

The errors of gradual escalation were compounded by the US failure to isolate the battlefield by cutting the Ho Chi Minh Trail, the main route by which North Vietnam infiltrated troops and supplies into South Vietnam. This enabled Hanoi to maintain and rebuild its forces in the South and thereby permitted those forces to recover from military defeats that might otherwise have made it impossible to continue the war. Allowing the Vietcong and PAVN troops to find sanctuary in Cambodia and Laos further enhanced Hanoi's ability to continue a war it might otherwise have lost. Gradual escalation therefore produced a stalemate on the battlefield in Vietnam and at the same time eroded support for the war in the United States. This policy finally was discarded after the Tet Offensive of 1968. This effort by North Vietnam to end the war resulted instead in a major US/South Vietnamese military victory; however, because of various public relations factors, this tactical military victory ended up as a strategic political defeat.

Between 1968 and 1972, the United States adopted a policy of Vietnamization, which in part was possible because Communist forces were badly weakened by the military defeat they suffered during Tet. Improvements and reforms in South Vietnam's government and armed forces fostered by Vietnamization further weakened the Communist insurgency and strengthened the position of the South Vietnamese regime. This was true despite the fact that, as part of Vietnamization, most US troops gradually were withdrawn from Vietnam. The improved position of the South Vietnamese regime forced North Vietnam to change its strategy, and in 1972 Hanoi launched an all-out conventional invasion of the South known as the Easter Offensive. Backed by massive US combat air support, South Vietnam's armed forces fought well and repelled the attack.

Finally, after the Paris Peace Accords of 1973, which included the major flaw of allowing more than 150,000 North Vietnamese troops to remain in South Vietnam, the United States in effect abandoned South Vietnam. This abandonment occurred because President Nixon was weakened and then forced to resign the presidency as a result of the Watergate scandal. Nixon's political decline and eventual resignation helped antiwar members of Congress reduce aid to South Vietnam and also end all funding for any US military operations anywhere in Indochina. Freed from interdiction by US air power, North Vietnam transformed the Ho Chi Minh Trail into an all-weather route, thereby significantly increasing its ability to move troops and supplies, including artillery and tanks, into South Vietnam.

In this burgeoning mix of adverse developments, the precipitous reduction in US aid to the South Vietnamese government was a major and probably the most important factor that led to South Vietnam's defeat. This occurred in 1975 when North Vietnam, its forces bolstered by retraining and new supplies of modern Soviet weapons, launched a second conventional invasion of South Vietnam. South Vietnam's armed forces were overwhelmed and the country fell to the Communists. An observation by Mark Moyar succinctly sums up that denouement: "No small nation could long survive the assaults of an enemy lavishly supported by two great powers unless it received substantial assistance from another great power."[1]

---

[1] Moyar, *Triumph Forsaken*, 184.

EPILOGUE

When he wrote *Vietnam: A History*, a volume published in 1983 and probably still the most widely acclaimed journalistic history of the Vietnam War, Stanley Karnow called his first chapter "The War Nobody Won." His point was to highlight the grim fact that after winning its war to control all of Vietnam at such dreadful cost, the country's Communist rulers in Hanoi imposed a brutal, corrupt, and economically inefficient regime on the people of the former South Vietnam. The demoralization this caused quickly spread from southerners who had opposed Communism to many of those who had embraced and fought for it. Karnow quotes a number of the latter, including a physician and longtime Communist who "burst out" with the following comment to him: "I've been a Communist all my life. But now for the first time I have seen the realities of Communism. It is a failure – mismanagement, corruption, privilege, repression. My ideals are gone."[2]

Coverage of the tyranny that Communism brought to a unified Vietnam is widespread and easily accessible elsewhere. It will suffice here to mention expressions of regret from two former Communist soldiers, one a Vietcong colonel and the other a PAVN colonel. In 1990 the former Vietcong officer bitterly complained that decades of struggle and talk of liberation had produced "this impoverished broken-down country led by a gang of cruel and paternalistic half-educated theorists."[3] Less bitter, perhaps, but reflecting no less disillusionment, is the regret of Bui Tin, the PAVN colonel who in April 1975 accepted the South Vietnamese surrender in Saigon. Living in exile in 2002, he wrote that "my saddest moments come when I think of my land, which is still so backward politically, and my people, who still, after all these long years of sacrifice and deprivation, have not found freedom."[4]

These comments, and many more like them about what Communism brought to the former South Vietnam – to say nothing of the genocide it brought to Cambodia – can and have been used by many commentators to reinforce the revisionist case at the expense of the orthodox narrative. But this author would like to shift the focus to an overlooked irony that lies at the very heart of the orthodox case: the assertion, covered at some length in Chapter 1 of this volume, that in 1954 the United States should have left South Vietnam to its fate because it was an entity lacking in legitimacy and

---

[2] Quoted in Karnow, *Vietnam: A History*, 37.   [3] Quoted in Sorley, *A Better War*, 384.
[4] Bui Tin, *From Enemy to Friend*, 144.

hence viability. The argument goes as follows: South Vietnam's non-Communist regime did not rest on an adequate social base; the elites who controlled it were hopelessly compromised by their association with the French and were thoroughly corrupt to boot; it was riddled with inequalities and injustices to the point where it was beyond redemption; and it existed only because the United States was propping it up. Thus South Vietnam, in one historian's trenchant phrasing, was a "pseudo-nation," a "counterfeit creation" of the United States.[5] In contrast, Ho Chi Minh and the Vietnamese Communists had wide and deep popular support and genuine nationalist credentials by virtue of their long and effective struggle against the French and the social reforms they carried out in the areas they controlled prior to 1954. Their successful melding of Marxism and nationalism gave them their strength and viability, and, perhaps more importantly, their legitimacy.

The problem with this analysis is that it misidentifies what actually was and was not viable. Looking at a world map today, one can find many nations with all the flaws of South Vietnam, and in many cases nations with flaws that are far worse. If South Vietnam inherently was a "pseudo-nation" doomed by its unfixable flaws, what are all these other countries doing on the map? And what happens if one looks for Marxist states built on the foundations that presumably gave Ho Chi Minh and North Vietnam their strength, viability, and legitimacy? It turns out they are almost nowhere to be found. During the Vietnam War, Communist regimes ruled one-third of the world's people; today only stagnant Cuba and dystopian North Korea still have Communist social and economic systems, neither of which is likely to serve as an example for any other country to follow.[6] Of North Vietnam's two great Communist benefactors, the Soviet Union is defunct, to be found not on a map but rather in what Leon Trotsky, once Lenin's right-hand man, called the "dustbin of history." The People's Republic of China is still on the map, but it is a Communist state in name only. The Chinese Communist Party still rules through its one-party dictatorship, but the PRC's socialist economy established under Mao Zedong lies along with the Soviet Union in the dustbin of history, having been replaced by a form of state capitalism. Thus in both the Soviet Union

---

[5] David Anderson, "Review by David Anderson," *H-Diplo Roundtable Review*, XI, no. 7 (2009), 7; quoted in Hess, *Vietnam: Explaining America's Lost War*, 41.

[6] China, Cuba, North Korea, Vietnam, and Laos are the five countries in the world that generally are considered Communist because Communist parties still rule there.

and the People's Republic of China, Communism self-destructed, albeit in different ways.

The Socialist Republic of Vietnam, like the PRC, is still on the map, and, like the PRC, it is still ruled by a one-party dictatorship that calls itself Communist. But Vietnam also has abandoned Communism, and its economy, like the PRC's, is a form of state capitalism. In another ironic twist, in both the PRC and Vietnam the transition from Communism to capitalism, beginning with the dismantling of the failed collective farm system, was carried out by the countries' respective ruling Communist parties. Vietnam's official name, the Socialist Republic of Vietnam, and its ruling party's official name, the Communist Party of Vietnam, are nothing but veils masking a one-party dictatorship ruling over a country with a state-capitalist economy.

What happened? It turns out that rather than countries like the much maligned South Vietnam, it was the Communism, in particular the Communist economic and social system, that was not viable. Communism did not disappear from the Soviet Union, China, and Vietnam, because of conquest or any other form of force. It dissolved on its own because it could not provide adequately for the people who lived under it, at least when measured against what capitalism could provide. The system based on a body of thought that stressed the primacy of economics in determining how societies are structured could not produce a workable economic system.

Marxism got things backward. According to Marxist theory, capitalism and its exploitation come to an end when the proletariat seizes power. This social class, exploited under capitalism, establishes a state called the dictatorship of the proletariat – that is, the rule of the majority – and that state begins the process of building a socialist economic system, which over time gradually evolves into communism. As society approaches communism, the economic system under which all contribute according to their ability and receive according to their need, the state gradually becomes unnecessary and, in the words of Marx and Engels, it ultimately "withers away." In fact, in China and Vietnam, and in a somewhat different way in the Soviet Union, it was communism that withered away while the dictatorial state survived.

The process of withering began in all three countries with growing and unsolvable inefficiencies inherent in state-planned, centralized economies. It continued and accelerated as the Communist parties of those countries began a series of reforms, beginning in the late 1970s in China and during the 1980s in Vietnam and the Soviet Union. In the end, the Communist economic systems crumbed; they "withered away." In China and Vietnam, the dictatorial one-party state remained, with the old Communist party still in control. In the Soviet Union, the old Communist state collapsed, and along with fourteen independent non-Russian countries, a non-Communist Russia (officially: the Russian Federation) emerged from under the Communist rubble. Then, after about a decade of turmoil in the Russian Federation, a strong, dictatorial Russian state filled the vacuum left by the defunct Soviet state.[7]

Precisely how all this applies to the orthodox/revisionist debate on the Vietnam War itself is open to debate. But it is fair to say that while Ho Chi Minh and his comrades won the battle to control Vietnam, they lost the war to establish Communism there. They lost that war for one of the fundamental reasons orthodox commentators use to decry the American effort to defend South Vietnam: Communism, it turned out, was not a viable way of life, but, to borrow words that have been used to describe and dismiss South Vietnam, rather a pseudo, counterfeit system. And that gives us perhaps the most compelling of many reasons one can cite to re-examine the Vietnam War.

---

[7] A fairly similar process to what happened in China and Vietnam occurred in Laos, where today a Communist party rules over a country with an economy that is largely capitalist. In Eastern Europe, all the Communist regimes collapsed and the socialist economic systems were replaced by capitalist ones. Unlike in most of the former Soviet Union, political democracy replaced the Communist dictatorships in most of Eastern Europe. Cambodia once again is a monarchy.

Suggested Readings

What follows is not a bibliography but rather a list of revisionist books and articles on the Vietnam War. This list includes many of the most influential revisionist works on the war as well as other revisionist works that are less well known but were valuable sources in the writing of *The Vietnam War Reexamined*. That said, it is highly selective – less than seventy entries – and can only serve as an introduction to the enormous and expanding corpus of revisionist works on the Vietnam War. The revisionist perspective includes a variety of conflicting viewpoints, depending on the specific topic under discussion. What places the works listed here inside the commodious revisionist tent is that each in one way or another supports the premise that the United States had options it did not employ that might have enabled South Vietnam to survive as an independent, non-Communist state, and at a cost far less than was suffered with the strategy that ended with South Vietnam's destruction. Each work listed here therefore, in its own way, supports a reexamination of the Vietnam War.

Andrade, Dale. "Westmoreland Was Right: Learning the Wrong Lessons from the Vietnam War." *Small Wars and Insurgencies* 19, no. 2 (June 1968): 145–181.
    and Lt. Colonel James H. Willbanks. "CORDS/Phoenix: Counterinsurgency Lessons from Vietnam for the Future." *Military Review* 86 (March–April 2006): 9–23.
Birtle, Andrew J. "PROVN, Westmoreland, and the Historians: A Reappraisal." *The Journal of Military History* 72 (October 2008): 1213–1247.
Brower, IV, Colonel Charles F. "Strategic Reassessment in Vietnam: The Westmoreland 'Alternative Strategy' of 1976–1968." Naval War College, June 1990. Available online: www.dtic.mil/dtic/tr/fulltext/u2/a227314.pdf
Bùi Tín. *Following Ho Chi Minh: Memoirs of a North Vietnamese Colonel.* Translated by Judy Stowe and Do Van. Honolulu: University of Hawaii Press, 1995.
    From Enemy to Friend; A North Vietnamese Perspective on the War. Translated by Nguyen Ngoc Bich. Annapolis: Naval Institute Press, 2002.

"How the North Won the War." Interview with Stephen Young. *Wall Street Journal*, August 3, 1995. Available online: www.viet-myths.netbuitin.htm

Cao Van Vien. *The Final Collapse*. Washington, DC: U.S. Army Center of Military History, 1985.

Cerami, Joseph R. "Presidential Decisionmaking and Vietnam: Lessons for Strategists." *Parameters*. Winter 1997: 66–80. Available online: http://strate gicstudiesinstitute.army.mil/pubs/parameters/Articles/96winter/cerami.htm

Colby, William. *Lost Victory: A Firsthand Account of America's Sixteen-Year Involvement in Vietnam*. Chicago and New York: Contemporary Books, 1989.

Correll, John T. "Rolling Thunder," *AIR FORCE Magazine*, March 2005, 58–65.

Davidson, Phillip B. *Vietnam at War: The History, 1946–1975*. Oxford and New York: Oxford University Press, 1988.

Dommen, Arthur A. *The Indochinese Experience of the French and the Americans: Nationalism and Communism in Cambodia, Laos, and Vietnam*. Bloomington and Indianapolis: Indiana University Press, 2001.

Dror, Olga and K. W. Taylor, editors and annotators. *Views of Seventeenth-Century Vietnam: Christoforo Borri on Chochinchina & Samual Baron on Tonkin*. Ithaca: Southeast Asia Program Publications, 2006.

Dunham, Major George R. and Colonel David A. Quinlan. *U.S. Marines in Vietnam: The Bitter End, 1973–1975*. Washington, DC: History and Museums Division, U.S. Marine Corps, 1990.

Ellsworth, Colonel John K. *Operation Rolling Thunder: Strategic Implications of Airpower Doctrine*. Carlisle Barracks, PA: U.S. Army War College, 2003.

Gacek, Christopher M. *The Logic of Force: The Dilemma of Limited War in American Foreign Policy*. New York: Columbia University Press, 1994.

Hammer, Ellen. *A Death in November: America in Vietnam, 1963*. New York: E. P. Dutton, 1987.

Higgins, Marguerite. *Our Vietnam Nightmare*. New York: Harper and Row, 1965.

Hoang Van Chi. *From Colonialism to Communism: A Case History of North Vietnam*. New York: Praeger, 1964.

Kamps, Charles Tustin. "The JCS 94-Target List: A Vietnam Myth That Distorts Military Thought," *Aerospace Power Journal*, Spring 2001: 67–80.

Kissinger, Henry A. "The Viet Nam Negotiations." *Foreign Affairs* 47, no. 2 (January 1969): 211–234.

  Ending the Vietnam War: A History of America's Involvement in and Extrication from the Vietnam War. New York: Simon and Schuster, 2003.

Krepinevich Jr., Andrew F. *The Army in Vietnam*. Baltimore and London: Johns Hopkins University Press, 1986.

Krulak, Victor H. *First to Fight: An Inside View of the U.S. Marine Corps*. Annapolis: Naval Institute Press, 1984.

Le Gro, Colonel William E. *Vietnam from Ceasefire to Capitulation*. Washington, DC: U.S. Army Center of Military History, 1981.

Lewy, Guenter. *America in Vietnam*. Oxford and New York: Oxford University Press, 1978.

Li Tana. *Nguyen Cochinchina: Southern Vietnam in the Seventeenth and Eighteenth Centuries.* Ithaca: Southeast Asia Program Publications, 1998.

"An Alternative Vietnam? The Nguyen Kingdom of the Seventeenth and Eighteenth Centuries," *Journal of Southeast Asian Studies* 29, no.1 (March 1998): 111–121.

Lind, Michael. *Vietnam, The Necessary War.* New York: Free Press, 1999.

Lomperis, Timothy J. *The War Everyone Lost – and Won: America's Intervention in Vietnam's Twin Struggles,* rev. ed. Washington, DC: Congressional Quarterly Inc., 1993.

Margolin, Jean-Lewis. "Vietnam and Laos," in *The Black Book of Communism: Crimes, Terror, Repression,* eds. Stéphane Courtois et al. Translated by Jonathan Murphy and Mark Kramer. Cambridge, MA, and London: Harvard University Press 1999, 568–570.

McMaster, H. R. *Dereliction of Duty: Lyndon Johnson, Robert McNamara, the Joint Chiefs of Staff, and the Lies that Led to Vietnam.* New York: HarperCollins, 1997.

Momyer, William M. *Air Power in Three Wars (WWII, Korea, Vietnam).* Washington, DC: Office of Air Force History, 1985.

Moore, John Horton, and Robert F. Turner, eds. *The Real Lessons of the Vietnam War: Reflections Twenty-Five Years After the Fall of Saigon.* Durham: Carolina Academic Press, 2002.

This volume, which contains contributions from participants at a conference that took place in 2000 at the University of Virginia School of Law, includes articles by both revisionist and non-revisionist authors. Among others, it includes contributions by Stephen J. Morris, Lewis Sorley, Robert E. Morris, Douglas Pike, Mark Moyar, and Robert F. Turner.

Moyar, Mark. *Phoenix and the Birds of Prey: Counterinsurgency and Counterterrorism in Vietnam.* Lincoln and London: University of Nebraska Press, 1997.

Triumph Forsaken: The Vietnam War, 1954–1965. New York: Cambridge University Press, 2006.

Ngo Quang Truong. *The Easter Offensive of 1972.* Washington, DC: U.S. Army Center of Military History, 1980.

Owens, Mackubin Thomas. "Vietnam as Military History." *Joint Force Quarterly,* Winter 1993–94: 112–118.

Palmer Jr., General Bruce. *The 25-Year War: America's Military Role in Vietnam.* Lexington: University Press of Kentucky, 1984.

Palmer, Dave Richard. *Summons of the Trumpet: A History of the Vietnam War from a Military Man's Viewpoint.* New York: Ballantine Books, 1978.

Palmer, Gregory. *The McNamara Strategy and the Vietnam War: Program Budgeting in the Pentagon, 1960–1968.* Westport, CT and London: Greenwood Press, 1978.

Podhoretz, Norman. *Why We Were in Vietnam.* New York: Simon and Schuster, 1982.

Robbins, James S. *This Time We Win: Revisiting the Tet Offensive.* New York and London: Encounter Books, 2010.

Sharpe, U. S. Grant. *Strategy for Defeat: Vietnam in Retrospect.* San Rafael and London: Presidio Press, 1978.

Shaw, John W. *The Cambodian Campaign: The 1970 Offensive and America's Vietnam War.* Lawrence: University Press of Kansas, 2005.

Smith, R. B. *An International History of the Vietnam War,* vol. 1: *Revolution Versus Containment, 1955–1961.* Blasingstoke and London: Macmillan, 1983.

    An International History of the Vietnam War, vol. 2: *The Kennedy Strategy.* New York: St. Martin's Press, 1985.

Sorley, Lewis. *A Better War: The Unexamined Victories and Final Tragedy of America's Last Years in Vietnam.* San Diego: Harcourt, 1999.

    "Reassessing ARVN (a lecture)." Available online: http://nguyentin.tripod.com /arvn-sorley-2.htm.

Staaveren, Jacob Van. *Gradual Failure: The Air War Over North Vietnam, 1965–1966.* Washington, DC: Air Force History and Museum Program, 2002.

Summers Jr., Harry G. *On Strategy: A Critical Analysis of the Vietnam War.* New York: Dell Publishing, 1984.

Taylor, Keith Weller. *A History of the Vietnamese.* Cambridge: Cambridge University Press, 2013.

    The Birth of Vietnam. Berkeley: University of California Press, 1983.

Thomson, W. Scott and Donaldson D. Frizzell, eds. *The Lessons of Vietnam.* New York: Crane, Russak & Co., 1977.

This volume includes papers and comments by more than thirty analysts, both revisionist and non-revisionist, who participated in a colloquium and a conference held at the Fletcher School of Law and Diplomacy of Tufts University during 1973–74.

Thompson, Wayne. *To Hanoi and Back: The U.S. Air Force and North Vietnam.* Washington, DC, and London: Smithsonian Institution Press, 2000.

Turner, Robert F. "Myths and Realities of the Vietnam Debate." Available online: www.viet-myths.net/turner.htm. This article originally was published in the *Campbell Law Review* 9, no. 3 (Summer 1987): 473–496.

    Vietnamese Communism: Its Origins and Development. Stanford: Hoover Institution Press, 1975.

Veith, George J. *Black April: The Fall of South Vietnam, 1973–1975.* New York and London: Encounter Books, 2012.

Walton, C. Dale. *The Myth of Inevitable U.S. Defeat in Vietnam.* London and Portland, OR: Frank Cass Publishers, 2002.

Ward, Lieutenant Colonel James R. "Vietnam: Insurgency or War," *Military Review* 69 (January 1989): 14–23.

Westmoreland, William D. *A Soldier Reports.* New York: Dell, 1980.

Wiest, Andrew. *Vietnam's Forgotten Army: Heroism and Betrayal in the ARVN.* New York: New York University Press, 2008.

    ed. *Rolling Thunder in a Gentle Land: The Vietnam War Revisited.* London and New York: Osprey Publishing, 2006.

This volume includes articles by both revisionist and non-revisionist authors. Among the contributors are Andrew Wiest, Lewis Sorley, and Bui Tin.

and Michael Doidge, eds. *Triumph Revisited: Historians Battle for the Vietnam War*. New York and Abingdon: Routledge, 2010.

This volume features both revisionist and non-revisionist authors, with Mark Moyar responding to comments on his book *Triumph Forsaken: The Vietnam War, 1954–1965*. Aside from Moyar, revisionist authors who contributed to this volume include Andrew Wiest, Keith W. Taylor, Robert F. Turner, Andrew J. Birtle, and Michael Lind.

Willbanks, James H. *Abandoning Vietnam: How America Left and South Vietnam Lost Its War*. Lawrence: University Press of Kansas, 2004.

The Tet Offensive: A Concise History. New York: Columbia University Press, 2006.

Woodside, Alexander. "Central Viet Nam's Trading World in the Eighteenth Century as Seen in Le Quy Don's 'Frontier Chronicles.'" In K.W. Taylor and John K. Whitmore, eds., *Essays into the Vietnamese Pasts*. Ithaca: Studies in Southeast Asia, 1995, 157–172.

Index

Maps are indicated by page numbers in *italics*.

Index